enough

SHARON JAYNES

HARVEST HOUSE PUBLISHERS
EUGENE, OREGON

Cover design and illustration by Connie Gabbert Design + Illustration

Portions of this book previously published as *"I'm Not Good Enough"... and Other Lies Women Tell Themselves*

Enough
Copyright © 2009/2018 Sharon Jaynes
Published by Harvest House Publishers
Eugene, Oregon 97408
www.harvesthousepublishers.com

ISBN 978-0-7369-7354-0 (pbk)
ISBN 978-0-7369-7356-4 (eBook)

The Library of Congress has cataloged the earlier printing as follows:
    Library of Congress Cataloging-in-Publication Data
Jaynes, Sharon.
    "I'm not good enough"— and other lies women tell themselves / Sharon Jaynes.
    p. cm.
    Includes bibliographical references.
    ISBN 978-0-7369-1870-1 (pbk.)
    1. Women—Religious aspects—Christianity. 2. Self-perception—Religious aspects—Christianity. 3. Self-esteem—Religious aspects—Christianity. 4. Christian women—Religious life. I. Title.
    BT704.J35 2009
    248.8'43—dc22
    2008028528

Contents

To my three nieces,

*Grace Anne Vick, Emily Edwards,
and Katherine Edwards.*

*Watching you become such incredible wives
and mothers has been a great joy.*

Thank you for allowing me to be a part of your lives.

PART 1

*the battle for
your thought life*

House of Mirrors

I have no greater joy than to hear that
my children are walking in the truth.
3 JOHN 4

*C*arrie brushed on the finishing touches of makeup before rushing off to the carnival with her girlfriends. Just a bit of lip gloss and one more swipe of the hairbrush and she was ready to go.

Carrie heard the car horn blow as the girls pulled into the driveway. She grabbed her sweater and yelled to her mom, who was still in the kitchen.

"Bye, Mom. I'll be home by eleven."

"Be careful," her mother called out.

Carrie, Katie, Clair, and Meghan scurried from booth to booth as the carnival barkers drew them in. They watched boys humiliate themselves trying to fire rifles at metal foxes running across a black backdrop, shoot basketballs into hoops that seemed strangely small, and bang a giant hammer to prove who was the strongest among the bunch. The girls tried their hands at throwing darts to pop balloons, casting rings over old milk jugs, and tossing balls in slanted straw baskets. After eating sticky pink clouds of cotton candy, the girls wandered around to various sideshows.

"Come one, come all," the barker called. "Step right up and see yourself as you've never been seen before. The House of Mirrors—sure to entertain and amuse. Step right up."

"Come on in, little lady," the shifty man with greasy black hair and a toothy grin said as he motioned to Carrie. She shivered and wanted to turn and run away.

"Let's go in here," Katie said. "This will be fun."

Carrie was whisked away with the crowd and pushed into the first mirrored room. Elongated reflections stared back, and the girls giggled at the taller, thinner versions of themselves. In the next room, they doubled over with laughter at their stubby arms and legs, expanded torsos, and chubby cheeks. They struck various poses and got a taste of what shorter, wider versions of themselves might look like.

The girls ran to a third room, but Carrie stayed behind. She was silent as she stood mesmerized at what she saw staring back at her. Words seemed to appear across her chest, fading in and out in various scripted forms. *Worthless. Unloved. Ugly. Stupid. Unacceptable. Unforgivable. Dirty. Unhappy. Failure. Not good enough.*

Was this a trick? Did the others see what she saw? How did they know? Tears trickled down her cheeks as buried memories surfaced before her.

"Carrie, come on!" Meghan called from down the hall. "Let's go to the bumper cars."

Carrie took a deep breath, put on her perma-smile, and wiped her eyes. No one noticed the smudged mascara trail down her cheeks or her puffy eyes. Like always, no one knew.

HOUSE OF MIRRORS

I was in the sixth grade when I first ventured into the House of Mirrors at my hometown county fair—a mere 12 years old. Like Carrie, my group of giggling friends ran from booth to booth, suckered into paying good money to play rigged games. For hours we gave cash to shady carnival characters in hopes of winning a stuffed purple polka-dotted snake, an oversized tie-dyed teddy bear, or a cheesy piece of jewelry we'd never wear. Personally, I stuck with Pickup Ducks—a sure win.

We soared into the air on the Ferris wheel to get an aerial view of our small-town lights, rode through the darkened House of Horrors, each with her latest crush, and plunged down the mountainous, rickety roller coaster with arms in the air. But of all the sideshows at the carnival, it was the House of Mirrors that captured my attention.

Like Carrie and her friends, we walked through mazelike halls, giggling at the distorted images of ourselves. I looked at the various versions of me and tried to decide which one I liked best. But deep inside, in a place no one knew existed, I was in search of another version of me. I did not like the one I knew best.

After writing the first edition of *Enough* called *I'm Not Good Enough...and Other Lies Women Tell Themselves* and receiving thousands of emails in response, I've realized women all around the world have grown up with a distorted view of who they really are. They look into the mirror and see words that don't match up with the truth about who God created them to be.

They look into the mirror of value and see the word *worthless.*

They look into the mirror of success and see the word *failure.*

They look into the mirror of intelligence and see the word *stupid.*

They look into the mirror of competence and see the word *inadequate.*

They look into the mirror of acceptance and see the word *rejected.*

They look into the mirror of confidence and see the word *insecure.*

They look into the mirror of comparison and see the word *inferior.*

They look into the mirror of performance and see the words *not good enough.*

They look into the mirror of sufficiency and see the words *not enough...period.*

Many women live in a house of mirrors, believing distorted interpretations of who they are—and the devil polishes that mirror of deception every day to keep it shiny

I know the House of Mirrors well. I grew up there. Lived there for years. For decades, feelings of inferiority, insecurity, and inadequacy held me captive to a "less than" life. I looked like I had it all together on the outside, but on the inside I was a cowering little girl hiding in the farthest corner of the playground, hoping no one would notice my reluctance to join in.

You might expect me to say, "But then I met Jesus and all my insecurities miraculously disappeared." Oh, I wish that were the case, but that little insecure, lost girl grew up to become an insecure Christian woman.

If you've read my other books, you know my story. But if we're new friends, you need to hear a little bit about how I got into my fix. Who knows? Maybe you'll see yourself walking the path with me.

BROKEN MIRRORS

I grew up in small-town America, in the eastern part of North Carolina. My father was the successful owner of a building supply company, and my mom was a hardworking arts-and-crafts shop owner. On the outside we looked like a typical American family with two kids and a collie named Lassie. We lived in a beautiful brick ranch-style home with columns supporting the elongated front porch and sixty-foot pine trees forming a shady canopy. But behind the peaceful exterior loomed a deep, dark secret.

My father drank heavily and often terrorized our home with violent outbursts, fits of rage, and verbal and physical abuse. I saw things a little girl should never see and heard words a little girl should never hear. Many nights I went to bed with the covers pulled up over my head and eyes squeezed shut in attempts to block out the visual images that accompanied the violent noises occurring on the other side of my bedroom wall. Some nights I snuck into my brother's room, and we hid in the security of his closet.

Many mornings I woke up to broken furniture, my mom with a black eye, and my crying father promising it would never happen again. But it always did.

My mom was a bitter, angry woman who struggled to put on a good face in public. Unfortunately, behind closed doors, her bitterness, resentment, and anger spilled over to her children. "You can't do anything right." "Why can't you be smart like your brother?" "You're so ugly." "You did a terrible job cleaning that bathroom. Go back and do it again." When she said, "What's wrong with you?" I remember thinking, *I don't know, but something is. I'm just not lovable.*

My father spent most of his time running his company or carousing with friends. And even though his place of business was only a few blocks from our home, his heart was miles away. A battle raged in my little-girl heart. Part of me longed to have a daddy who loved me, and part of me was afraid to even get near the one I had.

Even though I was actually cute as a little girl, I never felt pretty *enough*. I longed to be cherished or valued, but I always felt I was in the way—a bother. That nobody liked me, wanted me, or loved me. And if your parents can't love you, then who ever could? I surmised I was not only not pretty enough, but not smart enough, talented enough, or good enough to be the apple of anyone's eye.

When I was six years old, I skipped off to school with a new box of crayons, a Swiss–polka dotted dress, and fresh hope that I would be liked. But first grade only confirmed my fears. I was "not enough."

As soon as my first-grade teacher held up that initial spelling flashcard, I knew I was in trouble. Back then, my church-sponsored kindergarten focused on coloring, playing, and napping. But first grade was a whole new ball game with letters, numbers, and tests.

Remembering one spelling exercise makes my palms clammy even today. We lined up our miniature wooden chairs in a row like a choo-choo train. The teacher held up a spelling flashcard for us to identify the word. If we missed the word, we had to go to the caboose. I spent most of the first grade in the caboose. For some reason, I especially had trouble with the word *the*.

My older brother, who proved to be very smart, had had the same teacher five years earlier, and I guess she thought a glimmer of hope lurked somewhere in the gene pool.

I'll help her, my teacher must have thought.

She made me a name tag that read *the* and I had to wear it for two weeks. Students came up to me and asked, "Why are you wearing that tag?" "Is your name 'The'?" "You must be stupid." "What's wrong with you?"

Well, I learned how to spell the word *the*, but that's not all I learned. I learned I was stupid, not as smart as everybody else, and once again, not enough.

The strands of inferiority, insecurity, and inadequacy began to weave an invisible yet indelible grid system over my mind. Every thought I had, every comment by other people, and every social interaction had to filter through that sieve of deficiency before it was interpreted by my little-girl mind. By the time I was a 12-year-old, that filter was cemented firmly in place. I was a scared and scarred little girl who kept her mouth shut by day and her eyes squeezed closed by night.

A House of Mirrors became my home, full of mirrors misshaped by the words of others and interpreted by a needy little girl who just wanted to be accepted and loved.

At the age of 12, I became friends with a girl in my neighborhood, Wanda Henderson. We had known each other since first grade but truly bonded by the sixth. Wanda's mother took me under her wing and loved me as though I were her own child. She told me I did have a father who loved me, a heavenly Father who loved me so much He gave His Son for me. Mrs. Henderson knew what was going on in my home, and she knew about my wounded heart.

Eventually the Hendersons invited me to go to church with them. Amazingly, my family, with its multilayered dysfunction, went to church on Sundays. Yes, with all the alcohol, fighting, pornography, and infidelity that riddled our home, we went to a politically correct, socially prestigious church—fighting all the way to the front door. We heard ear-tickling, inoffensive sermons that were moral enough to make us feel we'd done our American duty but not spiritual enough to convict or transform us in any way.

But the Hendersons' church was different. They talked about having a personal relationship with Jesus Christ, a concept I had never heard before. I wanted what they had. I went to this church and drank in every word the pastor and teachers had to say about a Savior who loved me so much He gave His life for me on Calvary's cross so I could have eternal life. He paid the penalty for my sin. He loved me, not because I was pretty or accomplished, but just because I was His. I didn't have to earn God's love, I already had it—a foreign concept for sure.

Two years after my initial visit to this Bible-believing church, when

I was 14 years old, I gave my life to Jesus Christ. Again, you might expect me to say all my insecurities went away. But nothing could be further from the truth. I went from being an insecure little girl to being an insecure Christian. All those feelings of "I'm not enough" went right along with me into my adult years. Except now I had a new verse to the misguided song stuck in my head: "I'm not a good enough Christian."

A NEW MIRROR

Into my early thirties, despite my conversion at 14, I felt as though something was wrong with me spiritually—as if I had walked into a movie 20 minutes late, spending the entire time trying to figure out what was going on. I had a wonderful husband, an amazing son, and a happy home life. I attended Bible studies year after year, hoping each one would be the one to fix me. I even taught Bible studies at a scripturally sound church, and I surrounded myself with strong Christian friends.

But something was missing, and I couldn't figure out what it was. The dirge of "I'm not good enough" was a song I couldn't get out of my head. The lies of the enemy created limitation in my life. The belittling taunts of the devil were the barbed wire that fenced me in and kept God's best at bay. I wonder if you can relate. Do you have lies that tumble about in your mind no matter how desperately you want them gone? Do you have regrets piled high like books unread? If so, we're going to tackle that together.

> The lies of the enemy created limitation in my life.
> They were the barbed wire that fenced
> me in and kept God's best at bay.

The battle to change the song in my head began when I was in my mid-thirties, sitting under the teaching of an older woman in my church, Mary Marshal Young. She opened my eyes to the truths in Scripture about who I was, what I had, and where I was (my position) as a child of God. I had read those verses scattered throughout

Scripture before, but when she encouraged me to cluster them all together into one list, God began a new work in my heart.

You are a saint.

You are chosen.

You are dearly loved.

You are holy.

These truths were right there on the pages of my Bible in black and white, and a few in red.

You are reconciled through Christ's life.

You are justified by Christ's blood.

You are free from condemnation through Christ's death.

You have the mind of Christ.

You can do all things through Christ.

I knew the verses were the infallible Word of God, but I felt rather squeamish hearing them, reading them, believing them.

They didn't feel right.

They didn't sound right.

They made me downright uncomfortable.

But I had a choice to make. Was I going to believe God told the truth? I tried to learn the verses and cooperate with the Holy Spirit to change the way I thought about myself, but it was a struggle...a battle. And so I came up with a *battle plan*. And that, my friend, is what I want to share in the pages of this book. The battle plan for overpowering the lies of the enemy with the truth of God. We're going to discover how to silence the inner critic that holds us hostage—to silence the lies that steal our confidence. We're going to knock down the walls that keep God's best at bay and lean into the still, small voice that calls us to more.

There are many facets to knowing how to replace those lies with the truth. Where do the lies come from? How do we know if what we're thinking and telling ourselves is a lie or the truth? How do we get the lies out of our minds? How do we overcome the lies of the enemy with the promises of God? How do we develop new ways of seeing ourselves when the lies have been our truth for so long? How do we walk out of the House of Mirrors once and for all and into the unerring reflection of our true identity?

It's time to stop believing the lies about ourselves and start believing the truth, no matter how beautiful it may be.

God wants to show you truths about your true identity, His timeless sufficiency, and your preordained destiny that flesh and blood cannot reveal. Jesus sits by the well waiting for you to show up, to dip down deep and pour out the affirmation you're thirsting for. "Affirmations that call you to let go of the hindrances that hold you hostage, take hold of the promises that set you free, and live boldly with that faith you've always longed for."[1]

So let's hunker down and begin with the first question: Where do the lies come from?

2

Realize the Enemy's True Identity

*The thief comes only to steal and kill and destroy; I have
come that they may have life, and have it to the full.*

JOHN 10:10

Mary Beth stood before the bathroom mirror, brushing her
shoulder-length hair and staring at the reflection. It seemed
like only yesterday she was a carefree little girl swinging from
the monkey bars on the schoolhouse playground. Oh, how she longed
for the days when her greatest concern was which hair bow to wear in
her neatly tied ponytail.

"Mommy, watch this," echoed as the distant memories passed
before her.

Birthday parties with an increasing number of candles, dance recit-
als with flashing cameras, prom dresses with handsome escorts, cheer-
leading routines with enthusiastic fans, church youth group with open
Bibles, and teary-eyed parents driving away from her college dorm.
Then there was Bob.

"Bob," she whispered as tears pooled in her eyes.

Bob and Mary Beth met at a campus ministry her junior year. He
was everything she had hoped for in a husband: handsome, ambitious,
spiritual, and most of all, attentive. Both sets of parents beamed as they
watched the couple walk the red-carpeted aisle of their church after
pledging their lifelong love.

Fifteen years later, Mary Beth and Bob had a mortgage, three kids, a dog, busy schedules, and a loveless marriage. They were so busy taking care of life that they forgot to take care of love.

That's when Jim appeared. She recalled the day she ran into the grocery store to pick up a loaf of bread.

"Mary Beth, is that you?"

"Jim! It's so good to see you," she said as they met halfway down the aisle in a friendly hug. "Where have you been? When did you get back in town?"

"I've been working in Europe for the past ten years," Jim said, "but now I'm back for a while. Man, you look great. Didn't anyone tell you you're supposed to look older as you get older? I'd love to catch up. Do you have time to step over to Starbucks and grab a coffee?"

Mary Beth's heart quickened. How long had it been since anyone had told her she looked great? She couldn't even remember. "No, I'd better not. I need to get back home."

"Well, maybe next time. I just can't get over how good you look."

"Oh hush. You're silly. I'll see you around."

Over the next several months, Mary Beth and Jim bumped into each other several times. She even found herself applying lipstick and making sure her hair was in place before leaving the house just in case she saw him. Her mind began to daydream about what it would be like to share a candlelight dinner with Jim. She imagined him reaching for her hand or brushing a stray strand of hair from her face.

Mary Beth pulled up his Facebook page and sent a friend request. She looked at his photos and wondered what it would be like to be in them. Mary Beth knew in her heart that the imaginings were not healthy. That the "innocent" texts that followed their third meeting needed to stop. So she planned a special surprise for Bob, hoping a romantic evening would suppress or replace the longings she felt for Jim.

She recalled the evening. The kids were at her parents' for the night, the dinner was cooked to perfection, and a rose petal fragrance wafted throughout the candlelit dining room. All day long Mary Beth had prepared. Wearing the clingy low-cut dress was intentional, not to mention what was underneath. Her hair was just as Bob liked it, and her body was scented, softened, and waiting to be touched.

"Hello," Mary Beth answered when her phone rang.

"Hi, honey. Listen, I'm not going to be able to make it home on time tonight. I might not even make it home at all. I've got an emergency meeting with the board, and it looks like we could be on a conference call until morning. Seems like our China export deal is in jeopardy. We didn't have anything planned for tonight, did we?"

"No," was all she said.

"Okay, see you later." *Click.*

I can't believe he just did that, she thought in a huff. *All he cares about is work. I can't live like this any longer. This isn't a marriage; it's job share. I tried. It didn't work. I can't believe God wants me to live like this. I know He wants more for me. I know He wants me to be happy.*

Mary Beth picked up her cell phone and tapped in the numbers.

"Hello," Jim answered.

"Hi, Jim. This is Mary Beth. Are you still up for that cup of coffee?"

Many cups of coffee and planned meetings ensued after that evening. Three months later, Mary Beth and Jim consummated their affair.

Temptation had turned into consummation had turned into condemnation. The taste of forbidden fruit rotted in her soul, and she wanted to die.

Looking down at the bottle of sleeping pills her doctor had prescribed, she thought just how easy it would be to end it all...right now...today.

$$\bullet \ \bullet \ \bullet \ \bullet \ \bullet$$

I wish I could tell you this is a script from a soap opera or primetime drama, but it's not. It's a common tale I hear time and time again. The names change, but the story line remains the same. And it makes me mad. I'm not angry with the women who pour their hearts out to me, but I am mad at the enemy who lies to them, the world that deceives them, and the old preprogrammed thought patterns that refuse to let go. I'm fed up with the enemies who whisper that God is holding out on them, that they could be happy if...

IN THE BEGINNING

The first step in the battle for your thought life is to realize the enemy's true identity. He shows up in Genesis chapter 3.

The Bible begins with the words, "In the beginning God created the heavens and the earth" (Genesis 1:1). Five days after time began, the Creator of the universe gazed at all He had made and was not completely satisfied. Yes, as the sun set on each of the first five days on God's kingdom calendar, He said, "It is good." But something was missing. Something more. Someone more.

The stage was set for Act 6. The curtain rose. Everything had to be perfect for God's grand finale. The angels gathered round as God announced the final scene on the magnificent drama.

He began with an announcement: "Let us make mankind in our image" (Genesis 1:26). This being would be different from all the rest. With body, soul, and spirit, man would enter into a relationship with the Creator on a personal and intimate level. He would be just a little lower than the angels and rule over all the living creatures in the air, at sea, and on the ground. He would fill the earth with others like him and subdue its wildness. Man would be God's friend.

God knelt on the ground and gathered a handful of dirt. He spat on the dust and began forming the most magnificent creation to date. With His very fingertips, God fashioned man's inward parts: capillaries, nerve endings, brain cells, hair follicles, eyelashes, and taste buds. Meticulously and deliberately, the Artist created a masterpiece of divine design.

And as the lifeless form lay before the celestial audience, God placed His mouth upon the nostrils of man and breathed life into his waiting lungs. Man's heart began to beat, the lungs began to expand, and the eyes began to flutter open. And the curtain began to fall on this, the sixth day of creation.

"Wait!" the Creator said. "My work is not done. It's not good for man to be alone. I'll create a helper suitable for him. A companion like him, but oh so different."

God—the Us, the three-in-one—began to fashion the grand finale: woman.

Can't you just see it now? Can't you sense the excitement of the angels as they hovered low? From the very beginning of time, mankind was set apart. Man—both male and female—was uniquely designed for a specific purpose as God's image bearer to rule the earth.

But one among the onlookers that day watched with evil intent. Yes, he was among the created angelic beings, one of the most beautiful. But he wasn't happy with his position in the heavenly order. He wanted to elevate himself above God. And while he had been created to be a light bearer, his rebellion caused him to be thrown to Earth to become known as the Prince of Darkness.

And now there were these humans created in God's image. The enemy thought they were disgusting—he wasn't pleased. As soon as Adam and Eve stood on the stage, the Prince of Darkness began to devise their demise. If he was going down, he was going to take as many of these image bearers with him as possible.

Adam and Eve lived in a perfect world. All their needs were cared for. They had perfect communion with God and with each other. They were naked and felt no shame. The only restriction placed on them was that they were not to eat from the Tree of the Knowledge of Good and Evil in the middle of the garden. God warned Adam, "When you eat from it you will certainly die" (Genesis 2:17).

As they basked in the light of God's love, darkness slithered into the garden with his plan to steal, kill, and destroy the image bearers. And how did he do it? He did it with the most powerful weapon of all: lies.

NOW THE SERPENT

Jesus called him "father of lies" (John 8:44 NLT). Paul referred to him as the prince of the power of the air (Ephesians 2:2 NASB). In the book of Revelation (KJV), John called him "the devil" (12:9), "the accuser of our brethren" (12:10 NASB), and "the great dragon" (12:9). No matter what you choose to call him, the deceiver slithered into mankind's perfect world in the garden, selling his bag of lies. The meaning of the word *lie* is "a falsehood with the intent to deceive," and deceive he did.

Genesis chapter 3 begins with the words, "Now the serpent." The great deceiver clothed himself as a serpent and slithered up to Eve with a game plan to destroy God's image bearers. He didn't come with a sword or a gun or even a knife for his attack. He simply wielded lies.

The serpent knew Adam and Eve would not buy into a bald-faced denial of God, so he slipped into the garden with a twist and a turn of the truth. He began by posing a question: "Did God really say, 'You must not eat from any tree in the garden'?" (Genesis 3:1).

It was an invitation for Eve to enter into dialogue. He knew exactly what God had said. He was just trying to draw her into a conversation to confuse her and cause her to doubt God.

The devil can't take away the promises of God. He can't change the truth of who you are and what you have in Christ. But he can put a question mark at the end of those promises to cause you to question if His Word is really true for you. He can put a question mark at the end of God's commands in an attempt to get you to question if His promises are applicable for today.

Anytime you have a thought that begins with the words, "Did God really say…" you need to stop and ask yourself, "Where did that thought come from?" Most of our decisions that lead us in a path away from God's perfect plan begin with this question.

Here's what God did really say: "You are free to eat from any tree in the garden; but you must not eat from the tree of the knowledge of good and evil, for when you eat from it you will certainly die" (Genesis 2:16-17).

See how the deceiver twisted the truth? Put a question mark at the end of God's statement rather than a period.

Oh, sister, we've got to know who the enemy is and understand how he works. He does the very same with you and me that he did with Adam and Eve. He takes the promises of God, such as, *I am holy and dearly loved*, and twists it around in your mind to become, *Am I holy and dearly loved? Can I do all things through Christ who gives me strength? Am I free of condemnation?*

Friend, when you sense that question mark at the end of God's promises, grab it with both hands and yank it into an exclamation mark!

I am holy and dearly loved!

I can do all things through Christ who gives me strength!
I am free from condemnation!

Okay, I got a little excited and veered off topic of the first step in the battle plan for the mind. Here we go.

Notice the first three words of God's command: "You are free." God's command was not stifling, but freeing. Adam and Eve had incredible freedom in the garden, a literal cornucopia of goodness at every turn. They had a sense of significance as rulers of the earth; a sense of security in that all their needs were provided for; a sense of belonging with perfect union and communion with God and each other. They had only one restriction—just one. And that was the Achilles' heel Satan went for. Boundaries God had established to protect them, Satan used to provoke them. God wanted to protect them from dying; Satan wanted them dead.

To the serpent's question, Eve replied, "We may eat fruit from the trees in the garden, but God did say, 'You must not eat fruit from the tree that is in the middle of the garden, and you must not touch it, or you will die'" (Genesis 3:2-3).

Eve got it mostly right. God never mentioned not touching the fruit, but that seems like a pretty good idea.

Next, Satan didn't even try to disguise the deception. He told a flat-out lie. His next words were the original lie. "You will not certainly die" (verse 4). The very first lie, and one of the greatest still: *God is not telling the truth; sin has no consequences.*

And finally, he told the greatest lie of all—*you can be like God.* "For God knows that when you eat from it your eyes will be opened, and you will be like God, knowing good and evil" (verse 5). In other words, "God doesn't know what He's talking about. He's holding out on you. You don't need Him. You can be your own god. The forbidden fruit will give you everything you ever wanted and more!"

> Boundaries God had established to protect them,
> Satan used to provoke them.

Almost every temptation we will ever face will start with these two thoughts: "I'd be happy if…" and "Did God really say…?" "If you play along with his line of questioning, before long you'll find yourself naked and ashamed. You'll wind up disoriented and disconnected from the voice of God that longs to call you by name in the cool of the day."[1]

Eve rejected the truth and believed the lie. She believed she could be like God and in control of her own life. "When the woman saw that the fruit of the tree was good for food and pleasing to the eye, and also desirable for gaining wisdom, she took some and ate it. She also gave some to her husband, who was with her, and he ate it" (verse 6).

And as Eve sank her teeth into the forbidden fruit, it settled in her soul and fermented into shame and condemnation. Her husband also felt the sickening rot of sin settle in his soul. Suddenly shame and fear entered the world, and Adam and Eve hid from God like wayward children.

Satan is not very creative, but he is effective. And he has been lying to us ever since that time in the garden. Why? Because it works.

ENEMY NUMBER ONE

I don't like to talk about the devil. I really don't. But to understand the battle plan for changing the way we think, we must know who the real enemy is. Your enemy is not your mother who hurt you, your father who abused you, your ex-husband who abandoned you, your friend who betrayed you, your employer who belittled you, or your child who dishonored you. Christians often operate like "blindfolded warriors. Not knowing who our enemy is, we strike out at each other."[2]

Listen, if we don't know who the real enemy is, then we can't win the battle. And I want to win! I want you to win! That means we've got to take a look at the enemy. He isn't going to be the focus of this book. He doesn't have the leading role; Jesus does. But he does have a role. And he is real.

A Barna poll asked Christians what they believed about the devil. Forty percent strongly agreed that Satan "is not a living being but a symbol of evil." Nineteen percent said they "agreed somewhat" with that perspective. Only 35 percent said they believed Satan is real, and 8 percent were not sure what they believed about the existence of Satan.[3]

No war has ever been won in the history of the world without a clear understanding of who the real enemy is. And the battle for our thought life is no different. This is our starting point.

As I mentioned at the beginning of this chapter, the enemy has many names. The name Satan means "adversary, one who resists." He is a created being. Just as God created man, He also created Satan. Oh, He didn't create him as the Evil One we know today. He created an angel named Lucifer, which means "morning star." However, Lucifer, like man, had a free will. At some point he chose to rebel against God and was thrown from heaven with one-third of the angels. We aren't told the exact details of Lucifer's fall from heaven, but two prophets, Ezekiel and Isaiah, have alluded to it (Ezekiel 28:12-17; Isaiah 14:12-15).

One thing we do know for sure is that Jesus said, "I saw Satan fall like lightning from heaven" (Luke 10:18). Jesus was there. We must always remember that while Jesus came to earth in bodily form at a certain point in history, He was before history began. "In the beginning was the Word, and the Word was with God, and the Word was God. He was with God in the beginning" (John 1:1-2). Jesus was. Jesus is. Jesus always will be.

When Satan was thrown from heaven, he took one-third of the angels with him into the final condemnation coming in the last days (Revelation 12:3). He has many aliases: prince of demons (Matthew 9:34), the god of this age (2 Corinthians 4:4), the ruler of the kingdom of the air (Ephesians 2:2), the accuser (Revelation 12:10), the father of lies (John 8:44), deceiver (Genesis 3:13), the great dragon (Revelation 12:9), the ancient serpent (Revelation 12:9), the devil (Revelation 12:9), and Satan, who leads the whole world astray (Revelation 12:9). Each one of these names reveals an aspect of his nature and tactics.

"Scripture depicts him opposing God's work (Zechariah 3:1), perverting God's Word (Matthew 4:6), hindering God's servant (1 Thessalonians 2:18), obscuring the gospel (2 Corinthians 4:4), snaring the righteous (1 Timothy 3:7), and holding the world in his power (1 John 5:19)."[4] Satan cannot dwell in a true believer because a true believer is sealed by and inhabited by the Holy Spirit. However, he can taunt, tempt, and trouble a believer by putting ideas and thoughts into the mind. He masks his thoughts as our own thoughts to get us to act in disobedience to God's will. However, the devil cannot make us do anything. He can only make the suggestion. And God always provides a way of escape (1 Corinthians 10:13).

One of his names is "deceiver." A deceiver is someone who presents a lie in such a way that it sounds like the truth. He tries to make you believe something is true when it isn't. He also tries to make you think something isn't true when it is. He speaks in your own voice. The thoughts feel like you and sound like you. He can't read your mind, but he watches to determine your specific struggles. Those present struggles and weaknesses, along with past hurts and failures, become the raw material with which he customizes lies just for you. And if you don't have enough pain in your past, he'll fabricate some.

Once I was in a Bible study group of 12 women when we were sharing some of the struggles from our childhoods we were having trouble letting go. At one point, one of my friends, who had remained quiet from most of the session, began to cry.

"You all have had such hardships in your lives. My childhood was wonderful. I'm a terrible person, and I don't have anyone to blame it on."

At that moment, I realized we were all fighting the wrong enemy. We were placing blame on people in our past rather than the deceiver, who wants to keep us stuck there. Do not allow the deceiver to deceive you about who the real enemy is.

His goal is for you to think a thought is your thought. When you repeat it often enough, it becomes your reality. You think it's true, but it's not.

When it comes to the devil, you don't have to outmuscle him, outsmart him, or outshoot him to be free of his influence. You just have to "outtruth" him, and we're going to get to that in just a bit.

When You Least Expect It
Did you notice when and how the enemy attacked in Genesis

chapter 3? I imagine Adam and Eve were simply minding their own business, gallivanting around the garden. Perhaps they were climbing trees or playing in the grass with cheetahs. Then the serpent slithered onto the scene, appearing out of nowhere. He's crafty like that.

I remember a September Tuesday when I was out in my garden, so to speak. It was mid-morning and I was taking a walk through the neighborhood. The sky was a clear, humid-free Carolina blue and the breeze was fall-crisp. I even sang a bit when I thought no one could hear. I felt all was right with the world. But it wasn't. Six hundred and twenty-three miles northeast of my little slice of momentary paradise, all hell was breaking loose. After my jaunt through the neighborhood, I came into the house with both my landline and my cell phone ringing. "Have you seen what's happening?" my husband said with panic in his voice.

"No," I replied. "I've been out walking. What is it?"

"Turn on the television. Start praying!"

I turned on the television and stared in horror as I watched what millions of Americans were watching as well.

American Airlines Flight 11, a Boeing 767 with 92 souls on board, took off from Boston's Logan International Airport en route to Los Angeles. Hijackers took over the plane, and 47 minutes after take-off, Mohammed Atta crashed the jet into floors 93-99 of the North Tower of the World Trade Center in New York City. Seventeen minutes later, hijackers crashed a second plane, United Airlines, Flight 175, with 65 souls aboard, into floors 75-85 of the World Trade Center's South Tower.

America was stunned. Shocked. Panic-stricken.

There was more. A third flight with 64 souls aboard, American Airlines Flight 77, left Dulles International Airport outside of Washington, D.C. It was also hijacked and flown into the western façade of the Pentagon in Washington, D.C., killing 59 aboard the plane and 125 military and civilian personnel inside the building.

For the first time in history, all flights over the entire United States were grounded. Arrows on the map showing flight patterns across the country disappeared.

At 9:59 a.m. on September 11, 2001, the South Tower of the World Trade Center collapsed. Twenty-nine minutes later the North Tower collapsed. Approximately an hour later, the 40 passengers and crew of a fourth plane, United Airlines Flight 93, heard the news about what was happening in New York City and Washington, D.C. In the passengers' attempt to overcome the hijackers on their plane, the plane crashed into a field in Somerset County, Pennsylvania, killing all aboard.

During the 9/11 attacks in 2001, 2996 people were killed and more than 6000 others were wounded. What started as a typical day morphed into one of the most tragic days in our country's history. *God, I whispered, we never saw it coming.*

That's how the enemy always attacks, He reminded me. *When you least expect it.*

Oh, friend, we must be prepared. We can't let our guards down and dance flippantly through life as if the enemy doesn't exist. No, we do not need to be afraid of him—not in the least. But we do need to be aware of the devil's schemes to hijack our true identity and waylay our God-given destiny. We need to be prepared when he attempts to crash into our towers of truth to demolish our faith when we least expect it.

God made sure the enemy's strategy to deceive the first man and woman was recorded in detail so we can learn from their mistakes and be prepared when the enemy attacks us as well. From Genesis to Revelation we can examine what he does and how he does it so we won't be "unaware of his schemes" (2 Corinthians 2:11).

Satan still whispers his lies and hijacks destinies. His goal is the same as it was in the beginning—to steal, kill, and destroy (John 10:10). And he is always looking for an opportune time (Luke 4:13). Usually when we least expect it.

Here's the good news. Are you ready for some good news? The battle has already been won. Jesus came to destroy the devil's work (1 John 3:8), and destroy it He did. But it takes practice for your mind, will, and emotions to catch up and catch on.

A man in the Arizona desert came upon a diamondback rattlesnake. With a hoe from the back of his car trunk, he cut off its head. Amazingly, the headless snake continued to shake its rattle and lunge at him.

"What's worse," the man said, "even though I knew its head was cut off, that he was dead, I still flinched."[5]

Satan has already lost the battle, but he continues to shake his rattle to draw our attention away from the truth of his defeat. And although he has lost the battle and Jesus has crushed his head under His heel (Genesis 3:15), he wants us to think he's still in control.

Satan does not give up on you when you become a Christian. He doesn't throw up his hands and say, "Oh well, I lost that one. I guess I'll move on to someone else." Quite the contrary. He knows who you are, what you have, and where you are as a child of God. He knows you are chosen, accepted, adopted, appointed, valued, justified, reconciled, redeemed, righteous, free from condemnation, holy, sealed, complete, and completely forgiven. His mission is to keep you from believing it. And he uses the same manipulative craftiness he used in the garden. That's why it's so important to understand what happened with the first man and woman. When he tries the same tricks on us, we'll be ready.

Paul exhorts us to "put on the full armor of God so that [we] can take [our] stand against the devil's schemes" (Ephesians 6:11). The Greek word used for "schemes" is *methodeia*. It's a method—a step-by-step, progressive plan. If he has a plan, then we need a plan. But he's not the only enemy we face when it comes to the battle for seeing ourselves as God sees us.

ENEMY NUMBER TWO

My brother was about four years old when he decided to grab a box of matches and a handful of sparklers to see how they worked. He had heard sparklers worked best in the dark, so he went into the darkest place he could find at Grandma's house—her wardrobe closet.

Stewart snuck into the darkness, crouched among the dresses and coats, and lit the first match. Immediately, the metal sticks began shooting fiery sparks in all directions. Within moments, he noticed more than sparklers on fire. Grandma's clothes were in flames. (I'm happy to say Stewart wasn't harmed, unless you count the spanking he got from Grandma.)

Friends, we don't have to go into a closet to find the darkness. It's waiting for us the moment we step out the front door. Just turn on the television to listen to the six o'clock news, and you know it's true. The world is full of darkness at every turn. No, the devil is not our only enemy. The Bible tells us our struggle is against the world, the flesh, and the devil.

What exactly is "the world"? The Bible gives several definitions. Sometimes *world* refers to all the people on the earth: "God so loved the world that he gave his one and only Son" (John 3:16). In some instances *world* refers to planet Earth itself (Genesis 11:1). At other times *world* refers to the world's values and mores (Romans 12:2). The world can be defined as "the whole system of humanity (its institutions, structures, values, and mores) as organized without God."[6] The ways of a culture oppose God, and Paul referred to this worldliness when he said, "Do not conform to the pattern of this world" (Romans 12:2). In other words, don't get so comfortable with the current culture that you fit right in without being any different. Jesus said the world hated Him and we shouldn't be surprised if it hates us as well (John 15:18-19). Both reflect the world's values or ways of thinking.

The Bible also tells us "the whole world is under the control of the evil one" (1 John 5:19). We seem to be splitting hairs here. But when we consider the power of the enemy and the pull of world systems, they are almost one and the same. Right now, the world systems are being heavily influenced by the Evil One.

But here's the hope. Jesus said, "But take heart! I have overcome the world" (John 16:33). As long as we live in the world, we will feel its pull. But God assures us we have what it takes to "overcome the world" (1 John 5:4-5). We have the power of the Holy Spirit living in us and faith in the Savior who works through us.

The world's lies say:

- Your value is based on your accomplishments.

- Your spouse must complete you and make you happy.

- If your husband no longer makes you happy, it's okay to leave him and find someone who does.

- You deserve to be happy at all cost.

- If it feels good, do it.
- Sex is a basic need.
- Waiting to have sex until after you're married is not practical.
- Success is measured by how much money you make.
- Your life is your own. Do what makes you happy.
- The more money you have, the happier you will be.
- The prettier you are, the happier you will be.

What the world tells us changes from one season to the next. What is wrong on one day may be right the next. What is despicable one day may be totally acceptable the next. But God's truth never changes.

ENEMY NUMBER THREE

Of all the activities ten-year-old Miriam enjoyed, she loved riding horses the most. Charlie, her favorite horse, had a sleek chestnut mane, well-defined, muscular legs, and a fierce, strong will to match. Miriam felt powerful and self-assured when controlling this massive animal—except when he caught a glimpse of the barn. Whenever Miriam and Charlie returned from a jaunt in the woods, as soon as they got close enough for him to see the barn, he bolted homeward, forcing Miriam to hang on to the reins for dear life.

One day her riding instructor witnessed this strong-willed animal taking control of his master.

"Miriam! What are you doing?" she called out. "You cannot let that animal control you in that manner! Bring that horse back out of the barn this instant."

Dutifully, Miriam mounted Charlie and led him a distance away from the stalls.

"Now," the wiser, older woman instructed, "when you turn around and Charlie sees the barn and begins to run toward it, turn your reins all the way to the right. Do not let him go forward."

On cue, Miriam steered her horse toward the stalls. On cue, Charlie began to bolt.

"Turn him! Turn him!" the instructor shouted.

Young Miriam pulled the reins to the right as hard as she could until the horse's head was inches away from touching his right shoulder. But instead of obeying her lead, Charlie fought her with 950 pounds of bone and muscle. Round and round the horse and rider circled.

"Don't let go," the instructor shouted. "You must break his will!"

After ten long minutes of going in circles, Miriam and Charlie both grew exhausted and quite dizzy. He stopped circling. She stopped pulling.

"Now gently tap him to see if he will walk toward the barn instead of run," the instructor commanded.

Charlie did not bolt, but walked at a steady pace. Miriam had broken this beautiful animal's will and regained control of him as he submitted to his master.

I see myself in Charlie. I have the tendency to do what I've always done—to revert to old habit patterns and thought patterns.

Before we head into the second step in the battle for our thought life, we must look at one more enemy to ponder: the flesh. From the time we are born, we receive messages about ourselves—some true, some false. We go through our lives doing whatever we think necessary to feel safe, secure, and significant. Between the time we're born physically and the time we're born again spiritually, we form certain habit patterns and thought patterns. Our unique way of getting our God-given needs met by our own strength and our own means is our unique version of the flesh.

As with the word *world*, *flesh* has several meanings in the Bible. One meaning is simply our bodies—our literal flesh and bones. The Bible says, "The Word became flesh and made his dwelling among us" (John 1:14). Jesus came in bodily form—flesh and bones.

But another use of *the flesh* refers to our sinful thought patterns and actions that develop over time, our mechanism for getting our needs met apart from Christ. Once we become a Christian, the desire to do things our way and in our own strength apart from God does not instantly go away. No one pushes the delete button on our old programming—our old thought patterns and actions. We experience a struggle between the flesh, with its preprogrammed thought patterns and actions that seek to please self, and the spirit, with its new thought patterns and actions that seek to please God.

When we become Christians, we're born again and have a new spirit within us. We are saved from the penalty of sin. However, as long as we live in an earthly body, we will battle with the power of sin. Our old fleshly desires war against our new spiritual desires. While we fight battles with the world on the outside, we also fight battles with the flesh on the inside—our mind, will, and emotions.

Charles Spurgeon said, "Beware of no man more than yourself; we carry our worst enemies within us." Sometimes we can be our own worst enemy.

The flesh's lies will say:

I've got to look out for myself because no one else will.
I deserve to eat that bag of chips.
I'm going to get even.
I'm going to quit. This is too hard.
I want what I want, and I want it now.
I'm better than that person.
My parents didn't love me, so no one ever will.
I've worked hard all week. I deserve as much wine as I want.

WHO TOLD YOU THAT?

"Put on your shoes," Cissy told her four-year-old granddaughter.

"I don't want to," Sarah said.

"I don't care if you don't want to. We need to go. Put on your shoes."

Defiantly, the stubborn preschooler put her hands on her hips, looked up at her grandmother, and said, "You're not the boss of me!"

"Oh yeah?" Cissy said. "Then who is?"

"God."

"Well, I work for Him," Cissy assured her. "Now put on your shoes."

Sister, make no mistake about it: The enemy is not the boss of you! God is! No matter what he says to you, you don't have to listen.

We've already looked at what happened when the serpent slithered into the garden and drew Eve into dialogue with the words, "Did God really say...?" Part of the problem was that she didn't recognize the lie or the liar.

After Adam and Eve disobeyed God, they hid. I don't know about you, but I've hidden a time or two. Maybe we don't hide behind a bush, but we do hide behind our own justifications and rationalizations. God asked two questions in Genesis chapter 3. The first was, "Where are you?" and the second was, "Who told you that?" God still calls out to us, "Where are you?" And He still asks, "Who told you that?"

As we move forward in this battle plan for changing the way we think, and look closely at the various lies we tell ourselves, I want you to hear God asking you, "Who told you that? Who is saying those things to you? Is it the echoes of the world? Is it whispers of the past? Is it old flesh patterns ingrained in your mind? Is it the devil disguising his voice as your own? Who told you that?"

The world, the flesh, and the devil are so intricately intertwined it's difficult to tell them apart. The *world* constantly seeks to pull us away from God by appealing to our flesh. The *flesh* defiantly tends to default to old thought and habit patterns. At the same time, John says, "We know...the whole world is under the control of the evil one" (1 John 5:19). The three are in cahoots, and it doesn't really matter which one is influencing you to tell lies about yourself. They're all in it together.

We defeat the devil every time we choose to listen to God's truth rather than the enemy's lies. We defeat the world every time we believe the Bible words rather than culture's ever-changing belief system. We defeat the flesh every time we act in a way that lines up with our new, born-again identity rather than our old, self-centered programming.

Francis Frangipane said, "The greatest battle that was ever won was accomplished by the apparent death of the victor, without even a word of rebuke to His adversary! The prince of this world was judged and principalities and powers were disarmed not by confrontational warfare, but by the surrender of Jesus on the cross."[7]

The purpose of this chapter has been to expose the enemy's true identity. However, the enemy is never to be our focus. Our focus is on Jesus Christ—the truth giver, the way-maker, victorious Savior, God's only Son, who defeated the enemy on the cross. Jesus Christ reigns supreme, and ministering angels surround us on every side (Hebrews

1:14). "Greater is he that is in you, than he that is in the world" (1 John 4:4 KJV).

Now we know the enemy's true identity. But more importantly, we know the Savior who has defeated him.

3

Recognize the Lies

Then you will know the truth,
and the truth will set you free.
JOHN 8:32

*D*ear Sharon," the letter began, "I found your email address on your website. I was searching for some information on what the Bible says about affairs. Somehow I came upon your site. I feel like I am on the verge of destroying my life. My life with my husband has never been good—marginal at best. I find myself working hard on my appearance so other men will notice and desire me. We have four children, and I'm miserable. My husband is in the military and away at boot camp. I'm glad he's gone.

"I am on the verge of having an affair with just about anyone to escape my marriage. I don't want to look back on my life and think I could have been happy with someone else. I feel like I am trapped in a loveless marriage. I want a divorce."

Can't you just see the enemy rubbing his hands together like a nasty fly? I bet he shuddered when she clicked the send button on her computer and her email came my way. "Oh no," I imagine him saying. "This could ruin everything."

THE MIND IS A NOISY PLACE

If you poke around the Internet, you'll see claims that the mind has about 50,000 to 70,000 thoughts a day. That seems high to me, but let's just say it's close. That's a lot of chatter! About one thought per second every waking hour.

Another study showed that 95 percent of our thoughts are habitual, meaning they are the same thoughts we thought about yesterday. To top it off, for the average person, 80 percent of those thoughts are negative. Scientists say our brains are "designed to take in and register negative experiences more deeply than positive experiences."[1]

Again, I'm not sure I buy all the numbers, but let's still say they're close. And remember, this is for the average person. I don't know about you, but I don't want to be the average person. I want to be aware of my thoughts and not leave them to chance. If we allow our thoughts to go unchecked, most likely the repetition of negative self-talk and lies will form ruts in our minds. We'll think about them again tomorrow, and the next day, and the next.

RERUNS, REPLAYS, AND REPEATS

When you consider the words in the letter at the beginning of this chapter, you can imagine how this woman had been thinking these same thoughts day after day. She didn't wake up one day and come to those conclusions. Disappointment in her life and in her husband had created so much internal chatter that she wasn't even able to hear the voice of God telling her anything different.

The lies she believed weren't really that different from the lies Eve believed in the garden. *God is holding out on me...I would be happy if...I'm going to take control of this situation...I don't care about the consequences...I want more...I deserve more...Anything is better than this.*

I can see the footprints of the enemy, who has trampled over this woman's heart and whispered lie after lie after lie—and she doesn't even know it. That's what makes the lies so effective—the average person doesn't know how to detect them.

We've looked at the first step to changing the way we think: Realize the enemy's true identity. He is doing everything in his power to keep Christians from experiencing the promises of God and walking in power and purpose. His goal is for us to live self-centered, miserable, lonely lives. His chief objective is our utter destruction, and his modus operandi is telling lies.

Now let's look at the second step in the battle for changing the way we think—recognize the lie.

COUNTERFEIT CADENCE

The Bible says, "We are not ignorant of [Satan's] schemes" (2 Corinthians 2:11 NASB). His schemes include a step-by-step, progressive plan of one lie that leads to another lie that leads to another lie. The lies begin small with seemingly insignificant consequences and gradually grow large with more destructive repercussions.

I'm so stupid.

I can't do anything right.

I'll never change.

Everyone would be better off if I weren't even alive.

Those thoughts are scary, aren't they? The real danger is when we agree with the thoughts and make them our own. The only way to stop the cadence is to recognize the deceit in the score. But the only way to recognize the lie is to know the truth. We must know the truth so when a counterfeit comes along we recognize its lack of authenticity.

When someone is training to become a bank teller, he or she is taught how to recognize counterfeit money. However, the instructors don't teach what counterfeit bills look like; they teach what genuine currency looks like. They study the markings, the coloring, and the feel of real money, so when the counterfeit comes along, the teller can recognize it. D.L. Moody once said, "The best way to show that a stick is crooked is not to argue about it or to spend time denouncing it, but to lay a straight stick alongside it."[2] God's Word is the only straight stick—the only measuring stick that matters.

Again, Paul wrote, "We are not unaware of [Satan's] schemes" (2 Corinthians 2:11). If Satan came to you in a little red suit with a pitchfork and announced himself as the devil, you wouldn't believe a word he said. But he is cunning and disguises himself as an angel of light (2 Corinthians 11:14). When he deceived Eve, he even quoted Scripture—albeit twisted and distorted.

He has a collection of old tapes from your past, and he pushes rewind and play, rewind and play. Oh yes, he knows which buttons to push. He also uses personal pronouns like "I" instead of "you." The thoughts sound something like this: *I am a failure. I am a loser. I can't do anything right. I'm ugly.* The thoughts sound like you, feel like you, and before you know it, you think they *are* you. That's the reason it's so difficult to detect the lies. They sound just like us.

In 1 Chronicles 21:1, the writer notes, "Satan rose up against Israel and incited David to take a census of Israel." Of course, David thought it was his own idea, but the Bible clearly states it was not. He would have never counted his fighting men if Satan had stood before him and said, "Hey, buddy, I know God wants you to depend on Him and His power, but I think you should count those fighting men just to make sure. You never know if God is going to come through for you. This way you'll know just how strong your army really is."

The devil knew David would have thrown him out by his hairy toe if he'd shown up in bodily form, so the crafty manipulator put the thought in David's mind. David thought it was his own idea, and off he went. Nine months later, when the census was complete, David felt guilty for his disobedience. God forgave David, but he still had to suffer the consequences of his actions.

Satan knows exactly which lies to whisper in your mind. He has watched you over the years and is well acquainted with your insecurities, weaknesses, and vulnerabilities. Do you tend to get discouraged? He will plant seeds of discouragement in your mind. Do you tend to struggle with rejection and loneliness? He will put ideas about rejection and loneliess in your mind. It's up to us to recognize the lies so we'll know how to defeat them.

We saw in chapter 2 how Satan came knocking on Eve's door and sold her a bag of lies, which she bought into hook, line, and sinker. He then moved on to her children—namely Cain.

Cain was not a happy boy. He was angry because God had accepted his brother's sacrifice and not his. God confronted Cain about his jealousy and anger. Apparently, it was written all over his face! God said to him, "Why are you angry? Why is your face downcast? If you do what is right, will you not be accepted? But if you do not do what is right, *sin is crouching at your door; it desires to have you,* but you must rule over it" (Genesis 4:6-7, emphasis added).

Kenneth Barker tells us, "The Hebrew word for 'crouching' is the same as an ancient Babylonian word referring to an evil demon crouching at the door of a building to threaten the people inside. Sin may be pictured here as just such a demon, waiting to pounce on Cain—it desired to have him."[3] Unfortunately, Cain did not master it, but let the lie of the enemy control his actions—just like his momma did. When I think of the word *pounce*, I envision a lion ready to spring on his prey. Interestingly, Satan is also referred to as just such an animal: "The devil prowls around like a roaring lion looking for someone to devour" (1 Peter 5:8). The moment we give in to the lies, Satan immediately changes his strategy to become the accuser who hurls accusations of shame and condemnation.

We've got the tools to recognize the lies. We simply need to know how to use them.

THE CONTROL PANEL

On July 16, 1999, John F. Kennedy Jr., his wife, Carolyn Bessette-Kennedy, and his sister-in-law, Lauren Bessette, met their death in a watery grave in the Atlantic Ocean. John was piloting a single-engine aircraft, and they were only a few miles from their destination when something went terribly wrong.

The plane left New Jersey en route to a family gathering in Massachusetts in the dark of night, and had to cross a 30-mile stretch of water. Its initial descent varied between 400 and 800 feet per minute. About seven miles from the approaching shore, the plane began a series of erratic turns, descents, and climbs. Its final descent eventually exceeded 4700 fpm, and the airplane nose-dived into the ocean. The water swallowed the plane and the three passengers on board.[4]

Other pilots flying similar routes on the night of the accident reported no visual horizon while flying over the water because of haze. They couldn't see a thing.

One pilot explained that John most likely experienced the "Black Hole" syndrome. Pilots of small-engine planes use the horizon as a reference point. However, John probably lost sight of the horizon, and his eyes gave the brain no clue as to which way was up and which way was down. In this situation, if an airplane should turn slightly or nose down slightly, the body's inner ear compensates to make the pilot believe he's flying straight and level. If for some reason the pilot makes another correction, he can make a bad decision worse.

John wasn't flying under Instrument Flight Rules, but rather Visual Flight Rules. That means he wasn't trained to use the instrument panel properly, but simply learned how to fly by sight alone. John no doubt became disoriented and his mind lost its sense of perspective and direction. He had what we commonly call vertigo, and the flight pattern showed all the evidence of "mind wobbling and tortured confusion." John's instruments told him his wings were tilted (flying sideways), but he felt he was right side up. While John had all the instruments on board for a safe landing, he didn't know how to use them.

One pilot explained John's probable vertigo and disorientation this way: "And here is the crux of the matter; the pilot's emotions drowned out the flight instrument's story about banking and diving at high speed, and screamed out, 'No way! It can't be. I'm actually flying straight and level. I know it!'"[5]

A skilled instrument flyer knows he can't rely on his feelings and regains control of the airplane by depending on the instruments. Instructors call this lifesaving skill "recovery from unusual attitudes." "The real skill of instrument flying is truly depending on the instrument's readings rather than your feelings. Recovery from 'unusual attitudes' consists of one essential belief: your feelings cannot be trusted as the final authority on what the airplane is doing. Your mind is boss. The instruments are your window on reality and you desperately need to understand the data they provide."[6]

Friend, I hope you are tracking with me. This isn't just about flying an airplane; this is about maneuvering through your thought life. John had everything he needed to make a safe landing right there on the instrument panel in front of him. He had the tools, but he didn't know how to use them. John relied on his feelings rather than the facts. His feelings lied, and he and his passengers died.

We can learn how to fly through the storms of life with limited visibility. We can maneuver safely through unexpected turbulence and relational malfunctions. God has given us the tools to avoid becoming disoriented and going into a tailspin or nosedive. His Word is the Truth that guides us through the inky soup when the horizon is nowhere in sight. His Word is the instrument panel. However, if we rely on our feelings, we won't know which way is up and which way is down.

By knowing how to use the instrument panel—the truth found in God's Word—we can recognize the lies and move ahead to the next step.

Robert McGee, author of *The Search for Significance,* wrote, "One of the biggest steps we can take toward consistently glorifying Christ and walking in peace and joy with our heavenly Father is to recognize the deceit which had held us captive. Satan's lies distort our true perspective, warp our thoughts, and produce painful emotions. If we cannot identify those lies, then it is very likely that we will continue to be defeated by them."[7]

WHATEVER IS TRUE

Paul gave us a sieve through which to filter our thoughts in Philippians 4:8-9:

> Finally, brothers and sisters, whatever is true, whatever is noble, whatever is right, whatever is pure, whatever is lovely, whatever is admirable—if anything is excellent or praiseworthy—think about such things. Whatever you have learned or received or heard from me, or seen in me—put it into practice. And the God of peace will be with you.

That's a lot to think about when thinking about what you're thinking about. In this book we're focusing on just the first directive: "Whatever is true." Once we determine what is true, we can make decisions based on facts rather than feelings. Emotions are powerful. Feelings are fickle. The truth is unchangeably secure.

Let's say you have a thought about yourself or your circumstances, and you're wondering if it's from the world, the flesh, or the devil. The big question is, is it true? Of course, the next question is, how do you know if it's true? The answer is in whether it lines up with or is contrary to God's Word. If it doesn't line up with Scripture—what God says about you or your circumstances—then it's a lie. Don't ponder it, play with it, or banter it around in your head. Stop the chatter.

Paul doesn't just leave us with the qualifying list; he gives us the means to implement it. "Whatever you have learned or received or heard from me, or seen in me—put it into practice."

It takes practice. Practice, practice, practice! And look at the result: "And the God of peace will be with you."

Here's another idea. If you're not sure if a thought is from God or the world, the flesh, or the devil, attach "in Jesus's name" to the end of it. For example:

I'm such a loser, in Jesus's name.

Hmm. Something about that just doesn't fit, does it?

How about this?

I made a mistake, but I know God forgives me when I ask, in Jesus's name.

Now that lines up with the truth.

PAY ATTENTION TO YOUR THOUGHT LIFE

Every weekday morning my husband's alarm clock goes off at five thirty. He gets up, showers, shaves, brushes his teeth, gets dressed, and places his jingling keys in his pocket. He clears his throat, blows his nose, and, well, does other noisy things. When he opens and closes the door leading to the garage, the alarm in the bedroom beeps three times—loudly. This happens every day, and I don't hear a thing. I sleep right through it. My body has grown so accustomed to his routine that I don't even hear the noise.

It's the same principle for anyone who has ever moved into a condominium, apartment, or house near a train track. The first night when the train comes barreling down the tracks, it wakes you up from a dead sleep and you think, *What was I thinking moving here? I'll never sleep through the night again!* But then, after about a week or so, you don't even notice the train. Your body grows accustomed to the noise, and you sleep right through it.

We can grow so accustomed to the lies that we don't even realize the chatter is there. We've got to pay attention and think about what we're thinking about.

David talked to himself regularly. In one psalm he wrote, "Awake, my soul!" (Psalm 57:8). The Hebrew word translated "awake" could be translated, "Pay attention! Open your eyes! Pay attention, soul!"

Check out these conversations he had with himself about himself.

- Why, my soul, are you downcast? Why so disturbed within me? Put your hope in God, for I will yet praise him, my Savior and my God (Psalm 42:5).

- Yes, my soul, find rest in God (Psalm 62:5).

- My soul...forget not all his benefits (Psalm 103:2).

- Return to your rest, my soul (Psalm 116:7).

- Praise the LORD, my soul (Psalm 103:1; 104:1; 146:1).

We can get so used to the lies that we don't even realize they're there. So now it's time to wake up! Pay attention! Be on the alert! Watch out!

PREPARE FOR TAKEOFF

Here we go again, I mused as the flight attendant began her routine instructions. I grabbed the magazine tucked in the seat pocket in front of me and began flipping through the pages. The man to my right continued reading the headlines in the day's newspaper. The woman to my left was a first-time flyer and paid close attention.

I glanced around the plane and noticed very few people listening to the flight attendant's lifesaving instructions. And then it hit me. The frequent flyers paid little attention, not because we were being rude, but because we had heard it all before. The safety procedures were routine information. The hum of the flight attendant's voice merged with the whine of the engine. We ignored her. However, the newbies paid close attention. But you better believe that if the pilot announced midflight that a crash landing was imminent, all of us "been there, done that" passengers would be reviewing those safety instruction cards tucked in the seat pocket in front of us quicker than you could say, "Buckle your seat belts."

Friend, we're getting ready to head into familiar territory for some. I'll be reviewing safety instructions you might have heard before. But read these truths from the Bible as if you are in danger of a crash landing. We never know when life will hit turbulence. Scrambling for the life jacket and fumbling with the oxygen mask on the way down is not the answer. We can be prepared so that when the storms hit or the engines fail, we'll be ready to land safely.

As you begin the process of detecting lies in your thought life, look objectively at any thoughts and attitudes that don't line up with Scripture. When you recognize and expose the lie, you disarm its destructive potential. I pray God will open your eyes to the power available to each and every one of His children who believe the truth (Ephesians 1:18-19).

Buckle up. Let's get ready to fly.

Reject the Lies

For though we live in the world, we do not wage
war as the world does. The weapons we fight with
are not weapons of the world. On the contrary,
they have divine power to demolish strongholds.
2 CORINTHIANS 10:3-4

Several years ago, my husband, my son, and I went on an excursion out West. We flew to Nevada, rented a car, and then proceeded to log in 2500 miles in ten days. We bounced around in a helicopter over the Grand Canyon, hiked the trails in Bryce Canyon, floated down an icy river in Zion National Park, and got too close to buffalo at Yellowstone National Park. Our last stop was Jackson Hole, Wyoming—cowboy country.

On Saturday night, we joined the locals at the weekly rodeo. It wasn't difficult to tell the tourists from the townsfolk. We were among the few with baseball caps and tennis shoes in the midst of a herd of Stetsons and cowboy boots.

The cowboys' skills entertained those of us who thought a bronco was a four-wheel drive. Cowboys, young and old, rode bucking broncos, raced around barrels, and conquered angry bulls. But the most nerve-racking event was the lassoing contest.

Even if you've never attended a rodeo, you probably know how the calf-roping contest works. Two chutes are side by side. Behind the door of one chute awaits an anxious young calf. Behind the door of the second chute awaits an eager cowboy mounted on his horse. When the roper is ready, he calls for the chute operator to pull a lever and release the calf. The calf runs as though its life depends on it. After it has a head start, another lever is tripped and the horse and rider explode through the second chute.

From a standstill, the cowboy digs his heels into the horse's flanks and forces it into a gallop—full speed ahead. With swinging lasso in hand, he pursues the little calf at lightning speed. The calf knows exactly where the exit is on the other side of the coral, and it runs as fast as its little hooves can take it in that direction. The cowboy rides up on the calf's heels, throws the lasso around its neck, and pulls the rope taut, forcing the calf to come to a hault. Then the rider hops off his horse, flips the calf on its side, and wraps another rope around three of the calf's legs. The rider's horse assists by backing up to keep the rope tightly drawn. When the calf is secured, the roper throws his hands in the air and the time clock stops. The time for capture is posted as the crowd applauds.

This happened time and time again as we watched to see who could capture and restrain his calf the fastest. I'll be honest; I was feeling sorry for the little calves, even though they were released as soon as the time was logged. I didn't like watching this one little bit. A few times the calf escaped the lariat and made its way through the exit. The first time that happened, I clapped wildly, whooped, and hollered. Several people glared. My husband made me stop.

Then God nudged me to pay attention. I was watching a perfect example of what Paul meant when he said to "take captive every thought." Specifically, he wrote, "We demolish arguments and every pretension that sets itself up against the knowledge of God, and we take captive every thought to make it obedient to Christ" (2 Corinthians 10:5).

Those calves reminded me of the lies that sometime run across my mind. Lies such as, *I can't do anything right...Nobody likes me...I'm not qualified...I'm so stupid...I'll never be successful...I'll always be average.* As soon as one of those thoughts comes bursting through the doorway of my mind and enters the arena of my thinking, I need to ride up on that thought's heels, lasso it with the truth of God's Word, and throw it back in the dirt where it came from. And the sooner I do it, the better.

LASSO THE LIES WITH THE TRUTH

So far, we have looked at the first two steps for changing the way we think and seeing ourselves and our circumstances through the lens of God's truth.

- Realize the enemy's true identity.
- Recognize the lies.

Now let's look at the third step:

- Reject the lies.

Yes, a fierce battle for our thought life wages in our minds. Negative chatter distorts who we are and distracts us from our destinies. Let's go back to 2 Corinthians 10 and take a deeper look at Paul's words.

> For though we live in the world, we do not wage war as the world does. The weapons we fight with are not the weapons of the world. On the contrary, they have divine power to demolish strongholds. We demolish arguments and every pretension that sets itself up against the knowledge of God, and we take captive every thought to make it obedient to Christ (2 Corinthians 10:3-5).

Many of the thoughts that rumble and tumble about in our minds have been there for a long time. We might not even know when or how they started. These pervasive and persistent thoughts can become what are called "strongholds." The Greek word for "stronghold" is *echo*, meaning, "to hold fast." It looks like our English word *echo*, and has a similar connotation: to echo again and again in someone's mind. A derivation of that same word, *echuroma*, means "a stronghold, fortification, fortress." A stronghold is a thought pattern that forms a fortress around the mind, holding it prisoner to faulty thinking. It's formed brick by brick with repetitive faulty thinking or all at once by a one-time traumatic event, such as a rape, molestation, or abuse.

These thought patterns have the potential to grab hold of a mind and rule a life. Many strongholds are built for protection, but inevitably become prisons. "No matter what the stronghold may be, they all have one thing in common: Satan is fueling the mental tank with deception to keep the stronghold running."[1]

In the Old Testament, a stronghold was a fortified dwelling used for protection from an enemy. David hid in wilderness strongholds when he was running from King Saul (1 Samuel 22:4; 23:14). These were usually caves high on a mountainside or some other structure difficult to attack. In the Old Testament, God is called our stronghold. "The LORD is a refuge for the oppressed, a stronghold in times of trouble" (Psalm 9:9). In other words, He is a place of protection and security.

In the New Testament Paul uses the Old Testament imagery of a fortress to describe a structure that keeps the enemy *in* rather than a structure that keeps an enemy *out*. An ungodly habit or habitual way of thinking can become a habitation for the enemy.

When we talk about strongholds, we're not talking about random thoughts or occasional sins. A stronghold is a thought pattern or habitual sin. It's a fortress built with the bricks of thoughts and held together by the mortar of emotions. Strongholds become our perception of reality.

A stronghold might be a thought such as:

- *I'm no good.*
- *I'm damaged goods.*
- *Nobody loves me.*
- *Nobody cares about me.*
- *I can't do anything right.*

A stronghold might be an addiction such as:

- Shopping
- Alcohol
- Sexual promiscuity
- Overeating
- Drug use

The enemy locks you up in hopes you'll never reach for the key within your reach—only a belief away. But look at the preceding words: *We have divine power to demolish strongholds.* The word *demolish* implies a kind of destruction requiring tremendous power—divine power. One reason many Christians are held hostage to memories of past sins, abuses, and lies of the enemy is that they swat at strongholds as if they're mosquitoes rather than blasting them with the truth as if they're concrete fortresses formed by years of construction. We cannot destroy strongholds with our own strength even on our best days. The Holy Spirit can destroy strongholds with His power even on our worst days.

The power of the Holy Spirit is the Greek word *dunamis*, which is where we get the word *dynamite*. To paraphrase 2 Corinthians 10:4, "the weapons we fight with are not the weapons of the world. On the contrary, they have divine power to *dynamite* strongholds." In other words, blow them to smithereens.

> We cannot destroy strongholds with our own strength even on our best days. The Holy Spirit can destroy strongholds with His power even on our worst days.

I don't want to give the impression that tearing down strongholds and changing old thought patterns is easy. We can grow so comfortable with our strongholds we don't even realize they're there. That was the case with me. I walked around saved but enslaved for many years. I dragged the ball and chain of inferiority, insecurity, and inadequacy around with me everywhere I went. I grew so accustomed to my limp that I didn't even notice it was there. "That's just the way I am," I said, shrugging.

I was comfortable with my weakness and served Satan a cup of tea every time I believed him. I hid away behind the wall he had helped me build. No, tearing down a stronghold of ingrained faulty thinking isn't easy, but it is simple. Recognize the lie. Reject the lie. Replace the lie with truth.

Second Corinthians 10:5 goes on to say, "We demolish arguments and every pretension that sets itself up against the knowledge of God." I don't know about you, but on a few occasions (okay, on more occasions than I can count), I have argued with God and against the knowledge of God. Interestingly, many of those arguments began with, "Did God really say...?"

The Greek word for *arguments* is *logismos,* meaning "a reckoning, calculation, consideration, reflection." A calculated thought might be a conclusion that you are a failure, after you have failed at something. It seems logical and all adds up. Upon reflection, it may seem highly probable. However, that's not what the Truth says. That "logic" is against the knowledge of God. Regardless of your calculations, God says you are a saint who has been given every spiritual blessing in the heavenly places, a child of God, and an heir with Christ. You have perhaps failed in your behavior, but that does not make you a failure in your identity. You may have failed (verb) but you are not a failure (noun). The best course of action is to reject the lie as soon as it crosses the threshold of your mind.

DON'T BUY WHAT HE'S SELLING

In my early years of marriage, door-to-door salesmen still roamed the earth. Yes, it was that long ago. Once I had a vacuum salesman come to my door. In my naiveté, I did the unthinkable. I let him in. Before I could convince him I didn't need a new vacuum cleaner, he had his demonstration trash sprinkled all over my foyer floor. He went on and on about the danger of pesky dust mites and hidden allergens that were going to ruin my family's health. *What kind of mother was I, anyway? Didn't I want to keep my family safe?* Mercy!

Almost two hours after he first stepped across the threshold of my home, I finally pushed him out the door. "Oh, Lord," I moaned as I leaned against the closed and bolted door. "What in the world just happened?"

And then in that still, small voice I heard, *You let him in.*

Yes, my first mistake was that I let the salesman cross the threshold of my doorway and enter my house. Once he was in, it was difficult to get him out. It's the same way with our thoughts. Once we entertain a thought, once we allow the "salesman" to scatter his "trash" in our minds, it's hard to dismiss him or push the lie back out. The easiest place for victory is at the threshold of the mind; don't even let the thought in the door. Reject the lie.

It's been said that every spiritual battle is won or lost at the threshold of the mind. I think victory is possible once the thought has passed over the threshold, but it's a lot easier to kick it out right away.

We have the power to take every thought captive and to make it obedient to Christ. Satan will try to post bail and set the lie loose again, but we have the power and the authority to lock it up and throw away the key.

TAKE UP THE SHIELD OF FAITH

We often think difficult people or circumstances are the source of our problems. I love what one pastor said: "Your problem is that you don't know what the problem is. You think your problem is your problem, but that's not the problem at all. Your problem is not your problem and that's your main problem." Now chew on that for a while.

Paul put it this way: "Our struggle is not against flesh and blood, but against the rulers, against the authorities, against the powers of this dark world and against the spiritual forces of evil in the heavenly realms" (Ephesians 6:12). As long as we think our foe is a mere mortal, the enemy is sittin' pretty. But we've already realized his true identity. Now we're focusing on recognizing the lie and rejecting the lie.

This spiritual battle is described as a "struggle." It literally means "wrestling" or "hand-to-hand" combat.[2] In other places in the New Testament, Paul mentions this spiritual battle. He told Timothy to "fight the good fight of the faith" (1 Timothy 6:12). And he said of himself, "I have fought the good fight, I have finished the race, I have kept the faith" (2 Timothy 4:7). He encourages Timothy to endure hardship as a "good soldier of Christ Jesus" (2 Timothy 2:3).

Yes, Jesus won the victory over sin and death when He died on the cross and rose again. Satan was defeated, and we have been saved from the penalty of sin. However, until we leave this earth and the presence of sin, we continue to fight against the power of sin. A big part of that battle is recognizing the lies and rejecting the lies that hold us captive to a life that's less than God's best.

We don't need to be afraid of this battle. It's the devil who needs to be shaking in his boots—if he ever wears any. Once you know the battle plan, he hasn't got a chance. As a believer in Christ, you have the power of the Holy Spirit working in you and for you. But you must know how to access that power.

Paul concludes his letter to the Ephesians with these words:

> Finally, be strong in the Lord and in his mighty power. Put on the full armor of God, so that you can take your stand against the devil's schemes. For our struggle is not against flesh and blood, but against the rulers, against the authorities, against the powers of this dark world and against the spiritual forces of evil in the heavenly realms. Therefore put on the full armor of God, so that when the day of evil comes, you may be able to stand your ground, and after you have done everything, to stand. Stand firm then, with the belt of truth buckled around your waist, with the breastplate of righteousness in place, and with your feet fitted with the readiness that comes from the gospel of peace. In addition to all this, take up the shield of faith, with which you can extinguish all the flaming arrows of the evil one. Take the helmet of salvation and the sword of the Spirit, which is the word of God (Ephesians 6:10-17).

While Paul tells us to take up the full armor of God, the shield of faith captures my attention here. The belt, breastplate, and sandals or boots were worn continually in battle, but the helmet, sword, and shield were worn only when the fighting began. When speaking of the shield, Paul is describing a large Roman shield covered with leather, which could be soaked in water and used to put out flame-tipped arrows.[3] As Satan shoots his fiery lies, we can hold up our shield of faith (what we know to be true) to block the lies and extinguish their flames.

And we must block them right away. For example, when I make a mistake, Satan whispers the thought into my head, *I'm so stupid.* As soon as the thought enters my mind, I can do one of two things: I can believe the lie and make it my truth, or I can reject the lie by saying, "That's not true. That is a lie of the enemy. I made a mistake, but I have the mind of Christ."

One thing we can learn from Eve is this: Do not dialogue with the devil. Don't engage in conversation with him or argue with him. Once you start dialoguing with the enemy, it's hard to stop. And you will never come out unscathed. The best course of action is to reject the lie right away. I wish we could put the devil on a "do not call" list, but we can't. However, we can choose to not answer the phone.

I think a phrase from the 1990s should be resurrected. It went like this: "Talk to the hand, 'cause the face isn't listening." People held up one hand like a stop sign toward the person they were saying no to. The phrase meant, *I'm not listening to a thing you say.* We can say that to the devil when he tries to engage us in conversation to try to confuse us or condemn us.

Certain television jingles drive my husband crazy. As soon as a nanosecond of the offending commercial appears, he presses the mute button. And while I tease him for being a commercial phobic, you know what happens to me if I listen to the jingle? I end up with that silly song in my head for the rest of the evening. He has the right idea—mute it, delete it, don't give it a chance to enter your mind.

EXTINGUISH THE FIERY ARROWS

Rosa stood in line for nearly an hour waiting for everyone else to clear away. She was a beautiful Latina woman attending a conference where I spoke in Mexico City. With the help of an interpreter, Rosa poured out her heart. When she was in her twenties, she married and had two small children. Her husband was not pleased when she discovered she was pregnant with their third child. "You cannot have another baby," he said. "You must have an abortion or I'm going to leave you."

Rosa was torn. Like her husband, she did not want this baby. Her marriage was in shambles, their finances were in ruins, and she was exhausted trying to keep up with the two little ones she already had.

Her religious convictions told her abortion was wrong, but the fear of living without her husband's support drove Rosa to an abortion clinic. Then, before the procedure began, she changed her mind and ran from the building.

"I did not have the abortion," Rosa said with tears in her eyes, "but I wanted to. My daughter is now 21 years old and has been the joy of my life. Of all my children, she treats me the best. But I have carried this guilt around with me all these years. How could I have considered aborting her? What kind of person am I?"

Rosa broke down in sobs as I and the interpreter tried to comfort her. She had asked God to forgive her, and she truly believed He had. But she could not forgive herself. For 21 years, Satan had whispered a lie into her heart: *This is the child you didn't want. This is the child you almost killed. What kind of person are you?*

Rosa had believed the lie, but on that day, as we took our stand, Rosa held up her shield of faith and extinguished the fiery arrows.

"Rosa, do you believe God forgave you?"

"Yes."

"Do you believe that what Jesus did for you on the cross was enough to pay for the penalty of your sins?"

"Yes."

"Do you believe 1 John 1:9 that says if you confess your sins, God is faithful and just and will forgive your sins and purify you from all unrighteousness?"

"Yes."

"Sister, you are forgiven. The enemy is lying to you and whispering words of shame and condemnation. He is the accuser, but God has already stamped 'Not guilty' on your heart. The devil has been shooting his fiery arrows of shame right at you. Hold up the shield of faith and speak truth to the lies."

Rosa chose to reject the lie. She held up her shield of faith that day...and the next...and the next...and the next.

C.S. Lewis wrote, "Relying on God has to begin all over again every day as if nothing yet had been done."[4] Life is daily, and the victory over the lies can be too.

STAND UP TO THE BULLIES

Notice how many times Paul admonishes us to *stand* in Ephesians 6:13-14. "Therefore put on the full armor of God, so that when the day of evil comes, you may be able to *stand* your ground, and after you have done everything, to *stand. Stand* firm then..." No one can stand for us. We must stand on our own two feet and *stand up* against the enemy—and *we stand on* the Word of Truth to do it.

Being from North Carolina, I love the old black-and-white *Andy Griffith Show*. In one episode, the neighborhood bully is picking on Opie. This blond-headed newcomer taunts and makes fun of Opie until he feels like a total loser. He's ashamed of his own cowardice and embarrassed in front of his friends. After Andy, the wise father, figures out what is disturbing his moping son, he gives him a little lesson in standing up to bullies. The next day, when the bully threatens Opie, the little freckle-faced boy looks his opponent in the eye and refuses to crumble under his threats.

"Do you want to fight?" the bully taunts.

Opie doesn't say a word. He just puts up his fists.

"Oh yeah? Well, knock this rock off my shoulder and I'll—"

Opie knocks the rock off his shoulder before the bully has time to finish his sentence.

"Oh yeah? Well, step into this circle," the bully continues as he draws a circle around himself in the dirt.

Opie steps into the circle.

Suddenly, the bully grows nervous. "You better be glad I've got on my good pants," the bully says as he backs away.

Opie never had to throw the first punch. All he did was stand his ground and the bully backed away. Bullies don't like it when we stand our ground. Never have. Never will.

Paul said, "Now it is God who makes both us and you stand firm in Christ. He anointed us, set his seal of ownership on us, and put his Spirit in our hearts as a deposit, guaranteeing what is to come" (2 Corinthians 1:21-22).

In his book *The Reason for God*, Timothy Keller said this:

> If anything threatens your identity, you will not just be anxious but paralyzed with fear. If you lose your identity through the failings of someone else, you will not just be resentful but locked into bitterness. If you lose it through your own failings, you will hate or despise yourself as a failure as long as you live. Only if your identity is built on God and his love...can you have a self that can endure anything, face anything.[5]

Maybe you've been running from the bully for way too long. Go ahead and take your stand. He'll probably slink away because he has his good pants on.

REST ASSURED IN THE TRUTH

It was another crazy adventure my husband talked me into—down the treacherous, snake-infested Amazon River.

Steve and I sat anxiously in our seats. I wondered if I was going to be able to endure the ride, especially knowing my propensity for motion sickness. But we began nonetheless.

The guide strapped all passengers into the tiny boats and gave last-minute instructions. Of course, there were life preservers, but what good would they do in the rapids that threatened to suck their prey below the surface?

The crew boarded and began the journey down the mysterious Amazon. The calm, meandering waters quickly gave way to fierce torrents, rushing rapids, and rocky crags protruding from the foaming waters. Alternating between plunging into the water and flying into the air, the boat made its way through the first set of rapids. My body relaxed, thankful that was over. But several times along the journey, calm gave way to chaos as passengers maneuvered to keep the boats afloat. Often, I closed my eyes and waited for the turbulence to pass.

When we finally reached the end of our journey, I picked up my popcorn and walked out of the theater.

I wasn't really on the Amazon River strapped in a tiny boat. I was comfortably sitting in a cushiony chair in an IMAX theater watching a documentary about the Amazon River. On the five-story domed screen covering 6532 square feet of projection surface, large images put you in the center of the action, and the surround sound gave the illusion you were indeed wherever the screen said you were. It wasn't real.

Yes, I did get a bit queasy from the larger-than-life movement down the river, but I was never in real danger. Even though the producers and director tried their best to create a realistic experience, I knew it wasn't true. It was a movie. I would walk out unscathed.

That is the peace of walking, or in this case sitting, in the truth. When you recognize the lie and reject the lie, you will have peace.

- Realize the enemy's true identity.
- Recognize the lies.
- Reject the lies.

5

Replace the Lies with Truth

Brothers and sisters, whatever is true...
think about such things.
PHILIPPIANS 4:8

For 15 years, Leanne was emotionally and verbally abused by her mother. Every day she heard she was a stupid, worthless failure. Her mother told her she was ugly and fat and not good enough. "No man will ever want you," she said.

Leanne grew up afraid of women and hating herself. *Why can't I be different?* she wondered. She believed her mother's estimation of her and lived in silent defeat. Leanne grabbed attention and approval any way she could, and by the time she was 23 years old, she had three abortions on her medical record. The guilt and shame of those abortions compounded her feelings of worthlessness.

But something amazing happened to Leanne when she was 24. She accepted Jesus as her Lord and Savior and became a new creation. She knew God had forgiven her the moment she asked Him to—totally and completely. However, the enemy continued reminding her of the terrible mistakes of her past. *How could I have killed my children? What would my friends think if they knew the truth? I can never let anyone know about my past. Some things are simply unforgivable in human eyes.*

Leanne met and married a wonderful Christian man. They began their life of ministry as he pastored a church in a small community. God blessed them with three children, but still the shame of her past lingered.

"I felt so unworthy of my husband's love," she told me. "I felt I wasn't good enough to be his wife. I never told him about my past. It was a secret that weighed me down."

Leanne went to a women's retreat and picked up one of my books, *Your Scars Are Beautiful to God.* For the first time, she began to heal from the wounds her mother had inflicted on her little-girl heart. She realized it was the deceiver who taunted her with the lie that what she'd done was unforgivable. He was the one who heaped shame and condemnation on her anew every day. The enemy pushed rewind and play on the mental reel of her mother's words of discouragement, disparagement, and disregard.

She did something that made the enemy mad. She forgave her mother. Even though her mother had since died, she forgave her as if she were standing before her that very day.

Then Leanne imagined Jesus erasing all her faults, especially the ones her mother had so maliciously and meticulously written on the chalkboard of her mind. "All gone," she said. "I'm set free."

But one more step to Leanne's freedom was necessary. As long as she kept her past a secret, she would never be totally free. The enemy would continue to pull out the memory at the most opportune times. She knew she had to tell her husband.

"I prayed all day and night for the courage to tell my husband about the three abortions. Except for personnel at the clinics, no one in the world knew about the abortions but me. I had to tell my husband the secret so Satan couldn't use it against me any longer.

"Finally, I did it. I told him the truth. But he didn't react the way I imagined he would. He held me in his arms and cried. 'I can't believe you've held on to this for so long alone,' he said. He was amazing.

"I am no longer shameful. I am pure.

"I am no longer ugly. I am beautiful.

"I am no longer unlovable. I am dearly loved."

Leanne recognized the lies, rejected the lies, and replaced the lies with truth. She is now walking in the truth as a holy, chosen, dearly loved child of God.

We are now at our fourth step to changing the way we think and seeing our identity and our circumstances through the lens of God's Word—*replace the lies with truth*. Who better to teach us how to do this than Jesus Himself?

FIGHTING BACK WITH THE TRUTH

"Repent and be baptized!" the prophet called to those gathered around the Jordan River. People from all around Jerusalem and Judea came to hear this man called John preach about forgiveness and repentance of sins. They wondered if he could be the Messiah, but John assured them he was not. "I baptize you with water," he said. "But one who is more powerful than I will come, the straps of whose sandals I am not worthy to untie. He will baptize you with the Holy Spirit and fire" (Luke 3:16).

One day John saw Jesus emerge from the crowd. John held out his arms and proclaimed, "Look, the Lamb of God, who takes away the sin of the world!" (John 1:29). Jesus presented Himself for baptism, and as He came up from the water, the clouds parted, a dove descended, and God spoke: "You are my Son, whom I love; with you I am well pleased" (Luke 3:22).

It was a red-letter day on the kingdom calendar when the culmination of God's incredible plan of redemption was set into motion. And where was Jesus's first assignment? It was in the desert, face-to-face with His nemesis—the devil He came to destroy:

> After fasting forty days and forty nights, he was hungry. The tempter came to him and said, "If you are the Son of God, tell these stones to become bread." Jesus answered, "It is written: 'Man shall not live on bread alone, but on every word that comes from the mouth of God'" (Matthew 4:2-4).

Wait a minute. What does he mean, "If you are the Son of God..."? Didn't God just say in chapter 3, "You are my Son; whom I love..."? Yes, He did. Friend, the deceiver will do the same to you. When you begin to take hold of the truth of your true identity in Christ and the powerful promises of God, the devil will say to you, *If you were a child of God... Then He would answer your prayer.*

Then He would give you what you want.
Then He would make you happy.
Then He would make you successful.
Then He would...

The devil knows exactly who you are and what you have as a child of God. His goal is to cause you to doubt and question the truth.

How did Jesus defeat the devil? He pulled out the sword of the Spirit—the Word of God—and plunged it into Satan's lie. He recognized the lie, rejected the lie, and replaced the lie with truth.

Once again the devil taunted Him and took Him to the highest point of the temple. "If you are the Son of God," he said, "throw yourself down. For it is written: 'He will command his angels concerning you, and they will lift you up in their hands, so that you will not strike your foot against a stone'" (4:6).

Once again, Jesus recognized the lie, rejected the lie, and replaced the lie with truth: "It is also written: 'Do not put the Lord your God to the test'" (4:7).

Again, the devil took Jesus to a high mountain and showed Him all the kingdoms of the world and their splendor. "All this I will give you," he said, "if you will bow down and worship me" (4:9).

Again, Jesus wielded the sword of the Spirit, the Word of God. "Away from me, Satan! For it is written: 'Worship the Lord your God, and serve him only'" (4:10).

Defeated, Satan tucked his tail and slunk away to wait for an opportune time (Luke 4:13). Yes, he left Jesus alone that day, but he declared, "I'll be back." And come back he did.

While Jesus's temptations are similar to ours in nature, they were specific to His particular challenges. For example, Satan would probably not tempt you to turn a stone into bread; his temptations would be customized to fit your particular struggles. *If you were a child of God, wouldn't He send you a husband? Give you a baby? Make you successful? Heal your sickness?* Unless we intentionally overpower the lies with the truth, the lies will become our truth.

Jesus knew who He was. He trusted in God when He said, "You are my Son, whom I love; with you I am well pleased." So the question is, will we trust those words as well? Allow God to baptize you in the affirmation that you are His daughter, whom He loves; and with you He is well pleased.

Allow God to baptize you in the affirmation that you are His daughter, whom He loves; and with you He is well pleased.

Jesus won the battle in the wilderness by being preloaded with the truth. Oh, dear one, how foolish we are to think the garden is where our lives will be trouble free. Our circumstances do not determine a life of joy and victory. Jesus experienced victory in the desert. Eve experienced defeat in comfort and ease.

BELIEVING THE TRUTH

Lies can become a haunting hum in your head, like a song you just can't shake. And the best way to get the annoying tune out of your mind is to replace it with a new one. As King David wrote, "He put a new song in my mouth" (Psalm 40:3). If we've been taunted by the lies, we need to do the same.

One Christmas I had "Frosty the Snowman" stuck in my head. I don't know why. I don't even like the song. Every time I got quiet, that silly tune popped into my mind, and the next thing I knew I was humming it. I didn't want to; it just automatically came.

Finally, my husband said, "Sharon, if you want to get that song out of your head, you've got to start singing a new one."

He was right. I picked a new song to sing. Even then, I had to intentionally sing the new song to get rid of the old one.

As we've already seen, a battle is going on for our thought life, and this is where the fighting heats up. We've realized the enemy's true identity, recognized the lies, and rejected the lies. Now it's time to pull out the sword of the Spirit, the Word of God, and cut the enemy down to size. Jesus didn't win the battle by outsmarting or out muscling the devil. He won the war by out *truthing* him. If it worked for Jesus, it will work for you.

> Jesus won the battle in the wilderness by
> being preloaded with the truth.

One of the primary messages of the book of John is truth. *Truth* is one of the most repeated words spoken by Jesus and the most recorded word in John's Gospel—77 times in the New International Version. To cite a few examples (emphasis added)...

- The law was given through Moses; grace and *truth* came through Jesus Christ (John 1:17).

- Whoever lives by the *truth* comes into the light, so that it may be seen plainly that what they have done has been done in the sight of God (John 3:21).

- You will know the *truth,* and the *truth* will set you free (John 8:32).

- Jesus answered, "I am the way and the *truth* and the life. No one comes to the Father except through me" (John 14:6).

- [Jesus prayed], "Sanctify them by the *truth*; your word is *truth*" (John 17:17).

The truth waters us, feeds us, matures us, sustains us, frees us, heals us, cleanses us, transforms us, and empowers us. Many times Jesus began a statement with, "I tell you the truth." Why did He do that? I believe He was trying to get our attention, to emphasize His point, and to let us know He is trustworthy. He wants us not only to believe *in* Him, but to believe Him.

The voice you listen to will determine your destiny. When you choose to listen to the Truth, you will live a life based on truth.

DISCOVERING THE TRUTH

John begins his account of the gospel, "In the beginning was the Word, and the Word was with God, and the Word was God. He was with God in the beginning" (John 1:1-2). The Greek word for "Word" is *logos* and refers to the entire expression of God revealed to man. It is the direct revelation of God to man.

Another Greek word translated "word" is *rhema*. As *logos* is the entire Word of God, *rhema* is a passage of Scripture God quickens to your spirit. As we store up the *logos* of God in our hearts, God will open our eyes to understand a personal *rhema*. This may occur when you're reading the Bible or when the Holy Spirit brings a verse or passage you have previously read to mind. Jesus promised, "But the Advocate, the Holy Spirit, whom the Father will send in my name, will teach you all things and will remind you of everything I have said to you" (John 14:26).

When two people read the same passage of Scripture, one may see something that speaks to her about a specific situation she's experiencing while the other moves along unaffected. This happens often with my husband and me as we're reading the Bible or listening to a sermon together. I get all excited: "Man, did you hear that? Did you see that?" Steve just looks at me and says, "Sure, honey." Then I know I have just experienced a *rhema* from God specifically for me. At other times, Steve gets out his marker and with a gleam in his eye highlights a passage meant just for him. God is personal and intimate with each of His children, and He has specific revelations for anyone who takes the time to study His Word.

Now, let's go back to Paul's letter to the Ephesians, specifically focusing on the armor of God in chapter 6. We looked at how to use the shield of faith to reject the lies in chapter 4. Now let's pull out the sword of the Spirit and chase Satan off for good.

Paul writes, "Take the helmet of salvation and the sword of the Spirit, which is the word of God" (Ephesians 6:17). Guess which Greek word is used for "word"? *Rhema*—a particular word the Holy Spirit brings to our remembrance. But remember, for the Holy Spirit to bring a *rhema* to our remembrance, the *logos* has to first be deposited in our minds.

TELLING YOURSELF THE TRUTH

When God created man, He created us in three parts: body, soul, and spirit. The earthly body is the part we see and houses the five senses.

It is temporary and lasts for only a short time, though it will be transformed at the resurrection. The spirit is the inner man that communicates with God and lives for eternity. This is the part of us "born again" when we come to Christ.

The third part of man, the soul, is what makes up our personality. It is made up of three parts: mind, will, emotions. We receive information into our minds, we act on that information with our will, and we feel a response with our emotions. The brain is part of the body and is different from the mind. The mind uses the brain just as we use a computer to store, enter, and search for information.

Think of it like an apple. The peel is your body—the part you see. The inside under the peel is the soul—the mind, will, and emotions. The seed or core is the spirit—the part that determines the identity of the apple, be it Granny Smith or Red Delicious.

From the day we're born physically to the day we're born again spiritually, we develop habit patterns and thought patterns to get our God-given needs of safety, security, and significance met apart from God. These thought patterns are stored in our minds, on the hard drive, and become the operating system our actions and emotions depend on for direction. The input for the computer comes from the messages we receive and how we interpret the data.

When we become a new creation in Christ, no one pushes the delete button to remove the old ways of thinking; rather, we must participate with God to reprogram the computer, the mind. Paul teaches, "Do not conform to the pattern of this world, but be transformed by the renewing of your mind" (Romans 12:2). As we begin to recognize the lies, reject the lies, and replace the lies with truth, we will be renewing our minds to think biblically and truthfully. Once we change our thinking, our actions and reactions (or emotions) will also change. We cannot act differently than we think, so real change begins in the mind.

In my backyard, I have a small fountain without a plug or drain hole. Often it gets murky with leaves and other debris. Since I can't pull a plug to drain it, I had to come up with another way to clean it out. I simply put a hose in the fountain and fill it to overflowing with clean water. As the clean water fills the fountain, the debris-filled water spills over the edge. The clean water flows in and displaces the dirty water until it is crystal clear once again.

That's what happens as we fill our minds with the truth. It displaces and replaces the lies. The more we tell ourselves the truth, the less debris will muddy our thoughts. I've often longed for a plug to pull so the old thoughts could drain from my brain, but it just doesn't work that way. More often than not, though, God uses a truth to displace the lie rather than simply removing the lie and leaving an empty space.

Renewing your mind is somewhat like replacing wallpaper. Getting the old paper off is the hard part. When I replaced the wallpaper in my bathroom, it was an arduous and time-consuming task. I scored the paper with a sharp instrument, wiped down the wall with a stripping solution, and attempted to peel the old paper from the wall. But it didn't come off easily. I'd get so excited when I peeled off a large piece. I could feel those endorphins kicking in! But most of the time, I had to pick off the old paper little pieces at a time. With my fingernails and a putty knife, I picked at it for days. I knew if I left even a little bit of residue on the bare sheetrock, it would show up as a lump under the new wallpaper.

I wish I could tell you re-wallpapering your mind is easy, but it's not. Oh sure, sometimes you get a big piece to come off all at once. Or a great mental and spiritual breakthrough pulls down a big chunk of that old thinking. But most of the time it's a tedious process that takes patience and determination.

Psychiatrist Paul Meier conducted a study on the effect of meditation among seminary students. He concluded, "Daily meditation on Scripture, with personal application, is the most effective means of obtaining personal joy, peace, and emotional maturity...On average, it takes about three years of daily Scripture meditation to bring about enough change in a person's thought patterns and behavior to produce statistically superior mental health and happiness."[1]

You can hire someone to change the wallpaper in your house, but you can't hire anyone to change the wallpaper in your mind. You must do it yourself by rejecting the lies and speaking the truth about yourself to yourself. Author Seth Godin wrote,

People don't believe what you tell them.
They rarely believe what you show them.
They often believe what their friends tell them.
They always believe what they tell themselves.[2]

You and I will never change the way we think because someone tells us to. It will only happen when we tell ourselves the truth. Rehearse it. Speak it. Believe it. The thoughts you consume will eventually consume you. Make them count.

Let me make this clear. I am *not* advocating name it and claim it. I am not saying that if you repeat *I am a millionaire, I am a millionaire, I am a millionaire,* you will become a millionaire. Or that if you repeat *I am going to meet my future husband, I am going to meet my future husband, I am going to meet my future husband,* you will meet your future husband. This is not about visualizing or naming what you want in order to get what you want. That smacks of New Age teaching and distorts the true meaning of Christian faith—elevating man's desires above God's will. You will never see Jesus teaching about how to have a materialistic, carefree life. He preached quite the opposite.

The thoughts you consume will eventually consume you.

What I *am* advocating is repeating and rehearsing the truths about your true identity and the promises of God as found in the Bible. Realigning your thoughts with God's thoughts is the key to living fully and free.

One more thing: Replacing the lies with the truth is not about positive thinking. It's about truthful believing—lining up your thought life with God's Word. Positive thinking isn't bad, but that's not what we're talking about here. Oh, friend, believing the truth is so much more.

PRACTICING THE TRUTH

If you have believed the lies of the enemy rather than the promises of God for a long time, it will take consistent practice to reprogram your thinking. Sometimes we're hesitant to embrace the truth about who we are as children of God: holy, chosen, redeemed, and dearly loved. We find it easier to believe the lies, because they are what we've heard all our lives.

The more you rehearse thinking the truth about who you are, the more your thoughts will line up with who God says you are. The more you recite the promises of God, the easier it will be to make them yours.

I remember sitting with my country grandmother watching a program about Neil Armstrong walking on the moon. "That's a bunch of hogwash," Grandma spat. "There's no way that man walked on the moon. He's just walking around on some television set. I'll never believe that's real."

A man walking on the moon was just too far-fetched for Grandma Edwards. She never believed it was true. But it was. Some Christians think their new identity in Christ is too far-fetched to be true. They never do believe it's true. But it is. And even though the devil can do nothing to make your true identity less true than it is at the moment you come to Christ, he can try his best to keep you from believing it.

Paul reminds us an "incomparably great power" is available for those who believe (Ephesians 1:19). The truth is the truth, whether or not we believe it. However, the truth won't have power in our lives until we *do* believe it.

The way you think about yourself will become the way you see yourself, whether it's true or false. Eventually, you'll believe what you tell yourself. If you tell yourself negative, distorted statements about yourself, you will act in negative, destructive ways. If you replace the lies with the truth about who you really are, then you will begin to walk, talk, and live like the child of God you already are.

Your beliefs affect your behavior. You cannot act differently from what you believe. And it takes practice. When my son was four years old, we decided it was time to take the training wheels off his little red bicycle. With a mixture of fear and excitement, Steven mounted the seat with my hand on the back fender to help keep him steady. He placed his feet on the pedals and wobbled his way across the lawn as I ran alongside him to keep him from falling. After a few trial runs, it was time for me to let go. When he noticed I was no longer running beside him, Steven panicked and tumbled to the ground.

"I can't do it," he cried.

"Sure you can," I said, cheering him on. "Once you get the hang of it, riding your bike will be the funnest thing you do as a kid. Let's try again."

For about 30 minutes Steven attempted to steady the bicycle on his own. Finally, he threw the bike to the ground, stood with his hands on his munchkin hips, and announced in frustration, "I can't do it. This is not fun, and it will never be fun!"

We put the bike away.

You can guess what happened. Several days later, once the frustration had abated, Steven mounted the bike and tried again. This time his body worked in tandem with the bike, and he mastered the fine art of bicycle riding. The following weekend, when we went to visit his grandma, he insisted that we take his bicycle. For hours he peddled around her cul-de-sac. It was the funnest thing he ever did as a kid.

> Your beliefs affect your behavior.

Changing old thought and habit patterns isn't as easy as learning how to ride a bike. It takes more practice. At first we may fall and skin our knees, wobble instead of ride steady, and battle with frustration. But when we fall, we simply get back up and try again.

The four steps we've learned so far aren't magical, but they are biblical. The change won't happen overnight, but with practice, it will happen. Like an amputee who reaches to scratch his missing leg, we may have lingering remembrances of the life we've left behind. Does a recovering alcoholic never again long for the warm brown liquid to course down her throat and sting her senses? Does the previously promiscuous woman never ponder the thrill of seduction? Does the silenced gossiper never crave the sensation of owning the power of hidden secrets? The influence of the world never ceases to exist. The desires of the flesh never disappear completely. The lies of the enemy are never

totally silenced. But the more you practice recognizing the lie, rejecting the lie, and replacing the lie with truth, the more power you will
have to live the abundant life God planned all along. That's what happened with Suzanne.

CHANGING "I CAN'T" TO "I CAN"

Suzanne had been severely depressed and anxious for months. In
desperation, she checked into a hospital for treatment. Medication
seemed only to make her thinking cloudy, and she was having a difficult time focusing. It was hard to even remember which medication
to take, and she often found herself crying for hours at a time. "I can't
do anything right," she lamented. "I can't even remember which medication to take when."

Her sister emailed her a devotional I had written about replacing
lies with the truth. Suzanne knew she wouldn't be able to concentrate
long enough to read the entire piece, so she printed it off to read a little at a time. When she started reading, she couldn't put it down. I had
made a simple suggestion: "If you find yourself saying, 'I can't do anything right,' stop right there and ask if that thought is from God."

Suzanne knew God was about to tell her something significant.
Given the circumstances of the last month in the psychiatric hospital
and the new drugs she was on, no wonder she was finding it difficult
to do anything correctly. She read on.

> If you aren't sure if a thought is the truth or a lie, try this
> simple test. Add "in Jesus's name" to the end of it. For
> example, "I can't do anything right, in Jesus's name." Hmm.
> That just doesn't seem to fit, does it? How about, "I'm a
> loser, in Jesus's name." Nope that doesn't fit either. Now
> when you recognize that you are telling yourself a lie, stop
> and replace it with the truth."

Suzanne decided she would give it a try. She recognized that she
had been believing the lies of the enemy rather than the truth of God.
It made so much sense to her. She kept repeating the phrase, "I can't do
anything right, in Jesus's name," and finally understood this thought

could not be from God. With this realization, she felt the darkness start to lift and decided to try to accomplish something simple.

I'll sew a seam, she thought. She sewed the seam, and then turned it over to discover that she had missed an area. But rather than saying the usual, "I can't do anything right," she laughed at herself. Laughed for the first time in weeks. Then she said, *I'm going to try this again because I can do something right, in Jesus's name.*

And she did it.

The writer of Proverbs states, "As [a man] thinks within himself, so he is" (Proverbs 23:7 NASB). Suzanne began to see how God saw her, and it changed the way she saw herself.

Here's a bonus to the story. Suzanne had felt God had given up on her, but when her sister's email came at her very point of need, she knew He still loved her dearly and hadn't given up on her at all. He was right there prompting her sister to send the very message she needed to hear.

I'd like to close this section by going back to Philippians 4:8-9 (emphasis added): "Brothers and sisters, whatever is true, whatever is noble, whatever is right, whatever is pure, whatever is lovely, whatever is admirable—if anything is excellent or praiseworthy—think about such things. Whatever you have learned or received or heard from me, or seen in me—*put it into practice. And the God of peace will be with you.*"

- Realize the enemy's true identity.
- Recognize the lies.
- Reject the lies.
- Replace the lies with Truth.

PART 2

the lies women tell themselves

6

I'm Not Good Enough

LIE: *I'm not good enough.*

TRUTH: *I am good enough because Christ dwells in me and the Holy Spirit empowers me* (John 14:20; Acts 1:8).

For years I wrote inspirational stories and tucked them into a metal drawer. That's where the stories stayed—stuck between my files for appliance warranties and tax returns. I created Bible studies and stored them in a file cabinet. I even taught pretend three-point sermons in my head and to imaginary audiences. These were words I never planned on anyone ever seeing or hearing. Being an introvert, I loved the quiet of studying and crafting words. It was just a little something I did—something between God and me. Our little secret.

Then God started stirring up something in my soul I didn't particularly like. *What if these stories and Bible studies aren't meant to stay in a drawer or file cabinet? What if those lessons in your head are meant to be heard? What if I have been preparing you for what I have prepared for you?*

I stuck my fingers in the ears of my heart and loudly sang *lalalala-lalalala*, trying to drown out the still, small voice calling me to more. But I didn't forget it.

One year after I felt that initial nudge from God, I met a gal named Lysa TerKeurst, who was just starting a ministry in town. She invited me to join her at a recording studio to tell a few of my stories for the Proverbs 31 Homemaker radio spot. I took a deep breath, put on head-phones, and tried not to sound too stupid.

After we finished the recording, she said, "You know, I've been praying for about a year for a ministry partner to take over the radio segment of this ministry. I think God is telling me it's you."

"Thank you so much, Lysa," I replied. "But I assure you, I am not the right person for the job. I don't know anything about radio. My accent is too Southern. And, well, I could give you a lot of reasons."

The truth is, every insecurity I had ever felt erupted from my dormant volcano of self-doubt. *I'm not good enough* shouted at me to run as fast as I could and not look back. But a niggling feeling in my heart hinted God had set up this whole thing.

I'M NOT ENOUGH

"I'm not _____ enough." You can fill in that blank with *smart, talented, gifted, spiritual, outgoing, attractive,* or any number of positive attributes (and many of those we will cover in the pages of this book). But the root source of each one of those blanks is rooted in "I'm not good enough." Period. It's one of the enemy's favorite deceptions to hold God's children hostage to a life that is "less than." "I'm not good enough" is an insidious lie that keeps God's best at bay for many of His children.

The enemy tries to get us to focus on our flaws rather than on our faith. When we focus on our faults, we take our focus off God, who equips us; the Holy Spirit, who empowers us; and Jesus, who envelops us.

The Bible *does* say no one is good enough to earn his or her way into heaven (Romans 3:23). Salvation is a gift of God (Ephesians 2:8). However, many have taken the truth that they are not good enough to earn their way to heaven and transferred it to "I'm not good enough— period." But through the finished work of Jesus Christ, and His power working in you and through you, you are good enough to do everything God has called you to do and be.

> "I'm not good enough" is an insidious lie that keeps God's best at bay for many of His children.

Giving in to the lie of "I'm not good enough" will paralyze you. It's the coward's way out. I might have just hurt your feelings, but listen, I'm talking to myself too.

I was asked to speak to a group of teenage girls not too long ago. I thought, *I don't do teenage girls. They scare me. I'm not cool enough. They won't listen to me. I'm going to sound stupid.*

Friend, the book you're reading now is a revised and expanded edition of one I wrote more than ten years ago. And here I am admitting to you that I still struggle with this whole idea of being not good enough. Sorry. I haven't conquered it yet. God still stretches me and challenges me to see if I truly believe *He is enough* to work through me.

By the way, I did put on my cool jeans and my gladiator sandals and spoke to the girls. How did it go? I'm not sure. But here's what I do know. I am not responsible for the outcome of my obedience. That truth might be worth the price of this book right there. Say it to yourself often.

I am not responsible for the outcome of my obedience. God is.

Stepping out when "not good enough" is heckling at you to step aside is scary. Shrinking back and not moving forward is safer. But it is also boring—not the life to the full Jesus came to give. Henry Blackaby challenges us, "When God invites you to join Him in His work, He has assigned a God-sized assignment for you. You will realize that you cannot do it on your own. If God doesn't help you, you will fail. This is the crisis point where many decide not to follow what they sense God is leading them to do. Then they wonder why they do not experience God's presence and activity the way other Christians do."[1]

I don't want to be that person. I don't think you do either.

> I am not responsible for the outcome of my obedience. God is.

Courage and confidence follow obedience. I can't tell you how many times I've stood backstage at a conference with the words "I'm not good enough" screaming in my head. But when I step out in obedience, and do what God has called me to do, the power of the Holy Spirit overpowers the lies of the enemy, who told me to just go home.

THE GOD WHO FILLS IN YOUR BLANKS

Let's go back to that blank, the blank in "I'm not _____ enough." Moses was a man who felt he wasn't _____ enough. He had been adopted by the Egyptian pharaoh's daughter, raised in the palace, and educated in all the ways of the Egyptians. When he was 40, he came up with a plan to save the Hebrew nation. The plan failed and Moses bailed. He ran away to a desert place called Midian and became a sheepherder. When he was 80, God spoke to him through a burning bush and called him to go back to Egypt and lead His people out of bondage. But before Moses could deliver God's people, God had to deliver Moses. God had to set Moses free from the lies he had been telling himself for the past 40 years.

That's when the one-sided argument began. Moses told God He had the wrong man for the job. He wasn't brave enough, strong enough, smart enough, eloquent enough, charismatic enough, or confident enough.

At one point, Moses said,

> Suppose I go to the Israelites and say to them, "The God of your fathers has sent me to you," and they ask me, "What is his name?" Then what shall I tell them?

> God said to Moses, "I AM WHO I AM. This is what you are to say to the Israelites: 'I AM has sent me to you'...Say to the Israelites, 'The LORD, the God of your fathers—the God of Abraham, the God of Isaac and the God of Jacob—has sent me to you.' This is my name forever, the name you shall call me from generation to generation" (Exodus 3:13-15).

I go into great detail about Moses's encounter with God at the burning bush and the four lies that held him hostage in my book *Take Hold of the Faith You Long For*. Let me share just a smidgen here from that book about the name I AM, and how that name can rebuff the argument of "I'm not good enough."

> When God revealed His name I AM, He did so using a present tense Hebrew verb—an action word. He is a God

who acts on His people's behalf. He is a God who acts on *your* behalf.

God uses two forms of the same name in this passage. I AM is the name He refers to when speaking of Himself. LORD, or Yahweh in the Hebrew, is the third person form of the word and translated "He is." When God speaks of Himself, He says, "I AM," and when we speak of Him we say, "He is."

Originally, the Name was only four letters: YHWH. Later, scribes inserted vowels to form the word Yahweh. Some Bible translations render the same name as Jehovah. YHWH appears in the Old Testament more than 6800 times, and is found in every book except Esther, Ecclesiastes, and the Song of Songs. When you see the name LORD in all caps in the Bible, it is referring to Yahweh. When you see the word Lord in lower case, it is referring to another name for God—Adonai.

The Name YHWH was considered so holy to the early rabbinical scribes that they wouldn't even write the letters. They used "The Name," "The Unutterable Name," "The Great and Terrible Name," and "The Holy Name" whenever it appeared. You can imagine the Pharisees' surprise when Jesus said, "Very truly I tell you...before Abraham was born, I AM!"[2]

I AM says it all. He just is. Before there was anything, HE WAS. Scripture begins with the words, "In the beginning God..." (Genesis 1:1). He always has been and always will be.

I AM points to the very present tenseness or the IS-ness of God—the here-ness and nearness of God. HE IS your very present help in times of trouble. The writer of Hebrews tells us, "Without faith it is impossible to please Him, for he who comes to God must believe that He is and that He is a rewarder of those who seek Him" (Hebrews 11:6 NASB).

Moses was 80 years old when he had his argument with God at the burning bush. But what we'll see is that even the weakest knees in the hands of I AM become a mighty force to be reckoned with.

I'll go out on a limb and say that every single one of us, at one time or another, will struggle with feelings of inferiority, insecurity, and inadequacy just like Moses did. And the underlying statement feeding the sense of worthlessness is "I'm not _____ enough." You can fill that blank in with any number of qualities.

I'm not strong enough.

I'm not experienced enough.

I'm not talented enough.

I'm not brave enough.

I'm not pretty enough.

I'm not thin enough.

But here's what I want you to remember: Whatever you feel you are not, God is. Whatever you need, God is. He is the God who fills in your gaps; He is I AM who fills in your blanks.[3]

Once we let go of the lies that we are not enough and take hold of the truth that we are more than enough because of Jesus's presence and power in us, then we will be set free from the mealymouthed mentality and be on our way to experiencing the courageous confidence of an overcomer.

Here's what I want you to do. As you go about your day, I challenge you to "spot the nots" in your self-assessment. Sleuth for the "I am nots" in your thoughts and in your speech. For example, look out for words spoken or thoughts such as *I'm not smart enough; I'm not pretty enough; I'm not good enough.* Then once you "spot the not," "swat the not." That's right. Swat it right out of your vocabulary. Here's the deal: Whenever you say, "I'm not _____ enough," God says, "I AM."

When You Say	God Says
I AM not smart enough.	I AM
I AM not talented enough.	I AM
I AM not patient enough.	I AM
I AM not loving enough.	I AM
I AM not caring enough.	I AM
I AM not wise enough.	I AM

I AM not strong enough.	I AM
I AM not outgoing enough.	I AM
I AM not secure enough.	I AM
I AM not bold enough.	I AM
I AM not _____ enough.	I AM

Now go back and read that list again. But this time, read it out loud. Go ahead. Nobody's listening. But if they were, they'd be blessed too.

• • • • •

"Nots" swarm like flies on the unaware and unsuspecting. Let me encourage you to "spot the nots" in your life. Hunt them down. Sleuth them out. Spot them. And once you spot the nots, swat the nots right out of your mind. Get rid of them. If you have a pen in your hand right now, go back to that list and put a big X right through those "nots."

I AM is the God who is everything you need. He is the God who fills in your blanks.

YOU'RE IN GOOD COMPANY

"I'm not good enough" was the undercurrent of my entire existence until I finally realized who I was and what I had in Christ. Bible teacher Beth Moore said, "In the dead of the night when insecurities crawl on us like fleas, all of us have terrifying bouts of insecurity and panics of insignificance. Our human natures pitifully fall to the temptation to pull out the tape measure and gauge ourselves against people who seem more gifted and anointed by God."[4]

Many women are living in silent defeat, comparing themselves to other women who likewise are living in silent defeat. *I'm not a good mother. I'm not a good wife. I'm not a good Christian. I'm not a good witness. I'm not a good housekeeper. I'm not a good decorator. I'm not a good cook. I'm not a good...*

One by one the petals fall from the beautiful flower God created us to be. Like ticker tape, our fragmented pieces of confidence scatter over the streets as the parade passes by.

Unfortunately, I wasted many precious years held captive by the enemy's lies before I held up my chained hands to God and said, "I'm ready for You to cut me loose."

Consider this:

> Jacob was a liar.
>
> Moses was a stutterer.
>
> David was an adulterer.
>
> Rahab was a prostitute.
>
> Esther was an orphan.
>
> Balaam's donkey was…well, a donkey

And yet God used each one of them to further His kingdom. You're in good company. See, God doesn't call us because we are particularly gifted or talented. He uses us because we are obedient and dependent on Him. He doesn't call the qualified; He qualifies the called.

Gideon is another one of God's chosen leaders who argued that he wasn't good enough. One day he was threshing wheat in a winepress when an angel of the Lord came to him. "The LORD is with you, mighty warrior," the angel announced (Judges 6:12). Now, first of all, you don't thresh wheat in a winepress. You thresh wheat in an open field by throwing it up in the air. The wind blows the chaff away and the grain falls to the ground. So what was Gideon doing in the winepress? He was so terrified of his enemies, the Midianites, that he was hiding. And yet, when the angel of the Lord came to him, he addressed Gideon as "mighty warrior." No wonder Gideon said, "Pardon me?" (6:13,15).

As soon as God called Gideon to greater things, Gideon began making excuses, allowing his insecurities and inadequacies to set limitations in his life. Gideon argued, "How can I save Israel? My clan is the weakest in Manasseh, and I am the least in my family" (6:15).

But God looked beyond Gideon's insecurities. He knew who Gideon *could be* if he trusted in God's power to work through him. Author Renee Swope wrote,

> God wasn't limited by Gideon's limitations, and He's not

limited by ours either. He didn't want Gideon to depend on his own strength. God wanted Gideon to depend on His strength. God was going to conquer the Midianites, but He invited Gideon to join Him.

Perhaps it was because He knew that, while conquering the Midianites, Gideon would also conquer his personal enemies of doubt and fear. Often God will call you beyond your limitations to do something that requires faith. It's not so much about what He wants you to do as what He wants to do in you, as you depend on Him.

We'll also need to realize our family of origin does not define our true identity. Once we become daughters of the King, we have a royal inheritance that determines who we are. Gideon had to stop thinking of himself as the runt of his family and start seeing himself as a child of God, a mighty warrior in his Father's eyes. Whether we had a great family or not, our hearts will only find lasting confidence when we find our identity as children of God.[5]

What about women in the Bible? When you turn the pages from the Old Testament to the New Testament, you can tell something is going to be different for women. In the Old Testament lineages, women were rarely mentioned. However, in Matthew, the first book of the New Testament, five women are listed in the lineage of Jesus. Of course, Mary, the mother of Jesus, is there—a teenage girl from Bethlehem. But who are the other four?

> *Tamar,* who had an incestuous encounter
> with her father-in-law.
>
> *Rahab,* who had been a prostitute in Jericho.
>
> *Ruth,* who was a foreigner from a cursed people
> group in Moab.
>
> *Bathsheba,* who had an affair with King David.

I'm so glad these women were listed. This shows us we can never go so far away from God that His grace can't reach in to save us, and then use us. Each of these women would have probably thought they weren't good enough if they had known how God was going to use them in His kingdom. What a beautiful example of what Paul wrote to the Corinthians:

> Brothers and sisters, think of what you were when you were called. Not many of you were wise by human standards; not many were influential; not many were of noble birth. But God chose the foolish things of the world to shame the wise; God chose the weak things of the world to shame the strong. God chose the lowly things of this world and the despised things—and the things that are not—to nullify the things that are, so that no one may boast before him. It is because of him that you are in Christ Jesus, who has become for us wisdom from God—that is, our righteousness, holiness and redemption. Therefore, as it is written: "Let the one who boasts boast in the Lord" (1 Corinthians 1:26-31).

GOD'S POWER AT WORK IN YOU

The truth is, if you have made Jesus the Lord of your life, you have the power of the Holy Spirit living in you and working through you. Jesus said, "You will receive power when the Holy Spirit comes on you" (Acts 1:8). You have God's incomparably great power at your disposal. "That power is the same as the mighty strength he exerted when he raised Christ from the dead and seated him at his right hand in the heavenly realms" (Ephesians 1:19-20). The same power that raised Jesus from the dead is at work within us? Yep. The same power.

Did you notice when Jesus received His Father's approval at His baptism, it was before He had done even one miracle? So many Christians are trying to earn what they already have. You are already enough because of the finished work of Jesus.

Jesus said, "I tell you the truth [Don't you just love it when He says that?], anyone who believes in me will do the same works I have done, and even greater works, because I am going to be with the Father" (John 14:12 NLT). What does going to the Father have to do with the power we receive? Because once Jesus went to the Father, the Holy Spirit came to take up residence in believers. "If you love me, keep my commands. And I will ask the Father, and he will give you another advocate to help you and be with you forever—the Spirit of truth." (John 14:15-17).

Take a glove, for example. A glove is powerless sitting on a bedside table. But put your hand in the glove and it can do many things: play the piano, paint a picture, scrub a floor, plant a garden. But is that the glove or the hand in the glove doing the work? Of course, it is the latter.

You and I are nothing more than gloves—powerless on our own, yet powerful when filled with the Spirit. The glove can't do anything if it is merely near the hand. It must be filled with the hand, controlled by the hand. And it is the same for us. We have power to do everything God has called for us to do when we are filled with the power of the Holy Spirit.

When you hear the lie "I'm not good enough" weaseling its way into your mind, reject the lie and replace it with this truth: "His divine power has given us everything we need for a godly life through our knowledge of him who called us by his own glory and goodness" (2 Peter 1:3). Another translation says it this way: "For His divine power has bestowed on us [absolutely] everything necessary for [a dynamic spiritual] life and godliness, through true *and* personal knowledge of Him who called us by His own glory and excellence" (AMP).

UNSHAKABLE CONFIDENCE

It's time to see yourself as God sees you. No more House of Mirrors with a distorted image of who you are. This is how God sees you:

- You are a child of God—John 1:12

- You are justified completely—Romans 5:1

- You are free from condemnation—Romans 8:1

- You have the mind of Christ—1 Corinthians 2:16

- You have been made righteous—2 Corinthians 5:21

- You have been blessed with every spiritual blessing—
  Ephesians 1:3

- You are righteous and holy—Ephesians 4:24
- You have been redeemed and forgiven of all your sins—Colossians 1:14
- You are a dwelling place for Christ; He lives in you—Colossians 1:27
- You are complete in Christ—Colossians 2:10
- You are chosen of God, holy and dearly loved—Colossians 3:12
- You have been given a spirit of power, love, and self-discipline—2 Timothy 1:7
- You are a partaker of God's divine nature—2 Peter 1:4

And that, my friend, is only the beginning. Say these verses aloud. Rehearse them in your mind. Believe the truth about who you are. You are more than good enough because of who lives in you and works through you.

Paul said he "put no confidence in the flesh" (Philippians 3:3). In other words, he didn't think he was good enough because of any talent or ability he had. But his confidence came from who he was, what he had, and where he was as a child of God. Someone once said, "A man wrapped up in himself makes a pretty small package." But someone wrapped up in God is an amazing sight to behold.

I am not advocating self-confidence, but God-confidence—confidence in who you are because of what Jesus has done for you and the Holy Spirit can do through you. Jesus said, "I am the vine; you are the branches. If you remain in me and I in you, you will bear much fruit; apart from me you can do nothing" (John 15:5). Connected to the vine, you can do everything God calls you to do (Philippians 4:13).

Paul knew what he could accomplish on his own—nothing. Oh, he could be busy. We all can do that. But bearing "fruit that will remain" is another story.

A confident woman is one who walks in faith, knowing she is a holy, chosen, redeemed, dearly loved child of God, empowered by the Holy Spirit, equipped by her Maker, and enveloped by Jesus Christ.

LAME MAN DANCING

Two weeks after Lysa mentioned the idea of me joining her at Proverbs 31, and my immediate dismissal of the idea, my husband suggested a romantic vacation to the island of Bermuda—a paradise off the coast of Cape Hatteras, North Carolina. One evening Steve and I splurged at a fancy restaurant, complete with a four-man band playing music from the '40s and '50s. We had taken a few ballroom dance lessons, and Steve was itching to see if we could remember the foxtrot.

"Come on, Sharon," he urged. "Let's take a spin on the dance floor."

"No way," I said. "Nobody else is dancing. I'm not going to be the only one out there with everyone staring at me. And suppose we mess up? I'd be embarrassed. It's been a long time since we've practiced, and I don't remember all the steps. Let's wait until some other people are out there so we won't be so conspicuous."

After a few moments, the first couple took their place on the parquet. They squared their shoulders, pointed their toes, and framed their arms. In one fluid motion they graced the dance floor with perfect dips, sways, turns, and twirls. They looked good, and they knew it.

Nope. I was not going to embarrass myself. I hunkered down in my seat with renewed resolve. I was stuck there. I refused to budge.

Then couple number two joined couple number one. Their steps weren't quite so perfect, but they looked pretty good too.

"Okay, I'll go," I said. "But let's get in the back corner behind that big ficus tree so nobody can see us."

Off we went to try to remember the slow-slow-quick-quick of the foxtrot. The whole time I was hoping all eyes were still mesmerized on the polished artistry of couple number one.

As I dared look at the crowd, I noticed they weren't looking at couple number one, number two, or even wobbly kneed number three. All eyes were fixed on a fourth couple approaching the dance floor. The husband was in a wheelchair.

He was a middle-aged, slightly balding, large-framed man with a neatly trimmed salt-and-pepper beard. His dapper attire included a crisp white shirt, a snappy bow tie, and a stylish tuxedo. On his left hand he wore a white glove—I guessed to cover a skin disease. With a smiling wife by his side, the couple approached the dance floor with a graceful confidence and fashionable flair. Suddenly everyone else faded away, and they seemed to be the only two people in the room.

As the band churned out a peppy tune, the blithesome wife held her love's healthy right hand and danced. He never rose from the wheelchair that had become his legs, but they didn't seem to care. They came together and separated like expert dancers. He spun her around as she stooped low to conform to her husband's seated position. Lovingly, like a little fairy child, she danced around his chair while her laughter became the fifth instrument in the musical ensemble. Even though his feet never left their metal resting place, his shoulders swayed in perfect time and his eyes danced with hers.

My heart was so moved by this love story unfolding before my eyes that I had to turn my head and bury my face on Steve's chest so no one would see the tears streaming down my cheeks. As I did, I saw person after person dabbing linen napkins to dewy eyes. This portrait of love and devotion transfixed even the band members, now misty-eyed as well.

Finally, the music slowed to a romantic melody. The wife pulled up a chair beside her husband's wheelchair, but facing in the opposite direction. They held each other in a dancer's embrace, closed their eyes, and swayed back and forth, cheek to cheek.

Surprisingly, I no longer worried about whether anyone was watching me. I didn't care if my steps weren't perfect. I wasn't even concerned about being compared to and falling short of perfect couple number one.

The Lord spoke to my heart in a powerful way. *Sharon, I want you to notice who moved this crowd to tears,* He seemed to say. *Was it couple number one, with their perfect steps? Or was it the last couple that had no steps at all? No, My child, it was the display of love, not perfection, that moved the crowd. If you obey Me, if you do what I have called you to do, then I will do for you what that man's wife did for him.*

God reminded me He isn't looking for perfect people with perfect children, perfect marriages, and perfect lives. He is not searching for men and women with perfect steps to do great things for Him. He is looking for courageous believers who will rely on His power to work in and through them to accomplish all He has planned for them to do. He is scouting for followers who will obey Him regardless of their present fears or past failures. He is looking for men and women who know they are good enough because of His power working in them and through them.

Simply put, God had sent me a lame man to teach me how to dance.

God chooses to do extraordinary work through ordinary people who will bring glory to His name. Men and women who know they are not good enough in their own strength but are incredibly powerful in God's strength slay the giants of this world.

• • • • •

RECOGNIZE THE LIE: *I'm not good enough.*

REJECT THE LIE: *That's not true.*

REPLACE THE LIE WITH TRUTH:

His divine power has given us everything we need for a godly life through our knowledge of him who called us by his own glory and goodness. Through these he has given us his very great and precious promises, so that through them you may participate in the divine nature, having escaped the corruption in the world caused by evil desires (2 Peter 1:3-4).

7

I'm Worthless

LIE: *I'm worthless.*

TRUTH: *I am God's treasured possession*
(Deuteronomy 14:2).

April felt worthless, as though she had little value to God—or to anyone else, for that matter. She longed to know what God really thought of her, what He saw when He looked at her, or if He even saw her at all.

"Lord, please speak to me and tell me how You see me. Or if You see me," she prayed. "I feel so worthless."

A few days after April cried out to God, He reminded her of a special field day in elementary school. It was as if He had pushed the play button to project it on the movie screen of her memory. April was ten years old and lined up for the 100-yard dash on her Christian school playground. All the other kids had on their school-issued navy-blue uniforms, but she wore a pair of bright orange, green, and yellow striped culottes with a matching top.

The whistle blew, and April took off running as fast as she could. She left the other girls in the dust and crossed the finish line first.

From several yards away, April's big brother and his friends watched the event from the second-story window of the high school. "Did you see your little sister win that race?" one of the boys asked.

"Are you kidding?" he said. "I couldn't miss her with those stripes."

"Later, when he told my parents the story," April recalled, "he seemed so proud of me. He said, 'You should have seen her. There was a long line of blue and then a flash of color running way ahead of them. She was amazing!'"

April asked God what He was trying to tell her by bringing this childhood memory into view.

That is how I see you, He seemed to say. *You stand out above all the rest. You don't have to fit in with all the others and be what they say you should be. I am proud of you, just like your brother was proud of you that day. Don't be afraid of being different. I made you unique in every way. I love you just the way you are. You are a blue-ribbon winner. You are My treasured possession.*

GOD VALUES YOU

Demeaning words from childhood itch like phantom worth, amputated by careless parents, unthinking friends, tactless teachers, and imprudent peers. *We wanted a boy when you were born... You were a mistake; we never wanted children... We don't want you on our team... Is that the best you can do?... This seat is taken.* Words that echo, confirming what we already suspected—we're worthless.

Here's the truth. We all have defects and deficiencies. God knows every one of them; He even knows what caused them. And yet He chose you anyway. He chose you before you were born. Consider God's words to Jeremiah:

> Before I formed you in the womb I knew you,
> before you were born I set you apart;
> I appointed you as a prophet to the nations
> (Jeremiah 1:5).

Long before God created the earth, He had you in mind. He decided to adopt you into His family through Jesus Christ and make you the focus of His love. Why? Because it gave Him pleasure to do so (Ephesians 1:5).

Not only did God know you before you were born and choose you to be His child, He appointed you to bear fruit. Jesus said,

> You did not choose me, but I chose you and appointed you
> so that you might go and bear fruit—fruit that will last—
> and so that whatever you ask in my name the Father will
> give you (John 15:16).

Not only did God know you before you were born, choose you to be His child, and appoint you to bear fruit; He also planned the specific time and place in history for you to be born. Paul wrote,

> From one man he made all the nations, that they should
> inhabit the whole earth; and he marked out their appointed
> times in history and the boundaries of their lands (Acts
> 17:26).

How in the world could you or I ever be worthless? It's impossible. The mere fact that we were created to be image bearers of a holy God says otherwise. C.S. Lewis wrote in his work *The Weight of Glory*, "There are no ordinary people. You have never met a mere mortal."[1] And you are no ordinary mortal! You are a priceless treasure.

YOU ARE WORTH MORE

As a little girl, I never felt I was worth much. I remember my mom telling the story about when my older brother was born. "Your dad was so happy that day," she beamed.

"Why?" I asked.

"Because he had a son?" she answered with a hint of *you should know the answer to that question.*

My heart sank. I never heard stories about my daddy being happy the day I was born.

Then there was the definitive day in the eleventh grade that took my self-worth to an all-time low. It was over 25 years ago, and I can still remember what I was wearing: lavender bell-bottom hip-huggers, a bubble knit short-sleeve top, Dr. Scholl's wooden sandals, and a blue bandanna tied around my head of long, oily hair I hadn't had time to wash that morning. Don't laugh. This was acceptable attire for teens when I was in high school, except for the days when a special awards or recognition assembly was held.

In homeroom that morning, the principal announced over the intercom that an unscheduled assembly would take place at eleven o'clock to recognize students being inducted into the National Honor Society. That's when I understood why so many of my friends were dressed a notch above the norm. Their parents had received the secretive congratulatory call the night before and made sure their kids had washed their hair and left the frayed jeans in the drawer.

Four hundred teens found seats in the darkened auditorium. The principal made a speech of commendation from the podium. "We are here to recognize those students who have achieved academic excellence, upheld high moral principles, and represented our school positively in the community. Will the following students come forward when your name is called to receive a certificate and a candle to be lit by last year's inductees?"

The principal called each name, and I watched several of my friends walk across the immense stage. Then, to my horror and surprise, my name was called. *Why didn't my parents warn me*, I thought. *I look horrible*—and I did.

When the houselights went up, I panned the back of the room where proud parents snapped pictures and pointed out their progeny to others standing on tiptoe to catch a glimpse. *My* parents were not among them—they never were. Even though I held a candle in my hand, their absence snuffed out the light in my heart.

I later discovered that my dad had received the call from the school the night before, the call that would have made most parents proud. But he forgot to tell my mom. Even though they both worked across the street from the school, they didn't come to the ceremony. In my mind, their absence confirmed what I'd suspected for the past 17 years. *I'm just not worth the trouble.*

I didn't care about the certificate or the principal's accolades. What I really wanted was to know I had value to the two people who mattered most.

Perhaps you had painful experiences in your past that left you feeling worthless, but Jesus wants you to know you have great value. It took many years, but finally I took hold of Jesus's words: *You are worth more.*

"Are not two sparrows sold for a penny?" He asked His disciples. "Yet not one of them will fall to the ground outside your Father's care. And even the very hairs of your head are all numbered. So don't be afraid; *you are worth more* than many sparrows" (Matthew 10:29-31, emphasis added).

> You are worth more than the money in your bank account.
>
> You are worth more than the number of friends you have on Facebook.
>
> You are worth more than the number of followers for your Twitter account.
>
> You are worth more than the number of meetings and appointments on your calendar.
>
> You are worth more than your successes or failures.
>
> You are worth more than your level of education.
>
> You are worth more than the price tags in your closet.
>
> You are worth more than your accomplishments or lack of them.
>
> You are worth more than many sparrows.

Oh, Lord, help me to really get this, I pray.

• • • • •

Once a little girl named Martha Taft was asked to introduce herself to her elementary school classmates. She stood and said, "My name is Martha Bowers Taft. My great-grandfather was president of the United States. My grandfather was a United States senator. My daddy is ambassador to Ireland. And I am a Brownie."[2] Undoubtedly someone had taught little Martha that she had great value just the way she was.

GOD ESTEEMS YOU

In Jesus's day, women were treated as the dregs of society. They moved about as shadows rarely seen and seldom heard. Women were not allowed to talk to men in public—even their own husbands. If a woman spoke to a man in public who was not her husband, it was assumed she was having a relationship with him and grounds for divorce. Women were not allowed to eat in the same room with a gathering of men, to be educated in the Torah (the Scriptures) with men, or sit under a rabbi's teaching. She couldn't enter the inner court of the temple to worship with men. A girl was considered the property of her father. The ownership was passed to her husband when she married and to her son if she were widowed. Each morning a Pharisee began his day by thanking God that He had not made him a "Gentile, a woman, or a slave." Imagine being the wife and waking up to those words!

I could go on, but you get the picture. In my book *How Jesus Broke the Rules to Set You Free*, I showed that in every encounter Jesus had with a woman, He broke one of those cultural rules. Jesus came to destroy the works of the devil and elevate women to their rightful place as co-heirs with Christ. Oh, girls, you were so worth it.

The story of Jesus's encounter with the Samaritan woman at the well is just one story that shows how valuable women are to God. At Jacob's well, Jesus met a woman who had been married five times and was currently living with a man she wasn't married to. The story begins, "[Jesus] had to go through Samaria" (John 4:4). He didn't have to go because of geography, but because His heavenly Father had a job for Him to do. See, there was this woman...

Let's ponder how Jesus showed this woman she had great worth. Come sit well-side and listen in on Jesus's conversation with someone who felt of no value to anyone.

> When a Samaritan woman came to draw water, Jesus said to her, "Will you give me a drink?" (His disciples had gone into the town to buy food.) The Samaritan woman said to him, "You are a Jew and I am a Samaritan woman. How can you ask me for a drink?" (For Jews do not associate

with Samaritans.) Jesus answered her, "If you knew the gift of God and who it is that asks you for a drink, you would have asked him and he would have given you living water" (4:7-10).

Oh, how this woman wanted living water. She had been married and discarded five times, and the man she lived with now was not her husband. She was so ashamed of her life that she came to draw water midday, rather than with the other townswomen, who came in the cool of the morning. But the midday heat was better than the early-morning stares and whispers.

Now this Jewish man was talking to her, and she was uncomfortable. I imagine she spoke to Him with a bit of bitterness in her tone. Jesus ignored the sarcasm and cut right to the chase—living water.

> Jesus answered, "Everyone who drinks this water will be thirsty again, but whoever drinks the water I give them will never thirst. Indeed, the water I give them will become in them a spring of water welling up to eternal life." The woman said to him, "Sir, give me this water so that I won't get thirsty and have to keep coming here to draw water" (4:13-15).

Again, oh, how she wanted that water. How she longed not to have to endure the heat of the day and the loathing of the other women. He told her,

> "Go, call your husband and come back."

> "I have no husband," she replied.

> Jesus said to her, "You are right when you say you have no husband. The fact is, you have had five husbands, and the man you now have is not your husband. What you have just said is quite true."

> "Sir," the woman said, "I can see that you are a prophet. Our ancestors worshiped on this mountain, but you Jews

claim that the place where we must worship is in Jerusalem" (4:16-20).

She tried to change the subject to religion rather than relationship, but Jesus wouldn't let her. He loved her too much. She was worth too much.

> "Woman," Jesus replied, "believe me, a time is coming when you will worship the Father neither on this mountain nor in Jerusalem. You Samaritans worship what you do not know; we worship what we do know, for salvation is from the Jews. Yet a time is coming and has now come when the true worshipers will worship the Father in the Spirit and in truth, for they are the kind of worshipers the Father seeks. God is spirit, and his worshipers must worship in the Spirit and in truth."
>
> The woman said, "I know that Messiah" (called Christ) "is coming. When he comes, he will explain everything to us" (4:21-25).
>
> Jesus looked intently at the woman, and for the first time in His ministry, He told someone His true identity: "I, the one speaking to you—I am he" (4:26). Then leaving her water pot, she ran back to town and told the townsfolk about the Messiah she met at Jacob's well (4:28-29).

I love this story. This was a woman who felt worthless, but Jesus made sure she knew she was highly esteemed. She had been discarded by five men. And now she felt so little about her own self-worth that she was willing to live with a man without the commitment of marriage. But worthless is not how Jesus saw her. He had to go to Samaria—not because it was the best route, but it was the route God told Him to take. Jesus needed to talk to a woman there. She was worth the trip.

Don't for one minute think her nationality and gender were happenstance. They were both intentionally chosen by our intentional God—just another example showing that God's plan to set the captives free was for *all* who believed. She was worth it, and so are you.

Jesus spoke to this woman without a hint of condemnation or judgment. While she felt she was worthless, He certainly didn't think so. As a matter of fact, He applauded her honesty.

This is the longest recorded conversation Jesus had with anyone, and it was with a woman who felt she was worthless. Again, for the first time in His ministry, Jesus told someone His true identity—that He was the Messiah. "I, the one speaking to you—I am he" (John 4:26). Remember in chapter 5 when we looked at the name for God—I AM? In the Greek, the original language of the New Testament, the word *he* is not used in verse 26. Literally Jesus said, "I who speak to you am."[3] This goes back to the book of Exodus when God told Moses His name was YHWH—I AM.

This story is filled with hope for every woman who's ever felt abused, misused, or forgotten. It's for every woman who's ever felt worthless because of circumstance or happenstance. Jesus says, "Oh, girl, you are so worth it. You have great value to Me. I'm willing to go out of My way to lift you out of the well of worthlessness and onto the hill of highly esteemed."

WHEN YOU FEEL AS THOUGH YOU JUST DON'T MATTER

For more than a decade we were joined at the hip. Not a day went by when we didn't talk on the phone at least once.

But sometimes friendships come unhinged. People change. Perspectives change. Purposes change. Passions change. While nothing went terribly wrong, and no hurtful words were exchanged, the void was vast beyond bridging. I felt tossed away. Discarded. Of little regard. Erased as if I had never been. Worthless.

Perhaps you've felt that way at some point in your life. It's a hard "dis-ease" to define. To put your finger on and say, "Yes, that's where it hurts." For me, it was a niggling ache. A haunting hurt that shot straight through at unexpected times.

Why was I having trouble letting go? Why were my feet stuck in the sucking mire of memories? Me—the woman who taught others how to leave the past behind. "One thing I do: forgetting what lies behind and reaching forward to what lies ahead" (Philippians 3:13 NASB).

Yep. I memorized it. I taught it. I flashed it on the screen in Power-Point Technicolor.

But there was this...

I was reading a book by Canadian Mark Buchanan, *Your God Is Too Safe*, and he diagnosed my heart-sickness with one fell swoop of his pen. That "thing" I had been struggling with but couldn't define. *My own deepest heart wounds have been inflicted by people who never set out to hurt me. It was worse. At some point they stopped even caring that what they did would hurt me. I became beside the point. My existence ceased to matter. The importance I believed I occupied in the heart of the other, the place of cherishing I thought was reserved for me turned out to be a myth.*[4]

Just as clearly as a physician who delivers a diagnosis would, Mark laid bare the crux of my problem: *I became beside the point. My existence ceased to matter.* For me, it was the worst kind of pain. A malignancy that spread and gnawed on other areas of my life.

Now that I had a diagnosis, now that the dis-ease had a name, I was faced with a choice. That's what God does, you know. He doesn't reveal a soul-sickness just for the sake of revelation, but always to bring healing...repentance...to help make you well. When He reveals an infectious soul-sickness, one you've never noticed or could define before, it's as if He's saying, "Now is the time." When He shows you a lie that has become your truth, it's time to reject that lie and replace it with His truth.

Jesus understands what it feels like to be of "no consequence" to someone (or many someones). Your arrow of pain shoots straight through the heart, comes out the other side, and finds its mark in the pierced hands of Jesus, the pierced side of Jesus, the broken heart of Jesus. "By his wounds we are healed" (Isaiah 53:5).

He gets it. He wants you to let Him take it. Let it go—not just into oblivion, but onto Him. Into Him. Here's what Jesus wants *you* to know. Here is the truth:

You are of great consequence. You are significant. Your existence will never cease to matter. You have great worth.

Look at this graphic. What do you see? Answer before reading the next line.

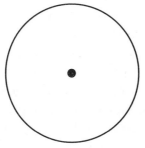

Did you say, "A dot?"

I did when someone asked me the same question.

But look at all that space around the dot! Inside. Outside.

Now think of the all-encompassing love of God. Above you. Beside you. Under you. You couldn't get away from it if you tried. That's the space inside the circle and outside the circle. That little tiny dot represents that person or the persons who have hurt you intentionally or unintentionally, the person or persons you've allowed to make you feel worthless. Why in the world do we look at the circle and see only the dot? Why don't we see the space?

Why in the world do we focus on the one person who has hurt us, or doesn't care about us, and not on all the people in our lives who do love us? On the God who loves us?

Here's what I'm challenging you to do: Stop focusing on the dot. Focus on the space around the dot. The dot is just that—a dot! She's a dot. He's a dot. God's love for you, and all the other people in your world who love you—including me—are the space.

> "On that day," Jesus said, "you will realize that I am in my
> Father, and you are in me, and I am in you" (John 14:20).

BATTERED AND BRUISED

The speaker came on stage and pulled out a $100 bill.

"Who would like this $100 bill?" he asked.

Hands shot up all around the room.

Then he crumpled the bill, threw it on the floor, and ground it with his foot. Holding up the dirty and tattered money, he then asked, "Now, who wants this $100 bill?"

The same hands went into the air.

"And that is why God still wants you," he said. "You may be battered and bruised. You may be tattered and torn. You may be crumpled and creased. But that doesn't change your value to God any more than what I've done changes the value of this $100 bill. You are still precious and valuable to God who chose you, redeemed you, and loves you as His own."

> As a father has compassion on his children,
>   so the LORD has compassion on those who fear him;
> for he knows how we are formed,
>   he remembers that we are dust (Psalm 103:13-14).

God understands that we are fatally flawed creatures, yet He deems us immeasurably valuable no matter how crumpled and soiled we are.

Paul wrote to the Christians at Corinth, "We have this treasure in jars of clay to show that this all-surpassing power is from God and not from us" (2 Corinthians 4:7). You and I might not look like much on the outside—we may appear as common clay jars—but inside are hidden, incredible treasures. Inside these old, cracked pots resides the most incredible treasure of all: Jesus Christ. And that makes us valuable.

WORTH MORE THAN A HERD OF PIGS

One of the ministries my husband and I are passionate about is Campus Crusade's production and distribution of *The Jesus Film* and *Magdalena*. *The Jesus Film* translates the gospel, primarily according to Luke, into the heart language of remote people groups all around the world. *Magdalena* translates the gospel as well, but tells the story from Mary Magdalena's perspective to show how much Jesus values women. Over two million people have made a decision for Christ because of these films.

An African tribe viewed *The Jesus Film* in their own language. As a follow-up, another ministry, Faith Comes by Hearing, provided the tribe with an audio Bible and a digital playback unit. A group gathered round to listen to the story of Jesus healing a demon-possessed man recorded in Luke 8:26-33.

> [Jesus and his disciples] sailed to the region of the Gerasenes, which is across the lake from Galilee. When Jesus stepped ashore, he was met by a demon-possessed man from the town. For a long time this man had not worn clothes or lived in a house, but had lived in the tombs. When he saw Jesus, he cried out and fell at his feet, shouting at the top of his voice, "What do you want with me, Jesus, Son of the Most High God? I beg you, don't torture me!" For Jesus had commanded the impure spirit to come out of the man. Many times it had seized him, and though he was chained hand and foot and kept under guard, he had broken his chains and had been driven by the demon into solitary places...
>
> The demons begged Jesus to let them go into the pigs, and he gave them permission. When the demons came out of the man, they went into the pigs, and the herd rushed down the steep bank into the lake and was drowned.

The tribal community was stunned when they heard this story. They knew the value of one pig, much less an entire herd. Why would Jesus do that? Why would He allow their entire income to be destroyed?

Many questions stirred among the listeners. Then the wise chief spoke. "Perhaps Jesus is showing us that one human soul is worth more than an entire tribe's economy."

I was silenced by his answer. That passage has been mysterious to me for many years, but God revealed the truth to an African chief hearing the story for the very first time. That chief understood just how valuable we are to God.

WORTH MORE THAN JEWELS

To celebrate our twenty-fifth wedding anniversary, Steve and I took a land-and-sea excursion to Alaska. The landscape was captivating as we traveled from the snowcapped mountains of Mount McKinley, through the majestic masses of ice at Glacier Bay, to the wildflower-covered tundra of lowlands.

Larry and Cynthia Price, our good friends from college days, took the journey with us, which was the best part of the trip. The first leg of the excursion was on land, and the second was by sea. While on the cruise ship, we docked at various Alaskan fishing villages to mill around the shops and get a taste of Alaskan civilian life. When the boat docked at Juneau, it seemed that everyone had lost their steam for wanderlust and opted to stay on the ship for the morning. But not me. I put on my jeans, slipped on my tennis shoes, and grabbed a credit card and ID. Off I traipsed to explore the shops and do what I do best—look for bargains.

I think I'll look into buying a tanzanite stone to go on my gold neck-lace, I thought to myself. *Everyone seems to be talking about the beautiful tanzanite here.*

I spotted a store with a banner that beckoned me with bright red letters: "End of the year closeout!" If I'm anything, I'm thrifty, so I decided this was the store for me.

I waltzed into Diamonds International with one purpose in mind—get a good deal. Right away I felt a bit out of place in my tennis shoes and jeans. The pristine showroom with crystal chandeliers, sophisticated suit-clad sales associates, and sparkling glass cases lined with jewels didn't give the impression of a discount store or closeout sale, but the sign said...

"May I be of assistance?" Gretchen asked. The sleek saleswoman with a European accent gracefully swept her manicured hand across the glass case. "Are you looking for something specific?"

"Yes," I answered. "I'm looking for a tanzanite slide for my necklace."

"Right this way," she answered as she elegantly glided across the room.

"Oh, I like this one," I said right away. "How much is it?"

"It retails for eighty-three, but our closeout price is forty-three."

Suddenly, I remembered I had a coupon for this store back on the ship, but I couldn't remember the details of the discount. "I have a coupon back on the ship. Should I go back and get it?"

"That won't be necessary," she replied. "We will honor it." Then she pulled out her calculator, began punching in numbers, and then lowered the price.

"Is it a special occasion, such as a birthday or anniversary?" she asked.

"Yes, it's our twenty-fifth anniversary," I replied.

"Then we can give you an even better price."

I was getting excited as the price continued to drop! Then the store manager came over to the case.

"Hello, ma'am," he said. "Have you been looking at this stone for quite some time?"

"Oh, no," I responded. "I just saw it a few minutes ago and decided I liked it."

"I'll tell you what," he continued. "I'll give you this tanzanite for twenty-seven if you promise to wear it to dinner tonight and tell everyone where you got it and what a great deal you got."

"That does sound like a great deal," I said. "Let's do it."

I pulled my credit card from my jeans pocket and the stone was mine. As Gretchen the European rang up the purchase, the store-owner filled out an appraisal. I thought it was a bit strange to fill out an appraisal for such a small amount, but, hey, what did I know? I got my purchase, stuffed it and the paperwork in my sweatshirt pouch, and headed out to peruse a few of the other jewelry stores.

I think I'll buy some earrings to match, I thought. As I went from store to store, I realized what a good deal I got at Diamonds International, so I decided to go back for another purchase. The wheeling and dealing followed the same pattern as before. They told me the suggested retail, then their closeout price, then the lower price because I was so special to them. Bottom line? Twenty-two. Sounded good to me.

We followed the same process. I gave the sales person my credit card and the manager began filling out the appraisal. But one small difference was that I looked at the credit card receipt before I signed it.

"Oh, I'm sorry, miss. You've made a mistake," I said when she handed me the receipt. "This says the charge is twenty-two *hundred* dollars instead of twenty-two dollars."

"That is correct," she said.

"No, you said twenty-two," I said with a voice that had suddenly jumped up two octaves. "You never said the word *hundred*!"

"Oh no, mademoiselle. The earrings are twenty-two *hundred* dollars."

I dropped the receipt as though it had suddenly burst into flames. "I don't want them. There's been a big misunderstanding!" Then a sinking feeling hit as I put my hand in my sweatshirt pouch and felt my previous purchase.

"What did I just buy an hour ago?" I asked as I pulled the stone from my pouch.

"That was twenty-seven *hundred* dollars," she clarified.

"I thought it was $27!" I shrieked. "You never said the word *hundred*! Not once!"

Thankfully, they took back the stone I had purchased and credited my account. I ran back to the ship as fast as my little tennis shoes could carry me and promised to never go shopping without an escort again! (At least not in Alaska.) Can you imagine if I had come home, opened my credit card bill, and seen a $4,900 charge rather than a $49 charge? Oh my. Steve affectionately calls that the day I went into Juneau, Alaska, and proceeded to spend my son's inheritance.

When we got home, I told my son the story. He didn't laugh like everyone else. He just looked at me dumbfounded and said, "Mom, didn't you pick up on the clues?"

"Like what?" I asked.

"Like, you were in *Diamonds* International. The stone was in 14 carat *gold*. It had little *diamonds* around it."

"Yeah, but they were very little diamonds!" I retorted.

"The manager wrote out an *appraisal*. He wouldn't do that for $27."

"But it was an end-of-the-season closeout sale," I argued.

Steven just looked at me and shook his head.

You know, Steven was right! All along, there were hints that the tanzanite was much more valuable than $27, and yet I refused to pay attention to the clues.

Oh, dear one, you are of great value to God. Have you been paying attention to the clues? You are His treasured possession. There's no closeout sale, end-of-the-year clearance, or discount coupon when it comes to your worth as a child of God. All through our lives, God gives us clues about our worth. The beauty of a sunset, the soothing sound of a baby's coos, the sweetness of a fresh strawberry, the warmth of a hug, the comfort of a phone call, the answer to a prayer. God loves and values you so much that He allowed and purposed for His only Son, whom He loved, to die on a rugged Roman cross to pay the penalty for your sin so you can spend eternity with Him. He didn't have to do that, you know. But He did because of your great worth to Him.

Here's another hint or clue of your value to Him—this book. I believe the reason you're reading this book is that God is giving you yet another hint of His great love for you and your worth to Him. Bought with a price...all sales final...no returns.

• • • • •

RECOGNIZE THE LIE: *I'm worthless.*

REJECT THE LIE: *That is not true.*

REPLACE THE LIE WITH TRUTH:

Look at the birds of the air; they do not sow or reap or store away in barns, and yet your heavenly Father feeds them. Are you not much more valuable than they? (Matthew 6:26).

8

I'm Such a Failure

LIE: *I'm such a failure.*

TRUTH: *I can do everything through Christ, who gives me strength* (Philippians 4:13 NLT).

June was a senior on the debate team when she presented a pro-life argument. She did her research and displayed amazing pictures of the development of a child in his mother's womb. She won the debate and received the highest grade possible. Six months later she had her first abortion.

Simply knowing the truth does not ensure that we will walk in the truth. A strong faith does not preclude weak moments. June knew the truth in her head, but she didn't have the courage to apply it to her life. "I could not speak what I supposedly believed any longer," June lamented. "I was a defeated failure." June went on to have two more abortions while attending college and eventually dropped out of school. Pregnant for the fourth time, she packed her bags and went home to her parents. As far as they knew, this was her first pregnancy.

This time, June knew she would have her baby—and she did.

Peter, the apostle, and June walked a similar path. While June denied her children the right to live, Peter denied his Savior's lordship. He made many mistakes, and he made them when they mattered most.

During the last meal Jesus celebrated with His disciples before He faced the cross, He warned them He would be leaving soon.

"Lord, where are you going?" Peter asked.

Jesus replied, "Where I am going, you cannot follow now, but you will follow later."

Peter asked, "Lord, why can't I follow you now? I will lay down my life for you" (John 13:35-37). "Even if all fall away on account of you, I never will" (Matthew 26:33).

Then Jesus answered, "Will you really lay down your life for me? Very truly I tell you, before the rooster crows, you will disown me three times!" (John 13:38).

But Peter declared, "Even if I have to die with you, I will never disown you" (Matthew 26:35).

I imagine Jesus simply looked at Peter with a knowing eye and a wounded heart. *Sure you will, buddy*, He must have mused. *You will die for Me, but not today.*

Peter was so sure of himself, and yet, before the sun rose over the horizon, he did the very opposite of what his self-assured, overconfident words proclaimed.

After Jesus's arrest, Peter followed at a distance and snuck into the high priest's courtyard where Jesus was being held.

"You are not one of His disciples, are you?" a girl asked at the door.

"I am not," Peter said.

"You are not one of His disciples, are you?" someone else asked as Peter stood warming his hands by the fire.

"I am not," Peter said.

"Didn't I see you with Jesus in the olive grove, and aren't you the fellow who cut off my relative's ear?" challenged another.

"I am not!" Peter said for a third time (John 18:25-27, paraphrased).

The moment the third denial escaped Peter's lips, a rooster crowed. As the new day broke over the horizon, Peter's heart broke over his sin. He wept bitterly over his cowardly actions. This brash, boisterous, demonstrative fisherman had cowered under the accusing gaze of a mere servant girl.

FAILURE IS NEVER FINAL

Three days after Jesus breathed His last earthly breath, the disciples received the news of the empty tomb from the women who had gone to visit the grave. Mark tells us an angel told the women to go and "tell his disciples and Peter" that Jesus was alive (Mark 16:7). I wonder why the angel singled out Peter. Could it be that God knew Peter would need an extra measure of grace and assurance because of his failure?

Can you imagine how Peter's heart raced as his feet ran to the empty tomb? I wonder what he was thinking as he kicked up the dust. Would he be ashamed to face Jesus if He were alive? Would he be grateful for another chance? Would Jesus even want to see him?

Peter did encounter Jesus after His resurrection. We don't know how many times they were together or when the conversations took place, but God does allow us to witness how Jesus embraced and restored this broken "rock."

After Jesus had appeared to the disciples and to many others, life seemed to go back to normal. Peter and John returned to what they had always done—fishing. One morning, as the sun rose over the horizon, their nets remained empty.

A man called from the shore,

"Friends, haven't you any fish?"

"No," they answered.

He said, "Throw your net on the right side of the boat and you will find some" (John 21:1-6).

As the nets began to fill, John remembered a similar incident that occurred three years earlier, and he realized the man on the shore was Jesus.

Peter jumped into the water and swam to shore while the others hauled in the miraculous catch. After dinner, Jesus pulled Peter aside and asked him,

> "Simon son of John, do you love me more than these?"
>
> "Yes, Lord," he said, "you know that I love you."
>
> Jesus said, "Feed my lambs."
>
> Again Jesus said, "Simon son of John, do you love me?"
>
> He answered, "Yes, Lord, you know that I love you."
>
> Jesus said, "Take care of my sheep."
>
> The third time he said to him, "Simon son of John, do you love me?"
>
> Peter was hurt because Jesus asked him the third time, "Do you love me?" He said, "Lord, you know all things; you know that I love you."
>
> Jesus said, "Feed my sheep" (John 21:15-17).

Jesus knew Peter would fail him, and yet his failure wasn't fatal. Jesus invited Peter to repentance and restoration. "I believe in you, Peter," He seemed to say. "Now get back to being a fisher of men rather than a fisher of fish."

June felt much like Peter. "I denied Jesus each time I walked through the door of that abortion clinic," she said. "But He has pulled me aside and asked, 'June, do you love Me?' And I have answered as Peter, 'Yes, Lord, You know that I love You.'

"I had felt my failure was too grave, that I was too far gone for God to forgive me," June explained, "but He showed me no place is so far away from His grace that He cannot save. My sin is never greater than God's grace."

DON'T SEW ON THE LABEL

Failure is never final. Failure is never fatal. We don't have to let our failure define us or confine us. We all struggle with feeling like a failure at one time or another—maybe as a mom, as a wife, as a friend, in ministry, at work, at holding our tongues, at loving the unlovable. Life brings us lots of opportunities to fail.

How often have I made a simple mistake, like driving away from the grocery store before putting my groceries in the car? Then I get home and the chatter begins. *I am so stupid. What's wrong with me? I'm such a failure.*

Renee Swope wrote, "When our thoughts heap condemning statements like these on us, we get buried in discouragement and defeat. Failure gets the final say. We become our own worst critic, and once again Satan loves it. Whether you are saying these things to yourself or you are repeating what someone else has said, once again they are exactly what the enemy wants you to believe."[1]

> We don't have to let our failure define us or confine us.

Accusation that leads to condemnation doesn't come from the Holy Spirit. Conviction that leads to repentance does (John 16:8). Accusation that leads to condemnation comes from the accuser (Revelation 12:10). Condemnation makes broad, sweeping generalizations about your character and identity, such as, *You're a failure...You're unreliable...You're a misfit.* Conviction from the Holy Spirit will be about a specific behavior and will never attach your identity to that behavior. *You lied to your coworker...You flirted with your neighbor...You shamed your child.* These statements are specific. Conviction's purpose is to conform you to the image of Christ. Condemnation's purpose is to contain you and rename you. Scripture assures us that the accuser will be completely defeated in the end, but until then, he accuses us before God day and night (Revelation 12:10).

When you slap a label on your identity other than who God says you are, the enemy takes a victory lap around your heart. Learn from your mistakes under the tutelage of the Holy Spirit, but don't get stuck there. Accept God's forgiveness and then move on.

Lysa TerKeurst writes about the limitations of living with the wrong kinds of labels. She explains how labels "imprison us in catego-ries that are hard to escape...Those labels start out as little threads of self-dissatisfaction but ultimately weave together into a straightjacket of self-condemnation."[2]

Many men and women failed in the Bible, and yet God did not label them according to their failure. David committed adultery, and yet God referred to him as "a man after my own heart" (Acts 13:22). Moses and Gideon both began as cowards, and yet God called them courageous. Peter denied he even knew Jesus, and yet Jesus labeled him "the rock."

Dr. Neil Anderson once said, "One reason we doubt God's love is that we have an adversary who uses every little offense to accuse us of being good-for-nothings. But your advocate, Jesus Christ, is more powerful than your adversary. He has canceled the debt of your sins—past, present, and future. No matter what you do or how you fail, God has no reason not to love you and accept you completely."[3]

If you have sewn the label of "failure" onto your heart like a kid with her name sewn into her clothes before going off to camp, cut it out or rip it off. Then sew on a new label with the truth of who you really are. You are a dearly loved, chosen, forgiven, redeemed child of God.

FAILURE MISBELIEF

It's easy to think one failure marks our identity as a failure. That's what the enemy wants us to believe. If he can make us feel as though we are a failure, then he's the winner. Never let failure have the final say.

Brennan Manning, in his book *Abba's Child*, wrote, "It used to be that I never felt safe with myself unless I was performing flawlessly. My desire to be perfect had transcended my desire for God...My jaded per-ception of personal failure and inadequacy led to a loss of self-esteem, triggering episodes of mild depression and heavy anxiety."[4]

> Never let failure have the final say.

Failure is just part of life, and the sooner we accept that we are flawed humans who depend on the perfect Christ, the sooner we put the taskmaster of perfection away. *I am not a failure, but I am a child of God who sometimes fails.*

What is failure, anyway, except a man-made yardstick for performance? God is much more interested in the process than the final product. If I obey God and lose the sale, I am still a success in God's eyes. "Do not throw away your confidence; it will be richly rewarded. You need to persevere so that when you have done the will of God, you will receive what he has promised" (Hebrews 10:35-36).

> God is much more interested in the process than the final product.

A moral failure is different. Sin is not a failure to measure up to a man-made yardstick of performance, but a failure to measure up to God's standards. Even then, God does not define us by the sin. "If we confess our sins, he is faithful and just and will forgive us our sins and purify us from all unrighteousness" (1 John 1:9).

WHERE ARE YOUR ACCUSERS?

The sun was just peeking through the securely locked shutters of Morah's bedroom window. The predawn stillness was broken only by the songs of early rising birds floating on the breeze. Morah was a tangle of sheets, arms, and legs as the man she loved lay sleeping beside her.

"Oh, Mathias," she whispered as her fingertips brushed a stray lock of hair from his closed eyes. "If only you weren't married. I know this is wrong, but I love you so. And I believe you when you say you love me as well. We are risking our very lives with these frequent trysts."

Morah's musings were suddenly interrupted by a banging on the door.

"Open up!" the gruff voice demanded.

"Who is there?" Morah cried as she scrambled to find her robe.

"Open up or we'll break down the door."

"What's all the commotion?" Mathias mumbled as he groggily sat up in bed. "What's going on?"

Before Morah could even think to answer, the angry mob of religious men broke through the simple lock and into the lovers' hideaway.

"What is the meaning of this?" Mathias barked. "What do you think you are doing?"

"What do you think *you* are doing, my friend?" the Pharisee countered. "That is the real question here."

"Morah, daughter of Omar, you are under arrest for adultery under the Law of Moses!" the moral police spat. "Get dressed and come with me."

The Pharisee tossed Morah her night robe, but failed to turn his head as she slipped her trembling frame from the cover of the sheets and into the thin cloak. He grabbed her by the arm and began dragging her to the door.

"Where are you taking me?" she cried.

"You'll find out soon enough," the Pharisee growled.

"What about Mathias?" the youngest man of the group inquired.

"Just leave him. We don't need him."

"Why don't you go back to your wife where you belong?" the Pharisee called over his shoulder as the group left the room. And with that, the conspiring mob continued their trek to the temple with the half-clad, trembling, weeping woman in tow. Two men flanked her on either side, dragging her through the early morning hustle and bustle of the city. The bait was hooked, and now it was time to reel in the catch.

A curious stream of townsfolk joined the parade. Jesus was already teaching in the courtyard with a group gathered at His feet. As always, His message and miracles drew large crowds. A distant rumble interrupted His gentle teaching as the angry mob and curious crowd approached. They marched right into the inner circle of the classroom and thrust the woman at the Master's feet.

Morah's unbound hair fell around her bare shoulders in disheveled disarray. Her shame-filled eyes stayed riveted on the earthen floor, refusing to meet Jesus's gaze. Then one of the men pulled her to her feet and displayed her for all to see.

She didn't need to look at the man before her. She recognized His voice. It was Jesus.

"Teacher," the pious Pharisee began, "this woman was caught in the act of adultery. The Law of Moses commands us to stone such a woman. Now, what do you say?"

Jesus didn't look at the woman's half-clad body as the others openly gawked. He looked into her soul.

Morah lifted her eyes and saw the face of love. *What do I detect in His gaze?* she thought to herself. It wasn't contempt, disgust, or condemnation, but rather compassion, concern, and pure, unadulterated love. Somehow, she knew this was the look she had been searching for her entire life.

As Morah considered the Pharisee's question, she understood Jesus's dilemma. If He set her free, the Pharisees would accuse Him of ignoring the Law of Moses and deem Him a heretic. If He sentenced her to death by stoning, His teachings of grace and forgiveness would be negated.

The religious leaders already held the stones in their clenched fists, anticipating His reply. Their hearts were as hard as the rocks they held in their hands. But rather than give a quick answer, Jesus moved His gaze from the trembling woman and stooped to the ground. With His finger, the very hand of God-made-man, He began writing in the dirt. A frigid chill swept through the Pharisees' pious robes. Suddenly they felt the rawness of naked exposure as Jesus's eyes looked up at each of them. Without a word, He uncloaked their sinful thoughts and desires. With one look from Jesus, they stood soul-bare and more exposed than the half-dressed woman before them.

Everyone held their breath. The silence was deafening. The tension was palpable. Finally, Jesus rose and delivered the verdict.

"If any one of you is without sin, let him be the first to throw a stone at her."

Then Jesus squatted once again and continued to write.

One by one the Pharisees unclenched their fists, dropped the stones, and filtered through the crowd. The older men who had accumulated a longer list of sins turned to leave first, with the younger ones not far behind.

The remaining crowd listened closely as the drama continued to unfold. After the last of the Pharisees cleared the scene, Jesus straightened up and asked her, "Woman, where are your accusers? Has no one condemned you?"

"No one, sir," she replied.

"Then neither do I condemn you," Jesus declared. "Go now and leave your life of sin."

The woman turned to leave, but not before picking up a discarded stone to take with her.

"To remember," she whispered.

I'm sure you recognize this story, based on the account of the woman caught in adultery recorded in John 8. She is one of the many nameless women in the New Testament. I've given her a name to help us realize she is one of us—a woman who had failed.

This woman was taken to Jesus in shame, but she received grace and forgiveness. The accusers went to Jesus in self-righteous piety, but skulked away condemned. The older ones with the much longer list of sins were the first to turn and slink away. I tell you the truth, the older I get, the more merciful toward others I become. In my early years, let's say in my twenties, I was much quicker to pass judgment on others. But the longer I've lived, the more mistakes I've made and the more clearly God has revealed my own shortcomings and failures. As John Wesley said when a drunk was led through town to be placed in the public stocks, "But by the grace of God, there go I."[5]

Notice that Jesus didn't say what she did wasn't wrong. He called sin a sin. But then He said, "Neither do I condemn you...Go now and leave your life of sin" (John 8:11). Jesus wants to give us a clean slate to start again, no matter how many times we fail.

Failure is a part of life. Everyone has failures, just different ones. The real tragedy is getting stuck there. Once again, we see Jesus demonstrating that failure doesn't have the final say when He is Lord of our lives.

FAMOUS FAILURES

Perhaps failure of a spiritual nature is not your issue. Perhaps it's failure of a marriage, of a job, or of a dream. If so, consider this:

- After Fred Astaire's first screen test in 1933, the director noted, "Can't act. Slightly bald. Can dance a little."

- Louisa May Alcott, author of *Little Women*, was encouraged to find work as a servant or a seamstress.

- Beethoven's violin teacher once told him he was a "hopeless composer."

- Walt Disney was fired by a newspaper editor for lack of ideas.

- Thomas Edison's teacher said he was too stupid to learn anything.

- Albert Einstein didn't speak until he was four years old and didn't read until he was seven. His teachers described him as mentally slow.

- Isaac Newton performed poorly in grade school.

- Henry Ford failed and went bankrupt five times before he finally succeeded.

- Babe Ruth set the home-run record (714), but he also once held the record for the most strikeouts (1330).

- Winston Churchill failed sixth grade.

- Dr. Seuss's first children's book, *And to Think That I Saw It on Mulberry Street*, was rejected by 27 publishers. The 28th publisher, Vanguard Press, sold six million copies of the book.

- In 1902, the poetry editor of the *Atlantic Monthly* returned the poems of a 28-year-old poet with the following note: "Our magazine has no room for your vigorous verse." The poet was Robert Frost.

- In 1889, Rudyard Kipling received the following rejection letter from the *San Francisco Examiner*: "I'm sorry, Mr. Kipling, but you just don't know how to use the English language."

- Agatha Christie had to wait five years before her first book was published.

- Beatrix Potter's *The Tale of Peter Rabbit* was rejected so many times, she decided to self-publish 250 copies. It has now sold over 45 million copies.

- Margaret Mitchell got 38 rejections from publishers before finding one to publish her novel *Gone with the Wind*.

- One basketball player missed 9000 shots in his career. He lost more than 300 games. Twenty-six times he was trusted to take the game's winning shot and missed. His name is Michael Jordan. He said, "I've failed over and over again in my life. And that's why I succeed."

These people refused to believe they were a failure simply because they had failed. We need to reject the lie of the enemy, who tries to kick us when we're down by telling us the lie. Failure can be the springboard for future success.

Once a little boy was practicing baseball by himself in the backyard. He threw the ball in the air, swung, and missed. Time and time again he missed the ball as it descended to the ground. Finally, he huffed and said, "Man, that's some pitcher." What a great perspective!

YOU'RE IN GOOD COMPANY

A common theme throughout Scripture is overcoming failure. Abraham passed his wife, Sarah, off as his sister because of fear (Genesis 12 and 20). Lot failed to stand up for what was right and offered his daughters to immoral men (Genesis 18–19). Jacob betrayed his father and stole his brother's blessing (Genesis 27). Moses struck the rock twice in anger when God commanded him to strike it once (Numbers 20:11). Aaron gave in to peer pressure and made a golden calf (Exodus 32). Miriam had a bout of jealousy and tried to usurp her brother's God-appointed position (Numbers 12). Jonah hopped on a boat and headed in the opposite direction when God called him to go to Nineveh (Jonah 1:1-3). Samson fell for the whims of a Philistine woman and gave away the secret to his strength (Judges 16). David committed adultery and murder and then tried to cover it up (2 Samuel 11).

You know what's amazing? Most of these men and women are listed as people of great faith who "conquered kingdoms, administered justice, and gained what was promised; who shut the mouths of lions, quenched the fury of the flames, and escaped the edge of the sword; *whose weakness was turned to strength*; and who became powerful in battle and routed foreign armies" (Hebrews 11:33-34, emphasis added). We have a great cloud of witnesses who can identify with failure. We are never alone in that regard.

Oh, friend, failure doesn't have to be fatal or final. During a time of failure, the enemy will tell you to quit trying, that you're hopeless, worthless, and powerless to succeed. Don't believe him. Reject the lie and replace it with truth. "No, in all these things we are more than conquerors through him who loved us" (Romans 8:37). "I can do everything through Christ, who gives me strength" (Philippians 4:13 NLT). God said, "My grace is sufficient for you, for my power is made perfect in weakness" (2 Corinthians 12:9).

Learn from your failure under the tutelage of the Holy Spirit, and then move on. Nothing makes the devil madder than a child of God who fails, gets back up, and tries again with the power of God moving him or her forward.

• • • • •

RECOGNIZE THE LIE: *I'm such a failure.*

REJECT THE LIE: *That is not true.*

REPLACE THE LIE WITH TRUTH:

I can do everything through Christ, who gives me strength (Philippians 4:13 NLT).

I'm So Ugly

LIE: *I'm so ugly.*

TRUTH: *I am God's masterpiece*
(Ephesians 2:10 NLT).

I was sitting in a crowded restaurant with my family when she walked by in her full-length, white satin ballgown delicately trimmed in lace and studded with tiny "jewels." Crinoline swished as she moved across the room. A rhinestone tiara sparkled on her head, and pearl-studded slippers accentuated her feminine feet. Golden ringlets framed her rosy cheeks, and puckered lips glistened with a hint of gloss. She knew she was beautiful, and she glanced around at the admiring smiles of onlookers as she walked through the crowd. She was three years old.

I'm not sure when the dream to be beautiful enters a little girl's mind, but I do know when the dream ends—when the preacher says, "May she rest in peace."

I remember sneaking into my mother's closet as a little girl and slipping my child-size feet into her size-seven high heels. I'd stand on my tiptoes on a chair, pull a hat off the top shelf, and plop it on my head like an oversized lampshade. Her satin evening jacket with sleeves that hung eight inches below my fingertips gave a nice, elegant touch to my outfit. A lady going to a party would never be caught without "putting on her face," so I crept into the bathroom, opened the forbidden drawer, and created a clownish work of art on the palette of my face. Red rouge circles on my cheeks, heaps of blue eye shadow on my munchkin lids, and smeared orange lipstick far exceeding the proper borders were finished off with a dusting of facial powder with an oversized brush.

From the time a little girl stretches on her tiptoes to get a peek in the mirror, she desires to be beautiful—perhaps like her mommy. But at some point, she looks in the mirror and doesn't like what she sees. The world screams messages from billboards, movie screens, and magazines about what beautiful is supposed to look like. Then we look in the mirror and say, "This isn't it."

This isn't just a first world problem. *National Geographic* reported that on the border of Burma and Thailand, members of the Kayan tribe begin their beauty rituals at age five by wearing brass rings around their necks. As they grow older, more rings are added, and eventually their necks elongate to look like a giraffe's. For these women, the shiny brass rings are the ultimate sign of female elegance and status. Maori women in New Zealand consider it beautiful to tattoo their lips dark blue. Young girls in the Karo tribe in southern Ethiopia allow their elders to cut scars onto their abdomens, which they believe will make them more beautiful and able to attract a husband. In a West African country, Mauritania, they believe bigger is better and have practiced the ritual of force-feeding young girls to plump them up.

Interestingly, Dove's global research found that only 4 percent of women around the world considered themselves beautiful.[1] That is up from 2 percent in 2004. Eighty percent of women agree that every woman has something about her that is beautiful, but do not see their own beauty.[2]

To be honest, I've always felt my nose was too big for my face and my tush too tushy for the rest of my body. When buying clothes, I'm always checking the mirror to make sure my pants don't make my backside look too big. You can imagine my shock the first time I went to South America to speak and saw tush enhancer undergarments in the store windows.

"What in the world is that?" I asked the interpreter.

"Oh, those are enhancers. To make women's backsides appear bigger."

My stars. All my life I'd been trying to make mine appear smaller and here they were trying to make theirs seem larger! We're a mess. When it comes to being beautiful, women are rarely content.

One of my friends' four-year-old granddaughter asked her, "Grandma, why is your bottom so big?"

"God gave me that," she said. "So wherever I go, I always have a nice cushion to sit on."

"I hope my bottom is as big as yours when I grow up," her granddaughter replied.

She could only hope.

I've gotten a little off track here, but not really. The point is, what is beautiful to one person or to one culture may not be beautiful to another. Who gets to decide? God does.

John Eldredge, in his book *Wild at Heart*, describes three longings that lie at the heart of every man: a battle to fight, a beauty to rescue, and an adventure to live. He also ventures to say that women have three longings of the heart as well: to be fought for, to share in an adventure, and to have her beauty unveiled.

> Not to conjure, but to unveil. Most women feel the pressure to be beautiful from an early age, but that's not what I'm unpacking. We also have a deep desire to simply and truly be the beauty and be delighted in. Most little girls will play dress up or wedding day. Or "twirling skirts"—those flowing dresses perfect for spinning around. Each one will put on her pretty dress, come into the living room, and twirl. What she longs for is to capture her daddy's delight.[3]

I read a quote once that said when a man looks in the mirror, he focuses on his best features. When a woman looks in the mirror, she focuses on her worst features. I don't know how men see themselves, but I do know most women focus on their negative features instead of their positive ones. If we look in the only mirror that matters, the Word of God, we will discover God thinks we're beautiful. A friend gave me a laminated card once with the following prayer: "Lord, help me see myself as You see me, no matter how beautiful it is."

STICKS AND STONES

When I asked my three-year-old little friend Brooke what she wanted to be when she grew up, she tossed her head back, flipped her hair over her shoulder, and simply said, "Beautiful." But at some point, every woman looks in the mirror and decides she's missed the mark.

I'll never forget the time I went to a doctor for a physical in the fifth grade. I can't remember if I was having a problem, but I do remember the doctor saying, "She's healthy, but she'll never be a beauty queen." That comment stuck. Self-diagnosis confirmed.

The world's ever-changing definition of beauty, our flesh's critical nature, and the devil's desire to destroy our healthy self-image all merge to malign a woman's perception of her own physical artistry.

My friend, Michele Cushatt, who is stunning, tells a story about a comment she overheard in college. I'll let Michele tell you the story as she shares it in her book, *I Am: A 60-Day Journey to Knowing Who You Are Because of Who He Is.*

> His name was, let's say, Mark.
>
> We were both sophomores at a Christian college in the Midwest. I didn't know him well, although on a small campus such as ours, everyone knew everyone. Drop eight hundred students in overpopulated dorms and intimate classrooms, and it doesn't take long for each of us to know who had sneaked out the night before and what family drama we'd left behind at home.
>
> Mark wasn't notable. Mildly attractive and well liked, connected to all the other attractive and well-liked people. Even in college, the high school hierarchy continued.
>
> I'd planned to go to medical school. But a come-to-Jesus altar call at a high school youth conference changed my trajectory. I wanted to go overseas, help the needy, tell people about Jesus. So I abandoned medicine and enrolled at

a Christian college, dreaming of Africa or Russia or some other place where I would change the world.

Instead, my world changed.

It happened a few weeks before Christmas break. Although I'd been in college for three semesters, I still struggled to find my place. I had great grades, plenty of friends. But the "freshman fifteen" turned out to be no joke, and I'd gain my full share of allotted pounds. If my self-perception hadn't already been skewed, I might've been able to accept my new physique, maybe take the necessary steps to change it. But for as long as I could remember, I'd never liked my appearance. Adding fifteen pounds to it only deepened my self-disgust.

This was the status of my self-esteem on the afternoon I overheard a male voice coming around a hallway corner: "Take Michele, for example."

At the sound of my name, I stopped. Held my breath.

The voice—which I recognized as Mark's—continued.

"She's one of those who'd be beautiful if she wasn't so fat. Know what I mean?"

I couldn't move.

I don't know what he said next, didn't stick around long enough to find out. Humiliated, I found my legs, ran to my dorm room, and wept.[4]

Several days later, Michele confronted Mark. He didn't see anything wrong with the comment and thought it was a compliment. Weeks later, when the semester was over, Michele packed her belongings and moved back home. She never returned to school.

I'm now forty-four years old. I have six children and a husband and wear a size eight(ish). But in the past two decades, I've been everything from a size two to an eighteen. At each size, regardless of how big or small, I didn't see myself as beautiful. Whether I passed a bathroom mirror or caught a glimpse of myself in a store window's glass, I still heard the same words: "You'd be beautiful if..."

You see, beautiful isn't about size. Nor is it about Mark. It's about how I see me. And what I choose to believe as a result.[5]

Now, I know we all want Michele to tell us Mark's real name so we can go and pay him a little visit. But we've all got Marks in our lives, don't we?

GOD'S MASTERPIECE

It was parents' night for my son's kindergarten class, and proud parents gathered in the classroom to find their child's seat. Rather than having names on the desks, a self-drawn portrait donned the front of each chair. The trick was figuring out which drawing was your child.

Steven's drawing had one really large eye with the other quite a bit smaller. His mouth slipped to the side of his face, and his ears were asymmetrical orbs attached to the sides of his head. The eyes were brown and the hair was blond. It was a toss-up, but we finally figured out which one was him.

Truthfully, Steven's portrait didn't look that much different from a Pablo Picasso original—whom Wikipedia lauds as one of the most influential artists of the twentieth century. On May 4, 2010, Christie's auctioned one of Picasso's paintings for 106.5 million dollars. Steven's work of art will never hang in an art gallery, but it is precious to me.

What's the difference? What makes one work of art worth more than another? Its worth is based on the artist who created it. And you, my friend, were created by the Almighty God—Elohim—the Creator God.

In the New Testament, Paul writes, "We are God's handiwork" (Ephesians 2:10). Other translation say we are His "masterpiece" (NLT), His "workmanship" (ESV), His "work of art" (NJB). The Greek word translated "workmanship" or "masterpiece" is *poiema*. The word describes something that is skillfully wrought, and artfully created. *Poiema* is where we get the English word "poem."

What God wants you to understand is that you are an epic poem—a work of masterful art. Jon Bloom, staff writer for DesiringGod.org wrote:

> Tiny, insignificant you are more glorious than the sun and more fascinating than Orion. For the sun cannot perceive its Creator's power in its own blinding glory, nor can Orion trace his Designer's genius in the precision of his heavenly course. But you can. You are part of the infinitesimal fraction of created things that have been granted the incredible gift of being able to perceive the power and native genius of God! And to you, and you only, is given a wholly unique perception and experience of God's holy grand *poiema*. There are some verses God will show only to you. What kind of being are you, so small and weak and yet endowed with such marvelous capacity for perception and wonder? This is not inspirational poster kitsch. This is biblical reality.[6]

A woman was and is one of God's most magnificent creations. She was and is the grand finale of God's creative genius and the inspiration for man's first poetry. After He created the land and the sea, the sun and the moon, creeping creatures on the earth, flying fowl in the sky, and swimming fish in the seas, He created man. But then He had one more masterpiece up His sleeve—the grand finale. God took a rib from the man and fashioned Eve. You, as a woman, are God's masterpiece.

Bruce Marchiano paints a beautiful picture of God's intentional artistry in creating Eve.

> He shapes her frame and shades her skin. He molds her mind and measures her structure. He sculpts the contour of her face, the almonds of her eyes, and the graceful stretch of her limbs. Long before she even spoke a word, he has held her voice in his heart, and so he ever so gently tunes its timbre. Cell by cell, tenderness by tenderness, and with care beyond care, in creation he quite simply loves her.[7]

Regardless of your self-perceived physical imperfections and culture-driven definition of your anatomical flaws, you are a magnificent creation of a masterful God. And you are beautiful.

David wrote the following as he marveled about how God put him together in his mother's womb.

> You created my inmost being; you knit me together in my mother's womb. I praise you because I am fearfully and wonderfully made; your works are wonderful, I know that full well. My frame was not hidden from you when I was made in the secret place, when I was woven together in the depths of the earth. Your eyes saw my unformed body (Psalm 139:13-16).

Like an artist who sees the finished work in his mind's eye, God saw your unformed substance and then began to fashion you from head to toe. He made no mistakes but planned each detail of your being. He is the masterful Potter who formed you and shaped your unique features. You are one of a kind.

I love that David said, "I know that full well." He had no doubt that he was a masterpiece created by God. No matter how you were conceived or came into this world, you were no mistake.

BARBIE IS NOT REAL

Have you ever wondered what Eve looked like? I must admit, I've always pictured her looking like Barbie. After all, isn't that what the artists always depict? Waist-length flowing tresses, hourglass figure, creamy smooth complexion, delicate feet begging for high heels—a perfect 10. Unfortunately, Barbie is the standard much of our society has depicted as ideal beauty. That standard for beauty is being passed along to children, as it is estimated 94,500,000 were sold in 2016,[8] which happens to be down from previous years.

But is the Barbie image that realistic? If you blew Barbie up to life-sized proportions, her measurements would be 36-18-33, and she would be five foot nine (websites varied on the bust size from 36 to 39 inches). The only blemish I can find is "Made in Japan" stamped on the bottom of her otherwise perfect foot. But, friend, she isn't real! She would barely have room for her liver in that tiny waistline.

My niece, Anna, told about a poignant moment with her eight-year-old daughter.

> I love myself but I hate my thighs. I do. I also hate my post-baby, three-times-C-sectioned tummy. No matter how many planks, sit-ups, or miles I run, it will never be like it was when I was in college. And that makes me sad, frustrated, and sometimes angry.
>
> When my sweet husband tells me I look beautiful, instead of just thanking him, I answer back with a caveat: "Thanks, but I look fat."
>
> I do this in front of my kids sometimes without realizing it. My boys always come back with, "No way, Mom. You look awesome" or "We think you're beautiful!"
>
> But my daughter is just quiet. Watching. Listening. Later she'll come up to me, hug me, and whisper, "I love you so much, Mommy."
>
> A couple of months ago, when she was all dressed up, I saw her looking at herself in the mirror. I stopped and said, "Lillian, you look absolutely stunning!"
>
> She turned around and said to me very matter of fact, "No I don't. I look fat."
>
> I gasped! *Doesn't she know how precious she is? Doesn't she know how beautiful she is? What a blessing she is? Doesn't she know what a miracle her very existence is?*
>
> And then I remembered all the times I answered her dad with the very same words. I was sad, ashamed, and most of all heartbroken. Lillian was eight years old. She understood that "fat" was how I felt about myself, so she decided she should feel that way too.

Lillian and I had a long talk that day. I told her what a blessing her life is, and how God made her special, unique, and beautiful. I also apologized to her, my two sons, and my husband for not loving myself like I should.

Lately, I've been saying "thank you" when I get compliments—something new to me—and it's made all the difference.

Now when I tell Lillian how gorgeous she is (which is all the time), she looks at me with her bright hazel eyes and says, "Thanks, Mommy! I think you're really beautiful too!"

Doris Mortman said, "Until you make peace with who you are, you'll never be content with what you have."[9] Until you understand that you are God's masterpiece, made in His image, you'll never be content with the features He's given you. Do you believe you are a happenstance mixture of your parents' genes, or do you believe you were intentionally woven and knitted together by God with a specific design in mind? What we believe about our origin greatly affects what we believe about our destiny.

You want to know the best beauty secret ever? You won't find it in a spa, at the cosmetic counter at the mall, or in a makeover article in a magazine. You will find it in the Word of God. We become more and more beautiful every time we sit at Jesus's feet. "We, who with unveiled faces contemplate the Lord's glory, are being transformed into his image with ever-increasing glory, which comes from the Lord, who is the Spirit" (2 Corinthians 3:18).

THE EYES OF THE BEHOLDER

In the book of the Bible called Song of Songs, we meet a king who is riding though his kingdom and spies a young Shulammite maiden working in the fields. He is captivated by her beauty and smitten by her form. Her hands are stained with grape juice from the vineyard, her skin is tanned from the midday sun, and her clothes are soiled from the dirt of the field, but the king sees beyond all that. While he is enthralled with her beauty, she begs him not to stare at her. She does not feel worthy of such attention. In our day, she would have probably said, "I'm so ugly."

No matter what she thought of herself, the king was mesmerized. Solomon adored her rosy cheeks, her long neck, her flowing hair, and her ruby lips. He adored the fact that she had all her teeth, shapely legs, and small breasts. He even thought her *poochy* tummy was adorable. He swooned, "You are altogether beautiful, my darling; there is no flaw in you" (4:7).

But what did she think of herself? Not very much. "Do not stare at me because I am dark, because I am darkened by the sun. My mother's sons were angry with me and made me take care of the vineyards; my own vineyard I had to neglect" (1:6).

She felt inferior to other women because of her weathered skin. It wasn't desirable in those days to be tanned by the sun. Lighter skin was considered exotic. Women went to great lengths to shade their skin from the scorching sun. But because she was forced to take care of her mother's sons' vineyards, she had to neglect taking care of herself. Amazingly, in the end, she began to see herself as her bridegroom saw her. Oh, that we would do the same.

Is the Song of Songs our song? For centuries, commentators have noted a parallel between the Lover and the Beloved to Jesus and His bride—the church. Jesus, the lover of your soul, looks at you and thinks you are beautiful—absolutely stunning.

A PORTRAIT OF BEAUTY

One summer I traveled to Paris and visited the Louvre art museum. At the end of a long corridor lined with famous paintings, a crowd gathered to capture a glimpse of the famous *Mona Lisa*. I jostled for position to catch a glimpse and was disappointed at what I saw. Honestly, to me she looked rather plain. What was the draw? I didn't understand until I heard the tour guide explain her history.

No one is really sure of Mona Lisa's true identity, but many think her to be Francesco di Bartolomeo di Zanobi del Giocondo's third wife, Lisa di Antonio Maria di Naldo Gherardini. (Try saying that three times real fast. No wonder most just say, "We don't know who it is!")

She was painted by Leonardo da Vinci between 1503 and 1507. The painting moved from King Francis I's castle, to Fontainebleau, to Paris, to Versailles, to Napoleon's estate, and ended up in the Louvre. However, on August 21, 1911, the *Mona Lisa* was stolen by an Italian thief. During that time, the Parisians placed another painting in her spot, but the citizens missed her terribly. Two years later, she emerged in Florence and was returned to Paris, where she remains in the Louvre behind bullet-proof glass.

Why is she loved today? Because once she was lost, but now she is found. She was stolen from her place of honor, but eventually returned to her rightful place of honor. No wonder she's smiling.

If you've come to know the saving grace of Jesus, this is your story too. Once you were lost, but now you've been found. Jesus paid the price for you and established you in your rightful place as a child of God. Maybe your portrait isn't in a museum, but if Jesus had a wallet, He'd have your picture in it.

"Let the king be enthralled by your beauty" (Psalm 45:11). That means He is captivated, fascinated, enraptured, smitten, spellbound, and taken with you. You are beautiful.

• • • • •

RECOGNIZE THE LIE: *I'm so ugly.*

REJECT THE LIE: *That's not true.*

REPLACE THE LIE WITH TRUTH:

We are God's masterpiece (Ephesians 2:10 NLT).

10

I Would Be Happy If...

LIE: *I would be happy if...*

TRUTH: *My joy comes from the Lord* (Psalm 126:3).

Do you want to hold her?" Karen asked.

I couldn't see the infant in question. Her mother had her wrapped up like a child about to enter a blizzard, though the room was warmed by the heat of fifty women and a table full of Crock-Pots and casseroles. I couldn't see her, but I knew that somewhere in the depths of that pink, fleecy cloth, little Makenna Purdue waited. At least five other women had held her already, and now it was my turn.

I was forty-one years old and I'd never conceived a child of my own. I'd never rested my hand on my stomach in awe of the life growing inside. I'd never had the privilege of bringing a miniature clone of myself to a Bible-study potluck and offering peeks and cuddles to my friends. So the question remained: Did I want to hold another woman's baby?[1]

As I read the words from my friend, Shannon Woodward, I understood exactly how she felt. I can still remember the day when the words *secondary infertility* were written on my medical record. An emptiness I had never experienced before blew into the place where my dreams had lived. *What have I done wrong? Why is God punishing me? Am I not worthy to raise another human being?* I prayed, repented of everything I could think of, fasted, and begged God to intervene. I changed my diet, had two exploratory surgeries, injected and ingested hormones, and had timed intimacy with my husband (which is anything but intimate). I was determined to outsmart the diagnosis.

But it didn't happen, and I understood the pain of empty arms and missing someone I'd never met. Our five-bedroom dream house was a daily reminder of beds that would not be slept in, toys that would not be scattered, and children who would not be tucked in at night.

Steve and I do have one amazing son. Steven Hugh Jaynes Jr. was born on a frosty February morning, and I never knew so much love could be wrapped in one tiny package. But God closed my womb for the possibility of siblings for him. Steven was conceived with no trouble whatsoever, and we were surprised and brokenhearted when we learned he would be our only child through natural means. But through the painful years of infertility, God unfolded a plan, a purpose, and a promise. He began to show me just what I needed to be happy: Him.

THE LIE IN THE GARDEN

Let's go back to the Genesis garden. Remember when the serpent slithered up to Eve and began to dialogue, beginning with, "Did God really say…?" Every one of his lies spring from the idea that happiness is just a decision away.

The enemy wants you to believe God is holding out on you. "You will not certainly die," the serpent said to the woman. "For God knows that when you eat from it your eyes will be opened, and you will be like God, knowing good and evil" (Genesis 3:4-5). Ponder those words. You. Will. Be. Like. God. You can be your own god.

Rather than being thankful for what we do have, we allow the enemy to point out what we don't have. Think about it. Eve had every tree in the garden at her disposal except one. Every tree. That is a cornucopia of choices. But rather than being thankful for what she did have, she bought into the lie and focused on what she didn't have. *I would be happy if…* Is any of this sounding familiar to you? It should. Satan uses the same tactics with us he used with Eve.

Eve had everything a woman could ask for: safety, security, significance, and love. It most likely never entered her mind that there could be something more...until the serpent made the suggestion. He implied that she could be more and have more if she would do the one thing God told her not to do. God's one restriction was for their protection. He told them, "When you eat from it you will certainly die" (Genesis 2:17). His desire was for her to have life and have it to the full. Yet she lost it all when she bought into the lie, "You will be happy if..."

THE GOD-SHAPED HOLE

No person, possession, place, or position will ultimately make you happy. Those things may give you moments or even periods of happiness, but ultimate, lasting joy can be found only in knowing Jesus. Why? Because God planned it that way. Solomon wrote, "He has also set eternity in the human heart" (Ecclesiastes 3:11). Another translation says it this way: "He also has planted eternity in men's hearts and minds [a divinely implanted sense of a purpose working through the ages which nothing under the sun but God alone can satisfy]" (AMPC).

I call this desire a "glory ache"—a longing to experience God's presence and work daily. We all have the ache, but not everyone knows exactly what the ache is longing for. So man tries everything under the sun, as Solomon describes in Ecclesiastes, to fill in the space at the end of *I'd be happy if...*

C.S. Lewis also wrote:

> We are half-hearted creatures, fooling about with drink and sex and ambition when infinite joy is offered us, like an ignorant child who wants to go on making mud pies in a slum because he cannot imagine what is meant by the offer of a holiday at the sea. We are far too easily pleased.[2]

I agree with Lewis's quote. However, I don't believe we are pleased with these God-substitutes for very long. No matter how much worldly success a man or woman has on this earth, I haven't heard of one yet who doesn't have a niggling feeling that there is something more. But still, we "fool about" hoping to land on the big "it."

It has been said that every person has a God-shaped hole that can be filled only by God Himself.[3] I've also heard it said this way: There is a God-shaped vacuum in the heart of every man that cannot be filled by anything or anyone, but only by God the Creator, made known through Jesus Christ.

Jesus spoke of this "hole" in John chapter 7.

> Now on the final and most important day of the Feast, Jesus stood, and He cried in a loud voice, If any man is thirsty, let him come to Me and drink!
>
> He who believes in Me [who cleaves to and trusts in and relies on Me] as the Scripture has said, from his innermost being shall flow [continuously] springs and rivers of living water.
>
> But He was speaking here of the Spirit, Whom those who believed (trusted, had faith) in Him were afterward to receive. For the [Holy] Spirit had not yet been given, because Jesus was not yet glorified (raised to honor) (7:37-39 AMPC).

"Innermost being" comes from the Greek word *koilia,* and means a cavity; the belly; the stomach; the womb.[4] A cavity is a hole or empty place. Jesus beautifully describes the living water of the Holy Spirit that will fill into and flow out of the spiritually empty place in every soul.

Once we discover the true joy and contentment that can be found only in Jesus, we become happier people. As a result, we are more pleasant to be around, and other areas of our lives seem to improve. But as long as we're trying to siphon our happiness out of our relationships, relationships will be arduous and illusive. We are placing a burden on other people they were not created to bear.

Here are some common I-would-be-happy-if lies:

> *I would be happy if I had a child.*
> *I would be happy if I had two children.*
> *I would be happy if I had a husband.*
> *I would be happy if my husband treated me better.*

I would be happy if I had a different husband.

I would be happy if I had more money.

I would be happy if I had a better job.

I would be happy if I had a bigger house.

I would be happy if...

I could fill the rest of this book with "I would be happy ifs." We can't explore all the lies of "I would be happy if," but let's look at just a few: money, marriage, motherhood.

Money

My husband loves golf, and when a salesman invited him to be his guest on one of Charlotte's most prestigious courses, Steve jumped at the chance. As they drove their cart up to the sixth tee, Steve took in the tree-lined fairway dressed in pink, purple, and fuchsia azaleas in full bloom. Six multimillion-dollar mansions surrounded the green. Swimming pools sat motionless, manicured lawns lay weedless, and $100,000 cars were parked in the driveways. Then Steve's host began to unfold the stories behind those walls.

"See that first house? Those folks are separated. The wife had two affairs, and her husband finally left. And that second house? The wife has caught her husband with a prostitute twice. She wants to divorce him, but she's recently inherited ten million dollars from her father and doesn't want her husband to get any of the money. She's trying to figure out the best way to get out of the marriage and keep her money. And that third house, the one with the yard that looks somewhat unkempt? That couple also got a divorce, and their house has been for sale for seven months." (Yes, the guy was gossiping. Not just a problem with the fairer sex.)

Steve was struck with the broken lives surrounding him. Later he told me, "These were people who had achieved everything they thought would ever make them happy, and they were miserable."

"Do you think they wanted more?" I asked.

"No, I think they wanted something different, but they don't even know what that different is."

David Myers, in his book *The American Paradox: Spiritual Hunger in an Age of Plenty*, notes that from 1960 to 2000, the divorce rate doubled, the teen suicide rate tripled, the violent crime rate quadrupled, and the prison population quintupled. There were increased rates of depression, anxiety, and other mental-health problems.[5] As a nation, we are three times richer than we were in 1950, but no happier. We give lip service to the adage, "Money can't buy happiness," but we buy into the lie that it can.

Eric Weiner describes the relationship between money and happiness:

> Recent research into happiness, or subjective well-being, reveals that money does indeed buy happiness. Up to a point. That point, though, is surprisingly low: about fifteen thousand dollars a year. After that, the link between economic growth and happiness evaporates. Americans are on average three times wealthier than we were a half a century ago, yet we are no happier. The same is true of Japan and many other industrialized nations. Think about it as Richard Layard, a professor at the London School of Economics, has, "They have become richer, they work much less, they have longer holidays, they travel more, they live longer, and they are healthier. But they are no happier."[6]

One of the wealthiest men in the Bible, King Solomon, concluded that the accumulation of wealth doesn't lead to contentment. "I have seen all the things that are done under the sun; all of them are meaningless, a chasing after the wind" (Ecclesiastes 1:14). He also said the pursuit of happiness apart from God is never satisfied: "The eye never has enough of seeing, nor the ear its fill of hearing" (Ecclesiastes 1:8). Those who seek to find their happiness in the accumulation of wealth will never get enough. A personal relationship with the Creator is the only true source of joy. Everything else is icing on the cake.

Timothy wrote:

> Godliness with contentment is great gain. For we brought nothing into the world, and we can take nothing out of it. But if we have food and clothing, we will be content with

that. Those who want to get rich fall into temptation and a trap and into many foolish and harmful desires that plunge people into ruin and destruction. For the love of money is a root of all kinds of evil. Some people, eager for money, have wandered from the faith and pierced themselves with many griefs (1 Timothy 6:6-10).

Some of the happiest people I have ever seen live in third world countries in mud huts. Money will buy a lot of stuff, but happiness is not one of them. Being smack-dab in the middle of God's will is.

Marriage

When I was five years old, I wrapped a long white sheet around my slender body and a bath towel around my head. Then I clutched a bouquet of plastic flowers to my chest and stood at the end of the long hallway of my parents' home. Suddenly, in my imagination, the sheet became a pearl-studded wedding gown with a satin train, and the towel became my lace veil.

I could almost hear the trumpets sounding and the organ filling the air with the wedding march as I proceeded to waltz down the hall. Yes, all eyes were on me as the guests stood to honor the bride. I had seen *The Sound of Music*, and I wanted to have a wedding in a great cathedral as Sister Maria (played by Julie Andrews) did. Oddly enough, I never did make it to the end of the hallway to see who the groom would be. That didn't really matter. This was my dream about becoming a beautiful bride—not about becoming a wife. (Several years later, it did matter who would be at the end of that hallway!)

Little girls (and big girls) dream about becoming a bride. One of my favorite dolls was a bride doll. Not all women reading *Bride* magazine are necessarily engaged. Yes, most little girls dream of one day wearing the long satin dress with a lacy veil and walking down the aisle to meet the man of their dreams. Then the little girl grows up and thinks, *I'll be happy if I'm married.*

The desire to be married has led to many women marrying someone they should have never been dating in the first place. Most of the emails I receive from women are about marital problems—by far. Listen, some of the most miserable and disappointed women I know are not single.

Yes, marriage can be wonderful. I love being married. But being married is not the golden ticket to happiness.

It has been said that a bride can't see past her wedding day and a groom can't see past the wedding night. Countless men and women walked down the aisle and said "I do," and then turned around and said "I don't."

 The devil will be quick to tell you a man will solve all your problems. He hates marriage, because he knows it's an earthly example of the heavenly relationship between Christ and His church. But he'll tell you the lie that a man will solve all your problems just to keep you from turning to Jesus to meet your greatest need.

Being married is not the ultimate source of happiness and joy. Being smack-dab in the middle of God's will is.

Mothering

The second most common email I receive is from distraught moms. Being a mom is hard; if it weren't, bringing a child into the world wouldn't start with something called labor! And yet, so many think if they could just have a child, they would be happy. Having a child does not ensure happiness.

Again, I love being a mom. The first book I wrote was *Being a Great Mom, Raising Great Kids.* But being a mom is not the ultimate source of happiness. Yes, children bring great joy, but they can also bring great heartache.

I have watched woman after woman throw her whole life into raising her children, sometimes at the expense of her husband, only to feel empty when the children leave the nest. Children were never meant to fill the God-shaped hole, and yet so many women try to fill it with a child.

One day, as I was studying the Song of Songs, I was struck by chapter 2, verse 1. I was reading it as if Jesus were the groom and I was His beloved bride (which I am). The bride said, "I am a rose of Sharon" (2:1).

God stopped me. *What is your name?* He seemed to say.

My name is Sharon, I replied.

Go look it up, He prompted.

When I looked up *Sharon* in my Bible dictionary, I discovered it meant "a fertile valley." Sharon was and still is a fertile valley in the Holy Land. Then God began to reveal His plan for me. Even though my medical chart said "secondary infertility," He made sure my name was Sharon—"fertile valley." And while my dream to have a houseful of children with Jaynes blood coursing through their veins didn't happen the way I had dreamed, God fulfilled my dreams by giving me a passel of spiritual children all around the world.

> He settles the barren woman in her home as a happy mother of children. Praise the Lord (Psalm 113:9).

Having children is not the ultimate source of happiness and joy. Being smack-dab in the middle of God's will is.

THE PURSUIT OF HAPPINESS

What do women really need to be happy? A man? A new house? Children? Financial security? A slimmer body? A wrinkle-free face? A new car? A fulfilling job? Successful adult children? Loving parents? Encouraging friends? A padded savings account? Good health?

We have only to look at the latest edition of *People* magazine or broadcast of *Entertainment Tonight* to know some of the unhappiest people on the planet are the most successful. They appear to have it all, but in reality, if you don't have Jesus you have nothing at all.

Friend, we will never find true happiness until the only word that comes after that ellipsis (…) is the name of Jesus. Don't be fooled. This is the truth.

Someone asked a wealthy man just how much it would take for him to be happy.

"Just a little bit more," he said.

Happiness won't be found by investing in the stock market, but by investing in people. It won't be found by spending money, but by spending time with family and friends. It won't be found by getting, but by giving. The Declaration of Independence declares the right to pursue happiness, but it fails to give the guidelines to make that possible.

Like trying to read a crumpled map from a glove compartment, we try to find the way to happiness. We hold the creased pages that have been taped together and run our finger along the highway, looking for shortcuts. Jesus said, "I am the way and the truth and the life" (John 14:6). He is the highway to holiness, the roadway to righteousness, and the pathway to peace.

Every year, almost 40 million Americans move.[7] Moves are work related, health related, or relationship related. Some are from downsizing, upgrading, or retiring. But mostly, people move because they think they will be happier somewhere else.

The truth is, as long as we live in this world, we will never be completely content. We are not made for this world. We were made for heaven. C.S. Lewis said, "If I find in myself a desire which no experience in this world can satisfy, the most probable explanation is that I was made for another world." And you were! But until we get to heaven where all our longings will be satisfied, God gives us glimpses of glory when we walk this earth with Him.

David prayed, "Satisfy us in the morning with your unfailing love, that we may sing for joy and be glad all our days" (Psalm 90:14).

THERE IS NO OTHER STREAM

In *The Silver Chair*, the fourth book in the Chronicles of Narnia, C.S. Lewis introduces a new character to the land of Narnia. Jill finds herself transported to Narnia as if she were caught up in a dream. The first creature she encounters is Aslan the lion—the Christ figure throughout the series. Aslan appears for a moment, and then stalks slowly back into the forest. Jill is terribly afraid of meeting up with the lion, but her increasing thirst drives her to search for water. Alas! Jill discovers a stream, but she has to pass by Aslan to reach it.

"Are you not thirsty?" said the Lion.

"I'm dying of thirst," said Jill.

"Then drink," said the Lion.

"May I—could I—would you mind going away while I do?" said Jill.

The Lion answered this only by a look and a very low growl. And as Jill gazed at its motionless bulk, she realized that she might as well have asked the whole mountain to move aside for her convenience.

The delicious rippling noise of the stream was driving her nearly frantic.

"Will you promise not to—do anything to me, if I do come?" said Jill.

"I make no promise," said the Lion.

Jill was so thirsty now that, without noticing it, she had come a step nearer.

"Do you eat girls?" she said.

"I have swallowed up girls and boys, women and men, kings and emperors, cities and realms," said the Lion. It didn't say this as if it were boasting, nor as if it were sorry, nor as if it were angry. It just said it.

"I daren't come and drink," said Jill.

"Then you will die of thirst," said the Lion.

"Oh dear!" said Jill, coming another step nearer. "I suppose I must go and look for another stream then."

"There is no other stream," said the Lion.[8]

Friend, there is no other stream to quench our thirst. Neither people, places, power, nor possessions will satisfy that longing deep in our soul for happiness. Only Jesus. He is the living water, the bread of life, the lover of our souls.

Augustine once said, "You have made us for yourself, O Lord, and our hearts are restless until they rest in you." It's time to rest.

· · · · ·

RECOGNIZE THE LIE: *I would be happy if* _____ .

REJECT THE LIE: *That is not true.*

REPLACE THE LIE WITH TRUTH:

The LORD is my shepherd; I have all that I need (Psalm 23:1 NLT).

I Can't Forgive Myself

LIE: *I can't forgive myself.*

TRUTH: *There is now no condemnation for me because I am in Christ Jesus* (Romans 8:1).

Dear Sharon,

I just read one of your devotions on receiving grace and forgiveness. You mentioned a woman who had three abortions and how she refused to forgive herself. That really touched me because, you see, 11 years ago I had an abortion. That is the first time I ever actually put that in writing. I had gotten way off track in my walk with the Lord and was angry at Him because of an extremely hurtful situation in my life. This was something I had prayed a lot about, and I blamed God for the way things turned out. It was a very dark time in my life, and I turned away from God to live a rebellious lifestyle. During that time, I got pregnant and had an abortion. No one knew...no one.

I wish I could go back and change things. I would willingly give my life to bring this child back, but I can't. I have asked God to forgive me, and I know that God's Word says He is "faithful to forgive my sins" and "will remember them no more," yet I can't forgive myself.

Unlike the woman in your devotion, I was a Christian when I had the abortion. I was very far from Him at the time, but I did know what I was doing was wrong. I think this is why it has been so difficult for me to accept His forgiveness. I listened to the voice of the enemy rather than the voice of God. The Holy Spirit was still trying to speak to me, but I chose not to listen. That's why I am having trouble forgiving myself. I think it is easier for someone to embrace His forgiveness when they first come to Christ, but I am struggling because I already was a Christian.

How can I forgive myself?

Sometimes the most difficult person to forgive is the woman we look at in the mirror each morning. Honestly, I believe it is easier to forgive others than to forgive ourselves. Shame and condemnation weigh heavy. The enemy's lies loom low. The ever-present reminder of what we've done echoes loud.

The enemy knows God forgave Kimberly the moment she asked. The devil can't do anything about that. But if he can keep her from feeling forgiven, then he's won. Let's not let him.

FORGIVING THE UNTHINKABLE

King David was a man who loved the Lord with all his heart. He was anointed as the future king of Israel when he was just a young boy, killed the Philistine giant Goliath with a sling and a stone when he was but a teen, and brought the ark of the covenant back to its rightful place in Jerusalem when no one else could. He was the most powerful and notable king in Israel's history.

God referred to King David as a "man after my own heart" (Acts 13:22). I can't think of a better endorsement than that. And yet David got caught up in his own press, believing he was above God's law.

About ten years after David was established as king, during springtime when the fighting men went off to war, he decided to sit out the battle. David stayed back at the palace rather than join his men on the battlefield. He wasn't where he was supposed to be, and he wasn't doing what he was supposed to be doing (which is a red flag for all of us).

One evening David decided to enjoy the cool night air and take a stroll on his flat rooftop. While glancing about his kingdom, he noticed his neighbor's beautiful wife bathing across the way. Rather than turn his eyes away, David watched the beautiful woman move the water over her naked body. He liked what he saw. He wanted what he liked.

"Who is that stunning woman?" he asked his servant.

"That, my lord, is the wife of Uriah the Hittite, one of your faithful soldiers."

"Send someone to bring her to me!" he commanded.

So in the heat of passion, David slept with his neighbor's wife and she conceived a child. When David learned Bathsheba was pregnant, he ordered her husband, Uriah, to come home for a respite in hopes he would sleep with his wife and believe the child was his.

While Uriah did return home as the king commanded, he would not indulge in the pleasure of sleeping with his wife while the rest of his men were fighting on the battlefield. "The ark and Israel and Judah are staying in tents," he said, "and my commander Joab and my lord's men are camped in the open country. How could I go to my house to eat and drink and make love to my wife? As surely as you live, I will not do such a thing!" (2 Samuel 11:11).

Uriah's loyalty derailed David's cover-up, so he ordered the commander of the army to put Uriah on the front lines and then withdraw the troops, leaving him open and unprotected. Uriah was murdered just as surely as if David had put his own sword through the soldier's heart.

I can still remember the first time I read this account. My heart broke at the thought that someone so close to God could fail so miserably. It was unthinkable. And then I began to see just how easily it could happen to anyone, even to me.

David kept his sin hidden like a cancerous mass that ate away at his very soul. In Psalm 38 he wrote,

> My guilt has overwhelmed me
>   like a burden too heavy to bear.
> My wounds fester and are loathsome
>   because of my sinful folly.
> I am bowed down and brought very low;
>   all day long I go about mourning.

My back is filled with searing pain;
 there is no health in my body.
I am feeble and utterly crushed;
 I groan in anguish of heart (verses 4-8).

David was literally sick because of his secret sin—held in the vise grip of guilt, unsure he could ever be free. Only later, when the prophet Nathan confronted him, did he truly confess his guilt, repent for his sin, and turn back to God. David didn't try to justify his actions, place blame on anyone else, or claim amnesty because he was king. He came clean and confessed, "I have sinned against the LORD." After David repented, Nathan proclaimed, "The LORD has taken away your sin" (2 Samuel 12:13).

David was a broken man who repented of his sin and then immediately received God's forgiveness and grace. He resumed his duties as king and proceeded to become one of the most powerful kings in Israel's history.

Mercy came with the key of forgiveness and flung the prison door open wide, but David had to take the necessary steps to shake off the shackles of shame and walk free into the kingdom of grace. It's the same for you and me. I wonder what would have happened if David had not accepted God's grace and stayed holed up in his room. I'm so glad he didn't. But so many do.

TAKE HOLD OF GRACE

No matter what we have done, God does not want us held hostage to feelings of guilt and shame. "It is for freedom that Christ has set us free" (Galatians 5:1). He longs for us to take hold of grace.

In no way do I want to diminish the seriousness of sin. Neither do I want to lessen the truth of grace. Our sinful state before we came to Christ is the very thing that separated us from God and drove Jesus to the cross. But when we come to God and confess our sins, the Bible promises, "He is faithful and just and will forgive us our sins and purify us from all unrighteousness" (1 John 1:9).

The Bible also goes on to say, "If we claim we have not sinned, we make him out to be a liar and his word is not in us" (1 John 1:10). I haven't met anyone who honestly believes they are without sin. However, I meet people every day who believe they are without forgiveness. Let's look at these verses.

The word *confess*—or *confession*—is most used in the Bible when it comes from the Hebrew word *yada* in the Old Testament, and the Greek word *homologeo* in the New Testament. Both mean "to acknowledge." To confess our sin is to acknowledge or agree with God about our sin. Also, both words imply repentance and being truly sorry for the sin. Repentance is turning away from the sin and turning toward the Savior. Another way to say it is to turn away from what is evil and turn toward what is good. Saying, "I'm sorry I slept with another woman's husband," and then continuing to do so, is *not* confession and repentance.

Remember, when the religious leaders took the woman caught in adultery to Jesus, He did not condemn her. He forgave her. But before she turned to walk away, Jesus said, "Go and sin no more" (John 8:11 NLT). That is the key to true repentance. It is more than being sorry that I got caught. It is a deeply sincere sorrow that I have sinned against God. It is a change of the mind that in turn changes behavior.

It is futile to think we can keep our sins to ourselves. God already knows every move we make, every thought we think, and every word we whisper. David said, "Where can I go from your Spirit? Where can I flee from your presence?" (Psalm 139:7). God sees it all. When we refuse to confess the sin, it can literally make us sick.

When we confess our sin, the next step is to believe God tells the truth. God said, "I, even I, am he who blots out your transgression, for my own sake, and remembers your sins no more" (Isaiah 43:25). Do you believe God tells the truth? That's the question, isn't it?

Jesus paid the penalty for your sin—past, present, and future. To say you believe God has forgiven you but you can't forgive yourself is like saying what Jesus did on the cross wasn't enough—that *you* have to do something more to add to that.

Bible teacher Beth Moore says, "Agreeing with God over our forgiven state is just as important as agreeing with God over our sin. If Satan can't tempt us to hide our sin and refuse to confess, he'll tempt us not to accept our forgiven and purified state. If we persist in feeling bad, we will think destructively and ultimately act on it. Don't let the devil get away with that!"[1]

To say "I don't feel forgiven" is to allow feelings to override the truth. Truth is truth whether we believe it or not. However, truth won't have power in our lives until we do believe it (Ephesians 1:19).

Receiving grace and forgiveness for the wrongs we've committed is an act of faith. Diane Dempsey Marr wrote, "It is difficult to fathom such extravagant, unconditional love, yet so many of us leave His gift unopened. We admire its wrapping or marvel at its enormity, but avoid getting too close. Something within us cannot grasp the idea that God meant this for us, and so we put conditions on accepting His gift."[2] Unconditional grace and love is so enormously generous that sometimes we have trouble believing it's for real. But it is.

It's true that no one deserves the grace and mercy of God, but for some reason, He has decided to immerse us in them. In *The Ragamuffin Gospel*, Brennan Manning explains, "To live by grace means to acknowledge my whole life story, the light side and the dark. In admitting my shadow side I learn who I am and what God's grace means. As Thomas Merton put it, 'A saint is not someone who is good but who experiences the goodness of God.'"[3]

What does God require? "If we confess our sins, [God] is faithful and just and will forgive us our sins and purify us from all unrighteousness" (1 John 1:9). Why should we require more from ourselves than our Creator requires from us? Your sin is not greater than God's grace. Never has been. Never will be. Confess your sin, accept God's forgiveness, and then move on (in the opposite direction of the offense).

> Forget the former things; do not dwell on the past. See, I am doing a new thing! Now it springs up; do you not perceive it? I am making a way in the wilderness and streams in the wasteland (Isaiah 43:18-19).

THE SHADOW OF SHAME

Two of Satan's greatest weapons against women today are shame and condemnation. Even though we know God has forgiven us, many rise each morning to put on the sackcloth and ashes of regret. Listen to what these women said:

> In my twenties I had three abortions. I have had the hardest time forgiving myself. In my Bible study, we were talking about sexual purity. A few of the women opened up and shared that they had had an abortion. I could not share with them that I had three. I am still having a hard time forgiving myself. I know in my heart that I am forgiven, but Satan keeps a hold of my mind in this department, and I keep feeling shame. I am now married and have three children. My little girl has suffered from seizures since she was five months old, and I sometimes wonder if God is punishing me. But even as I write this, God has reminded me that it is because of her struggles I have turned back to Him and rededicated my life to Christ. My daughter is the reason for my spiritual growth. That's not a punishment, is it? That is a blessing.

> A while back, I had an affair. I have asked God to forgive me many times. But Satan keeps reminding me of it. I know God and my husband have both forgiven me. But I go through periods of beating myself up. I need to learn how to let it go for good.

> My husband is a Christian, but has never been very affectionate. After my mother died, I fell apart. Several of my friends reached out to help me. One of those friends was an old high school boyfriend who was divorced. He was so caring and compassionate. One thing led to another, and we ended up sleeping together one time. I felt terrible after that and asked God to forgive me. It never happened again, and I am committed to staying with my husband. But I just can't forgive myself.

These are hard situations to let go, but we all have failures in our lives...just different ones. And the devil reminds us of them on a regular basis. He doesn't want you to ever be free. Remember, if you are feeling condemnation from past sins that you have already asked God to forgive you for, that is not coming from the Holy Spirit. It's coming from the devil, who doesn't want you to *feel* forgiven. Once you have repented and asked for forgiveness, in God's eyes it is finished, over and done with, wiped away. If feelings of condemnation persist, they are a result of listening to the lies of the enemy rather than the truth of God.

Admittedly, guilt is a powerful motivator. Parents use it, employers use it, teachers use it, friends use it, kids use it, and spouses use it. I am opposed to using guilt as a motivator because it is the very language of the enemy himself. I want to stay just as far away from Satan's native tongue as possible. When it comes to using guilt-infested words to motivate, don't speak them and don't receive them.

The feeling of not being able to forgive myself is steeped in self-loathing—anger with myself or blaming myself. It is one thing to take personal responsibility for our actions, which I believe we should do. It is another to take personal responsibility for our redemption, which we never could. Satan tries to keep us in a morbid mind-set of self-loathing. It's part of his job description. Satan knows the slightest whisper of guilt is easily received by a fragile heart pummeled by life. Do not let the enemy convince you to stay in the prison of guilt and shame. The sentence has already been served. You are free to go.

Paul wrote about the grace of God more than any other man who held the pen for the Holy Spirit. Before his name was changed to Paul, he was known as Saul—a zealous persecutor of the church and murderer of Christians. He tried to destroy the early church by dragging men and women from their homes, throwing them into prison, and organizing stonings.

> Satan knows the slightest whisper of guilt is easily received by a fragile heart pummeled by life.

Then one day, when Saul was traveling to Damascus to obtain letters from the high priest to have more Christians arrested, Jesus met him in the form of a blinding light all around him.

He fell to the ground and heard a voice say to him, "Saul,
Saul, why do you persecute me?"

"Who are you, Lord?" Saul asked.

"I am Jesus, whom you are persecuting," he replied. "Now
get up and go into the city, and you will be told what you
must do" (Acts 9:4-6).

Saul was dramatically changed by his encounter with the Light of
the World—Jesus. God changed his name to Paul, and he became one
of the greatest ambassadors for Christ in the New Testament.

I wonder how long it took Paul to accept God's grace and forgive
himself. We'll never know how long it took, but we do know he did.
"If anyone is in Christ," he wrote, "the new creation has come: The old
has gone, the new is here!" (2 Corinthians 5:17). Paul understood grace.
He believed in new beginnings, and he rejoiced that he was not the
same man he'd been before. God had wiped his slate clean.

Do you have past failures, regrets, or sins in your past that you're
still carrying on your shoulders? That's a heavy burden to bear, isn't it?
And so unnecessary. God is calling you right now to let it go. He has.
Don't give the devil one more moment of satisfaction by dragging the
past into your present.

THE RADIANCE OF REDEMPTION

Shame is a strong emotion brought on by lack of forgiveness from
yourself for yourself. Audrey was a woman who had committed adultery. God miraculously restored her marriage and covered her with
grace and forgiveness. Her husband, children, and parents forgave her
as well. But two years later, in a prayer meeting, she realized she had
never forgiven herself. She tells about a time, after a Valentine's dinner,
when a close friend prayed for her.

That Valentine's Day is marked in my heart forever. After
dinner, Dr. Don began ministering to all of us. As he was
praying for me, he identified acute grief that was locked
up deep in my heart. He went on to explain that we all go

through grief, but that this was something different. It was the result of extreme loss of something or someone, and this grief was locked inside. I looked around the room, and everyone was quiet. I then proceeded to tell the story of what had happened just two short years before. My grief was locked in because I hadn't yet forgiven myself for what took place. I was holding in the sorrow and pain and keeping it close to my heart. On the outside, few people would notice. God knew, however, and I quickly discovered that I was in the middle of yet another divine appointment.[4]

That night Audrey forgave herself and was released from her deep-seated grief. God removed her shame, and she is radiant today. As the Bible says, "Those who look to him are radiant; their faces are never covered with shame" (Psalm 34:5).

Jesus said, "If the Son sets you free, you will be free indeed" (John 8:36). No ifs, ands, or buts about it. It is a done deal. God forgives us the moment we ask. We can continue to condemn ourselves all the way to Peter's pearly gates, but it is a false accusation—one that undoubtedly Satan, the father of lies, has on an audio loop.

> Don't give the devil one more moment of
> satisfaction by dragging the past into your present.

The Bible says Jesus's sacrifice cleanses "our consciences from acts that lead to death" (Hebrews 9:14). "There is now no condemnation for those who are in Christ Jesus" (Romans 8:1). "See, I lay a stone in Zion, a chosen and precious cornerstone, and the one who trusts in him will never be put to shame" (1 Peter 2:6).

While we must accept God's forgiveness and forgive ourselves, we never truly forget. Honestly, I'm glad. If I forgot my sins and the pain attached to them, I would be more likely to make the same mistakes again. God removes the shame and the penalty, but memory helps us to never go down that path again.

Remembering our weakness also helps us to be more compassionate with others when they fall into seductive traps. I am much more merciful now than I was 30 years ago when my mistakes were fewer. Looking at others' mistakes on the backdrop of my own dark past makes them less visible to the judging eye.

THE FREEDOM OF FORGIVENESS

Here is the promise: "If we confess our sins, he is faithful and just and will forgive us our sins and purify us from all unrighteousness" (1 John 1:9). Have I said that already? Well, it deserves repeating.

God knows many of us will still feel the phantom pains of condemnation, even after we've asked for forgiveness. John wrote, "Even if we feel guilty, God is greater than our feelings, and he knows everything" (1 John 3:20 NLT). Our hearts might condemn us, but God is greater than our hearts. We might feel condemned, but simply put, it is not true that we are condemned.

Rejecting the lie of condemnation and replacing it with the truth of complete forgiveness and eradication of the offense is living in God's reality. It is also "the way to shut down debilitating self-criticism."[5]

Our self-condemnation cannot block God's forgiveness, but it can obstruct our walk in freedom. We will never be free of our past sins until we accept God's forgiveness and believe with our whole being that we are totally redeemed, completely restored, and eternally saved. The slate is wiped clean, the record expunged, and the sentence served.

Romans 5:1 states that we have been *justified* through faith. That is past tense. When Jesus said on the cross, "It is finished," He meant His work of redemption was complete. Satan lies to us, saying we must do more. So many Christians work hard to receive something they already have and to become someone they already are. Some engage in relentless activity to earn forgiveness or pay penance. But, dear friend, our striving will never be enough. If we could work hard enough to earn our forgiveness, Jesus wouldn't have had to die on the cross.

Imagine a brand-new home with beautifully placed brick, a securely shingled roof, and shiny wide windows. Imagine a manicured lawn, a welcoming front door, and a sprinkling of flowers under neatly trimmed shrubs. Oh, let's go ahead and put up a white picket fence with a winding sidewalk. Got the picture in your mind? Now, imagine a sign in the front yard that reads "Posted. Condemned. Keep Out." That would be silly, wouldn't it? Of course it would.

God holds the title deed to my life and yours. The truth is we are brand-new creations, not condemned structures about to fall apart. Take that sign down. It really looks foolish in a heart beautifully crafted by the Master Builder Himself.

THE BEAUTY OF REDEMPTION

Dear Sharon:

Last year, I saw your book in a Christian bookstore. The title, *Your Scars Are Beautiful to God*, touched me so much my eyes filled with tears. I thought to myself, *My scars are not beautiful to God*. I went home, but could not escape that title. The next day I went back and bought the book.

I am 61 years old. When I was 16, I had an abortion. I have carried those scars my whole life. I became a Christian and asked God to forgive me. I know He did, but I could not forgive myself. I continued to suffer from shame and deep sorrow. I never spoke about the abortion to anyone. It was too painful. When I brought your book home, I went into my room, shut the door, and asked God to help me get through the pages. As I read, I could feel His healing taking place.

In the story of Joseph, I found my answer. You mentioned that Joseph had two sons. The firstborn was named Manasseh, which means "God has made me forget all my trouble and all my father's household." The second was named Ephraim, which means "God has made me fruitful in the land of my suffering." You said, "It is the same with you and with me. God does not want us to simply forget the pain of the past. He wants us to be fruitful in the land of our suffering. Use it for good. Minister to others. Plant seeds of hope."

All my life I had buried the memories and tried to forget. This had never worked. The pain did not go away. Through the names of Joseph's sons, I realized that God did not want me to forget the pain of my past, but to be fruitful in the land of my suffering and allow Him to use what I have gone through for good.

I began writing in my journal all that I was learning about healing and forgiveness. The dam over my heart broke and words began to flow onto the pages. I poured out all the things I wanted to say to my child, and I believe she heard every word. The more I wrote, the more hope and joy I felt. I knew God was helping me express my pain for the first time. There were many tears but also much joy. I asked God to help me be fruitful through this experience and told Him I was willing to use my pain for a purpose.

Satan had created condemnation chatter in Carol's mind for years. Once she saw it for the lie it was, rejected the lie, and then replaced the lie with truth, she was free. Jesus wants the same for you and me.

"You cannot get beyond your own opinion of yourself—no matter how many good things God may say about you in His Word. Regardless of all the wonderful plans God may have for your life, none of them will come to pass without your cooperation."[6] God extends grace and forgiveness. It is up to you to accept and believe it. Live free. It's time to tell the devil, "Enough!"

"It has been said that 75 percent of all mentally disturbed people would be pronounced well if they could only be convinced that they are forgiven."[7] The enemy tells us we must pay a debt we never could. The truth tells us that God, through Jesus Christ, already has paid that debt on our behalf.

Imagine that you are hiding in a pitch-black, dark closet of shame. As you're crouched down on the floor, you bump into someone crouched down right beside you. You pull out a flashlight tucked in your pocket and shine the light. Behold, the person in the closet with you is Jesus! When you shine the light on His face, He simply says, "Friend, what are we doing here?"

Believe the truth of God's forgiveness, embrace the truth of redemption, and come out of hiding for good. You are forgiven and free.

• • • • •

RECOGNIZE THE LIE: *I can't forgive myself.*

REJECT THE LIE: *That is not true.*

REPLACE THE LIE WITH TRUTH:

If we confess our sins, he is faithful and just and will forgive us our sins and purify us from all unrighteousness (1 John 1:9).

I Can't Forgive the Person Who Hurt Me

LIE: *I can't forgive the person who hurt me.*

TRUTH: *I can forgive because Christ has forgiven me*
(Ephesians 4:32).

I was so confused. I was talking to God, but it seemed He wasn't talking to me. There seemed to be a barrier between us.

After my sophomore year in college, I decided to return to my hometown and work in a dental office. I had just received my dental hygiene license and loved working with patients. After my first year, something stirred in me—calling me back to school. I wasn't sure if it was loneliness tugging at me because all my friends were still away at college, or if it was God telling me I wasn't done. I prayed, but heard nothing. I didn't know where to go or what to do. Not to decide is to decide, so I stayed at my job and stuffed the idea down in my heart.

However, the following spring, the desire resurfaced. Once again, I prayed but felt no direction from God. After some months, I went to one of my mentors, Mr. Thorp, and asked him to pray for me.

"Let's read some Scripture about prayer before we pray," Mr. Thorp suggested. He turned to Matthew 6:8-15:

> Your Father knows what you need before you ask him. This, then, is how you should pray:

"Our Father in heaven, hallowed be your name, your kingdom come, your will be done, on earth as it is in heaven. Give us today our daily bread. And forgive us our debts, as we also have forgiven our debtors. And lead us not into temptation, but deliver us from the evil one. For if you forgive other people when they sin against you, your heavenly Father will also forgive you. But if you do not forgive others their sins, your Father will not forgive your sins."

Then he turned to Matthew 18:19-22:

"Again, truly I tell you that if two of you on earth agree about anything you ask for, it will be done for them by my Father in heaven. For where two or three gather in my name, there am I with them."

Then Peter came to Jesus and asked, "Lord, how many times shall I forgive my brother or sister who sins against me? Up to seven times?"

Jesus answered, "I tell you, not seven times, but seventy-seven times.

Finally, he turned to Mark 11:22-26:

"Have faith in God," Jesus answered. "Truly I tell you, if anyone says to this mountain, 'Go, throw yourself into the sea,' and does not doubt in their heart but believes that what they say will happen, it will be done for them. Therefore I tell you, whatever you ask for in prayer, believe that you have received it, and it will be yours. And when you stand praying, if you hold anything against anyone, forgive them, so that your Father in heaven may forgive you your sins."

Every passage Mr. Thorp turned to regarding prayer had verses about forgiveness either before it or after it. He stopped reading, looked me in the eye, and said, "Sharon, I sense that God is telling you that you have unforgiveness in your heart. Have you forgiven your father for what he did to you and what he withheld from you?" (Mr. Thorp had walked with me on my spiritual journey for the past ten years and knew very well what had gone on in my home.)

I was stunned. "Mr. Thorp," I respectfully replied, "I came here to pray about my future, not talk about my past."

"But, Sharon, God can't talk to you about your future until you obey Him regarding your past."

It was a rough morning, but a good one.

At that time in my life, I had been a Christian for seven years. My father had become a Christian just the year before. He had been a violent, heavy drinker with a rage disorder who gambled, indulged in pornography, and had affairs. Dad beat my mom, terrorized my brother, and treated me as if I were nonexistent. When he gave his life to Christ, he was truly a new creation. The change was and is one of the most miraculous transformations I've ever seen. Only the Almighty God could have orchestrated the twists and turns that led my father to the cross.

However, I had a niggling resentment toward my dad, which I clung to with a closed fist. Yes, I saw the change, but no, I didn't trust him. I didn't even like him. I still had nightmares, fits of fear, and trigger points of panic. Whenever Dad made a mistake— because lo and behold he still wasn't perfect—the bitterness of my childhood rose up like bile. God was speaking to me through Mr. Thorp, saying, *Now's the time to let it go.*

Mr. Thorp and I spent hours talking through the pain of my past and the purpose of forgiveness. We prayed. I cried. Finally, I cut my father from the noose of the past I held around his neck. In turn, God cut away the bitterness filling my heart and replaced it with a tender love of a daughter who saw her dad through the lens of grace. I was free.

Amazingly, after forgiving my father, my inability to hear from God was lifted. I knew exactly what I was supposed to do. I returned to school in the fall, and I met my husband-to-be six weeks later. I'm not saying when you forgive you're going to strike it rich or meet the man of your dreams. But I do know my refusal to forgive my earthly father hampered my communion with my heavenly Father. And that's exactly what the enemy wanted.

THE LIE OF THE ENEMY

We've all been hurt at one time or another. People disappoint us, disregard us, and devalue us. They misuse, abuse, and bruise us. Granted, some have been wounded more than others, but everyone will feel the pain of being hurt by another person.

The world, the flesh, and the devil will tell you that you have a right to hold that person accountable for the wrongs they've committed; to forgive would lessen the seriousness of the offense. "Don't do it!" the world cries. "He deserves to suffer," the flesh agrees. "He's a dirty, rotten scumbag, and you have every right to hate him for the rest of your life," the deceiver concurs.

But is any of that true? Yes and no. That person may very well be a dirty, rotten scumbag who doesn't deserve forgiveness. But the only person held prisoner by unforgiveness is the person who refuses to forgive. You deserve to forgive and be free of that person's influence. As long as you hold on to your hate, that person is still controlling you, and the devil grins from ear to ear. Ironically, most of the time the person we hold a grudge against doesn't even know it, and certainly doesn't care. It's like we're hitting our own head against the wall and saying, "Take this!" We're only hurting ourselves. I've often heard that unforgiveness is drinking a poison and waiting for the other person to die. Forgiveness is setting the prisoner free and realizing the prisoner is you.

The enemy says, "He doesn't deserve forgiveness!" In a way, he's right. You won't hear me say that many times, but he is. Yet here's the clincher: None of us deserves forgiveness, but God forgives us time and time again.

EXTENDING GRACE

In the last chapter we looked at how to *receive* forgiveness from God for our own mistakes, failures, and sins. We saw how to reject the lie of condemnation and replace it with the truth of grace. Now let's look forgiveness in the face and ask, *Can we extend that same grace to others?*

Forgiveness is a choice, a decision to hand the scalpel to God and allow Him to remove the tumor of offense from the heart of the wounded.

No one deserves forgiveness. I don't deserve it. You don't deserve it. Even the most repentant heart doesn't deserve it. Remember, grace, by its very definition, is a gift we don't deserve—it's unmerited favor from God (2 Timothy 1:9). We don't deserve it and can't earn it. Therefore, when we forgive, we are divinely imitating the Father. "Bear with each other and forgive one another if any of you has a grievance against someone. Forgive as the Lord forgave you" (Colossians 3:13).

The enemy knows the destructive potential of a bitter heart. That's why he tells us we can't let the bitterness go. We mustn't do it, he says. If we forgive, then we will somehow be letting the offender go free.

But that is a lie. We can do it. We must do it. If we don't, we will never be free.

Diane Dempsey Marr, in her book *The Reluctant Traveler,* said it well:

> Unforgiveness can be likened to a parasite; it feeds on the anger and hurt of its host, finding its most satisfying nourishment in human pain. It thrives on the cycle of replayed scenes, recalled anguish, and rehashed justification for holding fast to grudges. Essentially, unforgiveness grows plump on our desire for revenge.[1]

While most of us don't have a plan to exact revenge, we somehow think holding on to the unforgiveness is revenge enough. The irony is that the person we refuse to forgive most likely doesn't even care or know we're carrying the unforgiveness around. The only person being hurt when I choose not to forgive is me. The only person being hurt when you choose not to forgive is you.

And those replayed scenes Diane Dempsey Marr mentions? Who do you think is pushing the rewind and play buttons? I believe it is the devil, who wants to keep us bound to past hurts. But, friend, when we choose to forgive, God turns our pain into purpose, our hurt into hope, and our misery into ministry. No wonder the enemy trembles at the idea of a wounded soul forgiving the one who caused the pain.

WHEN IS ENOUGH, ENOUGH?

How much do we forgive? How many times? Does any offense warrant unforgiveness?

In Matthew 18:21-22, Peter asked Jesus, "Lord, how many times shall I forgive my brother or sister who sins against me? Up to seven times?"

Jesus answered, "I tell you, not seven times, but seventy-seven times."

Sometimes I think I like Peter's ideas better—seven strikes and you're out, buddy. But Jesus tells us to put no limit on forgiveness. He even gives us a story to drive the point home.

> The kingdom of heaven is like a king who wanted to settle accounts with his servants. As he began the settlement, a man who owed him ten thousand bags of gold was brought to him. Since he was not able to pay, the master ordered that he and his wife and his children and all that he had be sold to repay the debt.
>
> At this the servant fell on his knees before him. "Be patient with me," he begged, "and I will pay back everything." The servant's master took pity on him, canceled the debt and let him go.
>
> But when that servant went out, he found one of his fellow servants who owed him a hundred silver coins. He grabbed him and began to choke him. "Pay back what you owe me!" he demanded.
>
> His fellow servant fell to his knees and begged him, "Be patient with me, and I will pay it back."
>
> But he refused. Instead, he went off and had the man thrown into prison until he could pay the debt. When the other servants saw what had happened, they were outraged and went and told their master everything that had happened.
>
> Then the master called the servant in. "You wicked servant," he said, "I canceled all that debt of yours because you begged me to. Shouldn't you have had mercy on your fellow servant just as I had on you?" In anger his master handed him over to the jailers to be tortured, until he should pay back all he owed.

This is how my heavenly Father will treat each of you unless you forgive your brother or sister from your heart" (Matthew 18:23-35).

The first servant was forgiven a debt that would amount to millions of dollars by today's standards, and yet he refused to forgive a debt that would be equivalent to just a few bills. I am the wicked servant. God is the king. He has forgiven me of so much. How can I not forgive others?

Forgiveness doesn't mean we put ourselves in a position to be abused or mistreated again and again. If you're in an abusive relationship, it is very important to set up healthy boundaries or remove yourself from the situation. Many helpful books are available to assist with how and when to set boundaries for healthy relationships. One such book by Henry Cloud and John Townsend is simply titled *Boundaries*.

God's forgiveness should stir such love in us that we will long to forgive others in return. In Luke 7:36-50, a prostitute came to Jesus while He dined with a Pharisee. She wept, washed His feet with her tears, dried them with her hair, and anointed them with perfume. She was overcome with Christ's love and forgiveness. When the Pharisees questioned her acts, Jesus reminded them, "Whoever has been forgiven little loves little" (7:47). She had been forgiven much—and as a result, she loved much.

CUTTING THE PRISONER FREE

What exactly is forgiveness? Two Greek words translate the word *forgive*. The first is *charizomai,* from the word *charis,* which means "grace." This word appears 27 times in the New Testament. It means "to bestow a favor unconditionally; to show one's self gracious, kind, benevolent; or to grant forgiveness, to pardon." Believers are to *forgive* each other the way Christ has *forgiven* us, as found in Ephesians 4:32, Colossians 2:13, and Colossians 3:13. *Charizomai* indicates being gracious toward someone.

The other Greek word for forgiveness is *aphiemi.* It means "to let go from one's power, possession; to let go free, let escape."[2] Forgiveness is releasing someone from a debt, cutting someone loose, letting someone go, or liberating completely.

> The intent of biblical forgiveness is to cut someone loose. The word picture drawn by the Greek term for unforgiveness is unforgiven roped to the back of the unforgiving. How ironic. Unforgiveness is how we securely bind ourselves to what we hate most. Therefore, the Greek meaning of forgiveness might best be demonstrated as the practice of cutting loose the person roped to your back.[3]

Paul wrote to the Philippians, "Brothers and sisters, I do not consider myself yet to have taken hold of it. But one thing I do: Forgetting what is behind and straining toward what is ahead, I press on toward the goal to win the prize for which God has called me heavenward in Christ Jesus" (Philippians 3:13-14).

What exactly did Paul leave behind? I believe part of what he had to leave behind was the way he was unjustly treated and abused. Let's look at the cruelties he endured listed in 2 Corinthians 11:23-27.

> I have worked much harder, been in prison more frequently, been flogged more severely, and been exposed to death again and again. Five times I received from the Jews the forty lashes minus one. Three times I was beaten with rods, once I was pelted with stones, three times I was shipwrecked, I spent a night and a day in the open sea, I have been constantly on the move. I have been in danger from rivers, in danger from bandits, in danger from my fellow Jews, in danger from Gentiles; in danger in the city, in danger in the country, in danger at sea; and in danger from false believers. I have labored and toiled and have often gone without sleep; I have known hunger and thirst and have often gone without food; I have been cold and naked.

When I consider those words, I immediately think, *When did all those things happen to Paul?* If one of them had happened to me, I'd probably have a whole chapter in the Bible about it. But not Paul; he forgave the offense and the offender and moved on. Perhaps that's one of the secrets to his success in ministry. He forgave completely and moved forward quickly.

It's especially difficult to forgive when the people who hurt you seem to go forward as if nothing happened. *Don't you see the destruction?* we cry. *Don't you understand how you've shattered my life?* But with deaf ears and blind eyes, they go on with life as usual—eating, drinking, working, playing, and going to church—oblivious to the pain and anguish they've inflicted.

Sometimes when we forgive the offender, we must forgive the ignorance as well. As Jesus died on the cross, He prayed, "Father, forgive them, for they do not know what they are doing" (Luke 23:34).

A SHOW OF STRENGTH

When we hold a grudge against someone, the grudge ends up holding on to us. We emotionally strap the unforgiven onto our backs and lug them around wherever we go. We might not have had any control over the offense, but we do have control over whether we are going to allow it to control or color our lives from that point on.

Forgiveness is not a sign of weakness. It's a sign of strength. It took divine power to forgive my dad that day. It takes determination empowered by the Holy Spirit.

Forgiveness is not a feeling. It's an act of the will; you choose to forgive. You choose to forgive today, confirm it again tomorrow, and the next day and the next day and the next day until one day you realize you have no residual resentment at all.

I love that Paul said he was, "forgetting what is behind" rather than "I forgot what was behind." Forgetting is a present tense verb—a continual action. That means it's not a one-time-over-and-done exercise of the will. I am forgiving the offense today, and you know what? When the enemy reminds me of it tomorrow, I will forgive the offense again.

Forgiveness is not saying what the person did or did not do was right. It is simply saying we are taking the person off our hook and placing them on God's hook. We are cutting them loose from our back and giving the burden to God. We are no longer allowing them to hold us captive by our holding a grudge.

As long as we don't forgive, we are held in Satan's vise grip. It's the number one avenue by which Satan ensnares his prey. Paul wrote, "Get rid of all bitterness, rage and anger, brawling and slander, along with every form of malice" (Ephesians 4:31). Why? "In order that Satan might not outwit us. For we are not unaware of his schemes" (2 Corinthians 2:11).

Nothing will make a person more bitter than an unforgiving spirit. And nothing will dissolve bitterness quicker than a decision to forgive and let go of the offense. We cannot get better if we remain bitter.

Forgiveness is not

- Saying what the person did was not wrong
- Absolving the person from responsibility for his or her actions
- Denying the wrong occurred
- Pretending the abuse did not happen

Forgiveness is

- Letting go of your need for revenge
- Cutting the person loose
- Refusing to let bitterness and hatred rule your life
- Leaving the past behind by not allowing it to control your actions or emotions

Is someone strapped to your back? Most likely some of us have an entire busload of folks tied on there. No wonder we find the "great race of life" tiring and cumbersome! God never intended us to run with such a load!

Perhaps you're unsure if you have unforgiveness in your heart. Perhaps the unforgiveness has been there so long, it feels at home—like it belongs there.

Stop and pray Psalm 139:23-24: "Search me, God, and know my heart; test me and know my anxious thoughts. See if there is any offensive way in me, and lead me in the way everlasting." Let me share how that prayer changed Cary's life.

SET FREE

Cary lived with her father, mother, and two older brothers in a simple bungalow with concrete floors, no running water, and an outhouse in the backyard. While her father was a cold, violent man, her mother was loving and kind. In her earliest memory, she was three years old. Her parents had a violent argument and her dad punched a gaping hole in the den wall before screeching out of the driveway in his car, abandoning the family. A divorce followed.

When Cary was four years old, her father returned, beat up her mother, and ripped her crying children out of her arms. He forced them into his car.

"You can't take care of these children," he yelled. "You can't even drive a car. I've got a new wife who'll look after them better than you can. I'm taking them, and there's nothing you can do about it."

Cary's mother believed him, and she didn't run after them. Cary remembers peering out the rear window and seeing her mother's battered face as she stood in the doorway, crying, "At least leave me my baby girl." Cary's heart broke as her father drove out of the driveway and away from her world. Cary's stepmother was a cold, hard woman who showed little to no affection to her husband's three children. The trio lived for the weekends when they could go "home" to visit their mother.

Shortly after Cary arrived at her father's home, he began sexually abusing her. Confused and afraid, she didn't know how to say "no" or that she even could. Cary began wearing two to three pairs of pajamas to bed, even using safety pins to hold them together. Still her father violated his daughter time and time again.

Cary's brothers missed their mother terribly. She had remarried, to a violent alcoholic, and they constantly worried about her safety. At night, when their father and stepmother went out to dinner or to a movie, the boys called their mother's next-door neighbor. Their mother didn't have a phone, and the neighbor ran next door to get her so she could talk to her children. One night the call brought some news that shattered their world forever.

"Hi, this is Allen and Bobby. Can you go get my mom?"

"I'm sorry, boys. Didn't someone tell you? Your mom's husband shot her in the back today and then killed himself. Your mother's dead."

The one person who loved Cary the most was gone forever.

The sexual abuse continued. When Cary was 14, she gathered enough courage to lock her door. The next day, her enraged father took the door off its hinges and Cary lost all privacy or protection.

When Cary was 16, her father was in a car accident that caused him to be home during the day. Summer was approaching, and Cary was terrified of what he would do to her on the long summer days. Finally, she courageously told the authorities. They promised they would come and get her, but they never did. In desperation, she called the school guidance counselor and begged him to rescue her from this 12-year nightmare. The counselor did come, but because he didn't know what else to do, he took her to a juvenile detention center. The center was filled with girls being punished and one girl being protected—Cary.

The two months Cary spent at the detention center were the most secure of her young life. Bars kept the girls in and bars kept Cary safe. One Sunday, a Baptist preacher came to the detention center and presented the gospel of Jesus Christ. Even though she was not loved by her earthly father, Cary learned that she was loved by a heavenly One. At the close of the service, he asked, "If anyone would like to accept Jesus as their personal Savior, please stand." With tears streaming down her cheeks, Cary stood.

Three weeks after Cary's arrival at the center, an aunt who lived on the West Coast took her to live with her and her husband. Eventually, they adopted her as their own child. Cary believed she now had a chance to see what a real family was like. That dream was quickly shattered.

Cary adored her uncle and trusted him with all her heart. However, he destroyed that trust when he made sexual advances toward her two years after her arrival. Once again, a father figure violated her. Only this time, Cary knew she could have said no. But she didn't. She felt dirty, ashamed, and worthless. Cary went off to college, and like the woman at the well, she tried to fill her emptiness the only way she knew how—with men. She married at 18, but had the marriage annulled six months later. She married again at 20, but divorced after six years. She married again at 26, and divorced after 14 years. She married again at 40, but divorced three years later.

One night, she met Jesus at the well of His Word. She opened her Bible in search of verses on joy. *Surely the Bible can tell me how to find real joy,* she thought.

She turned to Psalm 16:11, "You will fill me with joy in your presence." Then to Romans 4:7-8, "Blessed are those whose transgressions are forgiven, whose sins are covered. Blessed is the one whose sin the Lord will never count against them." She flipped to John 15:11-12, "I have told you this so that my joy may be in you and that your joy may be complete. My command is this: Love each other as I have loved you." Then to 1 John 1:9, "If we confess our sins, he is faithful and just and will forgive us our sins and purify us from all unrighteousness."

The Holy Spirit opened her eyes to the truth that would set her free. *God, are you telling me that to find happiness, I must forgive?*

One by one, Cary began to pray about and forgive those who had hurt her. "Lord, I forgive my father for abusing me. I forgive my stepmother for not protecting me. I forgive Jake for killing my mother. I forgive Uncle James for seducing me." With each person Cary forgave, she felt the shackles of oppression drop from her arms, legs, and heart. Yet one person did not receive her forgiveness that night.

When I met Cary at a women's retreat, she listened intently as I spoke about running the race as Paul did. "We must forget the past: the good we've done, the bad others have done to us, and the ugly done through us," she heard me say. "We must find the hidden treasure, forgive those who have hurt us, and forgive ourselves."

See, that one person Cary had not forgiven was herself. She had made a series of bad choices throughout her life, and Satan reminded her of them daily. Finally, at the women's retreat, Cary had had enough. She decided to stop listening to the lies of the enemy and believe the truth of God. She accepted God's grace-gift of forgiveness and forgave herself.

And like the woman at the well, Cary left her water pot and brought an entire community to the One who told her about the living water that quenches so we will never thirst again. Today she is a speaker and Bible teacher who shares God's freeing truths with all who will listen.

SIX STEPS TO FORGIVENESS

Perhaps you've had enough and are ready to stop listening to the lies of the enemy—lies that tell you all the reasons not to forgive the people who have hurt you. Perhaps you're ready to start listening to the voice of truth assuring you of the freedom you'll gain when you do. Listen, forgiveness is hard work. Bitterness, anger, and hurt don't go away all at once. Forgiving is a process, but it begins with a decision to start. So let's start.

1. On a piece of paper, write the name of the person who hurt you.

2. Write down how the person hurt you (rape, verbal abuse, sexual abuse, neglect, betrayal, desertion, rejection).

3. Write down how you feel about that person. Be honest. God knows how you feel.

4. Decide to forgive. Forgiveness is not a feeling but a decision of the will. God will never tell us to do something without providing the power to obey. He has told us to forgive, and He will give us the power to do so, but it all begins with the decision to do so.

5. Take your list to God and pray. "Lord, today I choose to forgive _____ for _____. I have been terribly hurt [misused, abused], but I am not going to allow the offense to control me any longer. Just as You have forgiven me, I now forgive _____. I relinquish any need for revenge and place the consequences of this person's actions in Your hands. In Jesus's name I pray, amen."

6. As a visual exercise, destroy the list. Some have taken the list to a fireplace and burned it. Others have nailed the paper to a wooden cross. Still others have written the name of the person they're forgiving on a helium balloon and released it to heaven. However you choose, give the name to God.

If you prayed that prayer, I'm so proud of you. Let me give you a word of caution. When you see that person or think of that person, and those angry, hurt feelings rise to the surface, don't think you haven't really forgiven him or her. That's what the devil will tell you. I'm warning you right now, he will tell you that. When he brings up the offense, you need to remind him you have already forgiven the person. And while you're at it, remind yourself.

Remember, power follows obedience, and emotions or feelings usually lag behind.

BETH SET FREE

When Beth was ten years old, she was raped by James, a neighborhood boy. Beth's little heart was so battered and bruised that she transferred her hatred to all men and looked on them with disdain. It seemed as if this boy's face was on every man she saw, and none was to be trusted. She bore a fear that she would be raped again, and that terror stifled her relationships with men.

At a women's retreat where I spoke about the freedom of forgiveness, Beth decided to cut James loose. Did she feel like it? No. She simply decided she wasn't going to let the rape control her any longer, and forgiveness was the only way. Did he deserve to be forgiven? No, but she deserved to be free. It had nothing to do with him and everything to do with her. She gave the offender to God, taking him off her hook and placing him on God's. She felt somewhat better, but the true test was yet to come.

Several months later, Beth and her mother decided to have a yard sale. Her mother invited her neighbor to join them and combine their items. This happened to be James's parents, though they didn't know about the rape. It had been Beth's well-kept secret. While they were categorizing and pricing their items, James called.

"Hey, Mom," he said. "I went to your house and you weren't there, so I thought I'd try the Smiths" (not their real name).

"Yeah, we're here getting ready for a yard sale tomorrow," she said. "Come on over."

For a second, Beth didn't know what to do. An urge to run bubbled up within her. *By the grace of God, I am not going to let this control me any longer,* she silently prayed. *I am healed and set free, and there is nothing he can do to take that away from me unless I let him.*

When James came into the room, Beth smiled and said, "Hi, James. How are you?"

James was wearing a lewd T-shirt with an image of a girl pole dancing on the front. He refused to make eye contact with Beth. She wondered if he was ashamed. Now he was the one held captive by his actions.

"Before I became a Christian," Beth explained, "I would have lectured him on women's rights and used a lot of four-letter words. Then I would have gone in the house and cried. I would have cut myself because that was the only way I knew how to cope with the pain and shame of the rape. After I became a Christian, I probably would have been able to keep my mouth shut and prayed instead of cutting myself, but I certainly would have cried about it for days. But this time, it didn't even hurt. I was able to feel compassion for him. He's just lost like I was before I came to Christ, and I'm certain that I, just like him, left a trail of hurting people in my wake.

"It was at that very moment, standing among the clutter of the yard sale items, that I realized God had cleaned the clutter from my heart. I was totally healed. God had set me completely free from fear and anxiety over being raped again. Now I walk with courage and bravery into my past rather than pushing the feelings down and pretending they're not there. I am confident that He who began a great work in me is faithful to finish it!"

Someone once said, "We are most like beasts when we kill. We are most like men when we judge. We are most like God when we forgive."

• • • • •

RECOGNIZE THE LIE: *I can't forgive the person who hurt me.*

REJECT THE LIE: *That is not true.*

REPLACE THE LIE WITH TRUTH:

Bear with each other and forgive one another if any of you has a grievance against someone. Forgive as the Lord forgave you (Colossians 3:13).

13

I Can't Help Myself

LIE: *I can't help myself.*

TRUTH: *I am more than a conqueror through Christ Jesus, my Lord* (Romans 8:37).

Jennifer stood in front of the mirror staring at the overweight woman looking back at her. Just two years ago she'd lost 120 pounds, and now 80 of them were back. *I can't keep this weight off,* she thought. *I know what I'm supposed to do, but I just can't do it. I'm always going to be fat. I'm just going to accept it and quit trying. What's so bad about being fat anyway? I just can't help myself.*

Rachel loved Travis, she really did. Though they were both Christians, they found themselves staring at the ceiling in her bedroom after a night of passion that led to a morning of regret. *We've tried to remain pure,* she mused, *but we love each other so much. It's just natural to feel this passionately about the person you love. Once we start kissing, we can't stop. But I know it's wrong. I feel sick to my stomach every time we have sex. I just can't help myself.*

Martha could hear her six-year-old son crying in the next room. She was crying too. Her words of anger yelled at the top of her lungs just moments before bounced off the walls of their home. *Oh, God,* Martha prayed, *why can't I control my anger? Why can't I control the words that come out of my mouth? I'm destroying my family with them. I've tried to control my tongue, but the hateful words come out anyway. What's wrong with me? I just can't help myself.*

Maybe you've found yourself saying these same five words: "I just can't help myself." Or maybe you're given up and said, "That's just the way I am." If you have, you've been telling yourself a lie.

Yes, maybe *you* can't help yourself *by yourself*. But guess what? The power of the Holy Spirit working in you can. The key is, you must cooperate. Some say, "But I have prayed about it and it doesn't work. God doesn't care about me. He won't change me!" Oh, girl, God does care about you, and He has given you everything you need to change. "His divine power has given us everything we need for a godly life through our knowledge of him who called us by his own glory and goodness" (2 Peter 1:3). The one thing He won't do is *force* you to change anything. He has given us the dangerous gift of free will, but also the power of the Holy Spirit to follow through.

PAUL KNOWS JUST HOW YOU FEEL

Paul was a man who knew what it was like to struggle with the lie of "I can't help myself." Listen to what he wrote to the Romans:

> I do not understand what I do. For what I want to do I do not do, but what I hate I do. And if I do what I do not want to do, I agree that the law is good. As it is, it is no longer I myself who do it, but it is sin living in me. For I know that good itself does not dwell in me, that is, in my sinful nature. For I have the desire to do what is good, but I cannot carry it out. For I do not do the good I want to do, but the evil I do not want to do—this I keep on doing. Now if I do what I do not want to do, it is no longer I who do it, but it is sin living in me that does it.

> So I find this law at work: Although I want to do good, evil is right there with me. For in my inner being I delight in God's law; but I see another law at work in me, waging war against the law of my mind and making me a prisoner of the law of sin at work within me. What a wretched man I am! Who will rescue me from this body that is subject to death? (Romans 7:15-24).

Paul was a mess and he knew it. I've been right there with him, haven't you? I've known I needed to exercise, but taken a nap instead. I've known I needed to talk to the woman beside me in the airplane, but opened a book and read. I've known I should give my husband grace, but given him the cold shoulder and turned my back to him in bed. What a mess. In each case, I could have made a different choice, but I chose not to.

How do we move past the lie of "I can't help myself"? Paul was so excited to tell us the answer to that question that he couldn't even wait until Romans chapter 8, but blurted it out at the end of chapter 7. "What a wretched man I am! Who will rescue me from this body that is subject to death?" he cried. And then came the answer: "Thanks be to God, who delivers me through Jesus Christ our Lord!" (Romans 7:24-25). Exclamation marks all around!

CHANGING "I CAN'T" TO "JESUS CAN"

Before we come to Christ, we really can't help ourselves. Oh sure, we can make positive decisions and choose to act properly some of the time. But the apostle Paul tells us, "The mind governed by the flesh is death, but the mind governed by the Spirit is life and peace. The mind governed by the flesh is hostile to God; it does not submit to God's law, *nor can it do so*. Those who are in the realm of the flesh cannot please God" (Romans 8:6-8, emphasis added). "Nor can it do so" is strong language.

Once we come to Christ, we can no longer truthfully say, "I can't help myself. This is just the way I am." The truth is, that's just the way you *were*. You now have the power of the Holy Spirit living in you. You can do all things God calls you to do through Christ, who strengthens you. You are no longer a slave to sin. You now have a choice.

In our own strength, we don't have the power to consistently make choices that line up with our new born-again spirit. Left on our own, we will continue to do what we don't want to do and not do what we want to do. Poor choices sneak up and bite us in the back to sabotage our best efforts. It is only through the power of the Holy Spirit that we are able to turn "I can't" into "with God's help, I can."

"I can't help myself" is a lie. Send that lie through the shredding truth of "I can do all things through [Jesus Christ] who strengthens me" (Philippians 4:13 NASB). But remember, God has given you the gift of free will—the will to choose. The first step to overcoming the lie of "I can't help myself" is to realize you are responsible for your choices.

As I said before, we cannot act differently from what we think. So the first step in changing a behavior is changing the way you think— rejecting the lies and replacing the lies with the truth.

From the time you are born, your thoughts create neurological pathways in your brain like little roads. As you continue to think certain thoughts, those roads become four-lane highways. With time, the highways get paved and repaved with layers and layers of mental asphalt. These thoughts might not produce actions and habit patterns you even like, but you're comfortable with them.

When you come to Christ, God says, "I am doing a new thing!" (Isaiah 43:19). But sometimes that "new thing," even though it's a good thing, may feel uncomfortable because it's a different thing. Choosing to abstain from undesirable behavior may feel uncomfortable. Putting down the spoon or putting the cork back in the bottle is hard when it's a new roadway. Saying "no" to your usual "yes" may feel uncomfortable. No one likes road construction. But as you choose to reject the lie of "that's just who I am" and replace it with "that's who I was," you will be creating new neurological pathways over time.

> Saying "no" to your usual "yes" may feel uncomfortable.

YOU ARE A CHOICE MAKER

Let's go back to the three friends we met at the beginning of this chapter and look again at their struggles. What is the truth of their situations, and how can they change the messages they're telling themselves? Suppose they said the following:

Jennifer: *It's silly to think I can't lose weight. Of course I can. I can stop buying potato chips and cookies. I can order salads at fast-food restaurants instead of hamburgers and French fries, and I can start walking every day again. I can do it. I've done it before. My body is the temple of God, and I need to take better care of it. I can do all things through Christ, who gives me strength.*

Rachel: *It's ridiculous to think I cannot control my passion with Travis. We didn't suddenly end up in bed. It took many steps to get here. The kisses, the touches, the walk from the den to the bedroom. We can stop this. God, I repent right now of this sin in my life. I dedicate my body to You and pray that You give me the strength to resist temptation. I will guard my heart and stop putting myself in a position to fail. I can do all things through Christ, who gives me strength.*

Martha: *It's foolish to think I can't change the way I speak to my family. I will start each day dedicating my words to God. Set a guard over my mouth, Lord; keep watch over the door of my lips. When I feel as though I'm about to scream, I will walk out of the room and calm down. May the words of my mouth and the meditation of my heart be pleasing in Your sight. I can do all things through Christ, who gives me strength.*

When we tell ourselves we can't help ourselves—that's just the way we are—then we see ourselves as victims. As long as we see ourselves as victims, being controlled by someone or something else, we will never change. But when we see ourselves as choice makers, we can ask God to give us the power and determination to resist temptation.

Satan knows if he can convince us we can't help ourselves, we will remain in bondage to the lie. The truth is, I can choose to believe differently, and by the power of the Holy Spirit living in me, I can choose to act differently. Choice. Free will. God took a great risk when He gave that gift. How we use it will determine if we live in freedom or in slavery to poor choices.

There is always a choice. The world says we have no control over many sinful behaviors. "I was born this way." Born this way? Yes, you were born bent toward sin; we all were. But that doesn't mean you must *stay* that way. We also have a choice to respond according to our old flesh patterns or to our new, born-again, Spirit-led patterns.

Continuing to walk in a specific sin pattern or in specific poor choices can lead to the development of a stronghold, like we talked about in chapter 4. But remember, we have weapons with "divine power to demolish strongholds" (2 Corinthians 10:4). Sometimes the fight begins with one courageous choice.

"But I've tried and I just can't change," you might say. Listen, just because you couldn't do something before doesn't mean you never will be able to. Remember this from chapter 8: Failure is not final. Failure is not fatal. Get back up and try again. And here's what God wants you to know:

> Do not fear, for I am with you;
> do not be dismayed, for I am your God.
> I will strengthen you and help you;
> I will uphold you with my righteous right hand
> (Isaiah 41:10).

DESIRES ARE NOT NEEDS

Mary Elizabeth was strolling down the cookie aisle at Walmart with her three-year-old daughter, Sarah, riding comfortably in the "front seat" of the shopping cart. Suddenly, Sarah spied a box of sugar cookies, coated with pink icing and decorated with multi-colored sprinkles.

Her eyes brightened with enthusiasm as she put on her best cherub face. "Mommy, I *want* those cookies."

"Oh, Sarah," replied her mom, "we don't need any cookies today. We have plenty at home. Maybe another time."

Ten minutes later, as Mary Elizabeth passed through the checkout line, Sarah tried again. "Mommy, I *need* those cookies."

"No, Sarah, you don't need those cookies. We have plenty at home, and I'm not buying cookies today."

Finally, as they pulled out of the Walmart parking lot, Sarah gave it one last try. "Mommy, I think *God* wants me to have those cookies."

I laughed as my friend told me her story, but it was a nervous laugh. For just a moment, I saw myself riding through life in a shopping cart, pointing at first one thing and then another, whining, "I want...I need...God wants me to have."

Part of our problem with "I can't help myself" is that we've somehow twisted our minds to think our wants and desires are needs. Misbeliefs such as *I need another glass of wine* or *I need a new dress* aren't true. Those aren't *needs*, but *wants*. These misbeliefs come from the world, the flesh, and the devil. They come straight into our homes through television commercials that tell us we "need" to have a certain car to be happy, a particular shampoo to get a man, a specific salad dressing to have a smiling family around the dinner table. *You need it and you need it now!* the media shouts. But the truth is, you don't.

The writer of Proverbs said, "Like a city whose walls are broken through is a person who lacks self-control" (Proverbs 25:28). In other words, a person without self-control is like a house with all its windows and doors knocked out—without protection from all sorts of dangers and abuses.

ENGAGING THE POWER OF THE HOLY SPIRIT

If you were going off to war, and knew you'd be put on the front lines and probably wouldn't be coming back home to your family, what would you tell them? Think of the final instructions you'd give your children, the affirmation of your love you'd whisper to your spouse, and the words of endearment you'd share with your friends.

Jesus was in that very situation as He shared His last meal with the disciples in the upper room. All along, He had given them clues about how His earthly life would end and the purpose for His brief life here on earth. But they didn't understand. They refused to believe their king would be anything other than worshiped as He had been when He rode into town on the back of a donkey and was hailed with palm branches and praise.

I imagine during their last meal together, Jesus went through a mental list of what He needed to tell His friends before He went to the cross. John records those precious moments in John 13–17. Those words are some of the most endearing of Scripture and ones I read time and time again. I encourage you to read those chapters and place yourself in that room with Jesus, for you, dear one, are one of His disciples, and the words Jesus shared with the Twelve are meant for you as well.

Let's look at one word of comfort and instruction regarding a special parting gift Jesus was leaving His trusted friends. He said:

Very truly I tell you, whoever believes in me will do the works I have been doing, and they will do even greater things than these, because I am going to the Father. And I will do whatever you ask in my name, so that the Father may be glorified in the Son. You may ask me for anything in my name, and I will do it.

If you love me, keep my commands. And I will ask the Father, and he will give you another advocate to help you and be with you forever—the Spirit of truth. The world cannot accept him, because it neither sees him nor knows him. But you know him, for he lives with you and will be in you. I will not leave you as orphans; I will come to you.

Before long, the world will not see me anymore, but you will see me. Because I live, you also will live. On that day you will realize that I am in my Father, and you are in me, and I am in you. Whoever has my commands and keeps them is the one who loves me. The one who loves me will be loved by my Father, and I too will love them and show myself to them (John 14:12-21).

Did you catch that the Holy Spirit had been with them, but now He was going to be in them? What difference do you think that would make in someone's life? What difference has that made in your life?

Jesus gave them the promise of the Holy Spirit, and then He told them the purpose of the Holy Spirit.

But very truly I tell you, it is for your good that I am going away. Unless I go away, the Advocate will not come to you; but if I go, I will send him to you...

I have much more to say to you, more than you can now bear. But when he, the Spirit of truth, comes, he will guide you into all the truth. He will not speak on his own; he will speak only what he hears, and he will tell you what is yet to come. He will glorify me because it is from me that he will receive what he will make known to you. All that belongs to the Father is mine. That is why I said the

Spirit will receive from me what he will make known to
you (John 16:7,12-15).

Once again, after Jesus's death and resurrection, He left the disciples with final instructions before taking His seat at the right hand of
God in paradise—and it involved the Holy Spirit. He had given them
the promise and the purpose, and now He told them to wait for the
power.

> Do not leave Jerusalem, but wait for the gift my Father
> promised, which you have heard me speak about. For John
> baptized with water, but in a few days you will be baptized
> with the Holy Spirit...But you will receive power when the
> Holy Spirit comes on you; and you will be my witnesses in
> Jerusalem, and in all Judea and Samaria, and to the ends of
> the earth (Acts 1:4-5,8).

A few days later, the Holy Spirit fell on the disciples and transformed
a bunch of bungling cowards into powerful, prophesying preachers.
They commanded the lame to walk, cast out demons, preached to the
masses, confronted angry crowds, and laughed in the face of death.

They changed the world.

On that glorious day at Pentecost, when the Holy Spirit fell on the
worshiping believers, a new day was unleashed for the church. The
Holy Spirit now resides in every person who has accepted Jesus as Lord
and Savior (Romans 8:9). The Spirit of the living God has empowered
us with the same power that raised Jesus from the dead.

Then why don't we exercise that power? Because we don't believe.

In developing countries, it is not unusual to hear of miraculous
healings, signs, and wonders, and even the raising of the dead. No one
told them those things don't happen anymore. Praise God for that!
They believe in the power of the Holy Spirit in their lives and expect
God to show up when they call on His name. Oh that we would put
our sophisticated, overeducated minds aside and go to God as children
who believe He is who He says He is and does what He says He will do.

When we come to Christ, we are given the Holy Spirit as a deposit of our heavenly inheritance (Ephesians 1:14), as a seal upon our hearts (Ephesians 1:13), and as a permanent resident within us (Hebrews 13:5). But we have the choice to stumble about in our own strength, saying "I can't," or embrace the power of the Holy Spirit and say, "I can."

PUT UP A FENCE—REMOVE THE PATH

One Sunday my pastor had to do some housekeepin' fussin' at our congregation before he started his sermon. It was a "Visitors, close your ears" moment as Jimmy interrupted the service for an important message from our neighbors.

See, right beside our church property is a city park. On Sundays, when our parking lot is full, we tend to use the city park lot for our overflow parking. The only problem is the folks going to the city park don't like it that those daggum *church* people are taking their parking spaces.

It is not nice of us. Really. I'm sorry. I've done it too.

And while our sweet pastor calmly asked the congregation, once again, to *stop parking in the city parking lot* (he didn't yell, but I bet he wanted to), folks still do it.

As soon as Jimmy finished his announcement and began his sermon, God had a sermon just for me. He wasn't finished with me and the forbidden parking lot issue. *That's what happens when you make a path or keep a path open,* He seemed to say. *You're going to walk down it eventually.*

See, although we've been warned, scolded, and pleaded with not to park next door, a little path is situated through the bushes, from the city park's parking lot to our church's parking lot. The bushes are trimmed on both sides, cobblestones are carefully placed, and a nice little bit of concrete forms a gently curving sidewalk. Someone keeps the bushes clipped and the grass maintained. The breezeway almost beckons us (me) to break the rules.

Now let's go down a different path. Let's call the path sin, or maybe it's just a bad habit you say you can't help indulging in. Let's say you've decided that once and for all you are not going to park yourself in the parking lot of that behavior.

You're not going to stop by Dunkin' Donuts and eat a half dozen chocolate-covered donuts in one sitting.

You are not going to sleep with that boyfriend—ever again!

You're not going to date that guy you know is bad for you—ever again.

You're not going to look at that website.

You're not going to flirt with the married guy in the next cubicle.

You're not going to gossip about other people.

You're not going to drink alcohol because you know you have a problem.

You're not going to _____.

Hundreds of vices could be put in that sentence.

But then there's a nice little path you've kept open...just in case. You wouldn't call it "just in case." You wouldn't say it out loud.

The guy's number is still in your contacts list on your smartphone.

You still think about what that guy in the next cubicle would like when you get dressed for work in the morning.

You still pull up that website when you hope God isn't looking.

You still pull up a chair when someone begins to gossip.

You still take the route home from work that goes right by Dunkin' Donuts.

You keep a bottle in the cabinet...just for company.

The path beckons you. And as long as you keep the breezeway open, you'll probably breeze right through it...eventually. The answer? Remove the path. Put up a fence with no gate.

Remove the contact.

Change the job.

Get rid of your computer.

Take a different route home from work.

Remove the bottle.

Make the path impassable, implausible, and impossible to take, and put up a gateless fence instead. Jesus said if your eye causes you to sin, pluck it out (Matthew 5:29). That's pretty dramatic. I'm not telling you to pluck out your eye, and Jesus wasn't saying that either, not literally. But He was telling us to remove the cause of the temptation. Remove the path. Put up a fence.

Do you need to put up a fence where you now have a path? I erected a fence the moment I pressed the send button when I told this story about the pastor's sermon in a blog post. As soon as I had told someone about my parking dilemma, I never parked in the city parking lot again. Just telling someone about the struggle often helps with accountability. And you don't have to do it alone. You have the power of the Holy Spirit working in you and through you. Don't believe the devil for one second when he says you're helpless and hopeless to act any differently than you are today.

CELEBRATE THE VICTORIES

It was a long day with a longer to-do list. I was chipping away at it, but running out of emotional and physical steam. What I *needed* was tea...a large sweet tea without ice. No use wasting space with frozen water.

I hopped in the car and headed to Chick-fil-A. As I pulled into the parking lot, I heard a noise that made my stomach churn.

Flap. Flap. Flap.

I got my tea from the cheery gal at the window and headed to a parking space.

"Excuse me, ma'am," a perky blonde called out behind me. "Do you know you have a flat tire?"

"Yep," I replied. "Just figured that out."

So what? I had a flat tire. That's not a very exciting story. But what happened next is what I want to share with you.

I turned into a parking space and called AAA—"Triple A." Then I pulled up a book on my Kindle app on my iPhone, unwrapped my straw, and took a sip of tea.

An hour later, Alfredo showed up to change my tire. Two hours later I left the Chick-fil-A parking lot and headed home. Now, this still might not sound like a very exciting story to you, but for me, it was a small victory.

Here's what I didn't do:

I didn't cry.

I didn't fuss at God.

I didn't fall apart because the air in my schedule leaked out with the air in my tire.

And that, my friend, was reason to celebrate!

See, my default mode would have been to do all three: cry, fuss at God, and fall apart. I would have said, "I just can't help it. I'm an emotional person. I feel deeply." Then I'd go home in a bad mood for my husband to endure.

That would have been my natural response. My knee-jerk reaction. My default mode. My "I can't help it" moment.

But not today. So I celebrated that one moment of that one day when I responded well.

Driving back home and thinking about this one small attitudinal victory, I thought about a passage in the Bible I had just studied. (This is when my son in his teenage years would roll his eyes and say, "Do you have to relate everything to the Bible?" Well, yeah. I guess I do.)

See, in 1 Samuel 14, King Saul and his men were battling the Philistines. His son Jonathan and his armor bearer left 600 soldiers relaxing under a pomegranate tree and went up to face their enemies alone. The duo killed about 20 men in an area of about a half an acre. Then God threw the Philistines into confusion, and they started killing each other. It was a small victory, but a victory nonetheless. But rather than celebrate the win, Saul made a decree that the men couldn't eat until they achieved total victory. Total. All the enemies destroyed.

Jonathan didn't get the memo about the moratorium on food. And as the army walked through the woods, he dipped his staff in a honeycomb and had a sweet treat. His eyes brightened, and he was refreshed. The other men were weak from hunger, and in no condition to fight.

Jonathan's dad was furious. Almost killed the boy. Almost lost the war. He was not a good king.

Oh, friend, too many of us are waiting until we have total victory in our lives before we celebrate. We wait for perfection, which will never come. We beat up on ourselves for our missteps and mishaps. All the while we miss dipping into the honeycomb of celebration God provides.

You'll never have total victory this side of heaven, but you will have some. You'll still slip up and do what you vowed not to do and not do what you vowed you would do. But you will have victories. Many of them.

Don't miss them!

See them!

Seize them!

Celebrate them!

Celebrate the times when you don't yell at the kids. Hurray! Celebrate the times when you don't respond to the sarcastic cashier with a sarcastic word right back. Praise God! Celebrate the times when you don't fall apart because your schedule does. Do the happy dance! Celebrate the times when you didn't eat that extra bowl of ice cream. You go, girl! Celebrate the times when you stubbed your toe and didn't say a curse word. Well, praise God for that!

> Even though you may not respond to all of life's foibles and fallouts in a God-honoring way, take a moment to celebrate the times you do.

Pick up the honeycomb. Taste and see that the Lord is good.

Pat yourself on the back.

Raise your hand in a high five.

Give yourself a thumbs-up.

God is changing you, transforming you, and remaking you every day. Celebrate the progress. Even though you may not respond to all of life's foibles and fallouts in a God-honoring way, take a moment to celebrate the times you do. You knew you could do it!

• • • • •

RECOGNIZE THE LIE: *I can't help myself.*

REJECT THE LIE: *That's not true.*

REPLACE THE LIE WITH TRUTH:

God is faithful; he will not let you be tempted beyond what you can bear. But when you are tempted, he will also provide a way out so that you can endure it (1 Corinthians 10:13).

14

My Life Is Hopeless

LIE: *My life is hopeless.*

TRUTH: *My God can do exceedingly and abundantly above all I can ask or think* (Ephesians 3:20 NKJV).

I've prayed for a certain man my whole adult life. Let's call him Richard. However, as I type these words today, I haven't seen any softening of his heart for the things of God. Some would look at Richard and say, "Why bother?" He's a mess. He's hurt a lot of people, but none more than himself.

From the outside, Richard looks beyond repair, but I know better. Over the years, I've seen little glimmers of hope, only to be snuffed out by poor decisions. At one point he decided he would follow Christ! But that lasted only a few years, and then he went back to his old ways, becoming worse than he was before. He left his family and denounced his faith.

Alcohol. Women. Anger. Hate. Unemployment. Failed relationships. Richard's roller-coaster life was having fewer highs and lower lows. He was on a downward spiral, headed toward an abyss of clinical depression and hopelessness.

Then one day I got a call telling me Richard was in jail.

I went online and looked up the arrest report in the county where Richard was incarcerated. It was hard to fathom that this could be the same man I'd known since childhood. But it was.

Let me pause to tell you a little side story. God and I have this thing about the number 8:32. John 8:32 is my life verse and was the personalized license plate on my car for about 20 years. I can't tell you how many times I've looked at a digital clock on any given day and read 8:32. It's almost like a little wink from my heavenly Father, just letting me know He sees me, that He loves me.

So back to Richard's story. The second day after his arrest, I went back to the website and read the details of the police report. Arresting officer. Nature of the offense. Location of the arrest. Place of incarceration. Time of arrest. It was the time of arrest that shot right through me—8:32.

Oh, friend, that was no coincidence. The officer could have easily rounded the time to 8:30. But no, it was 8:32. God was saying to me at that moment, *I see him. I love him. I've got this. He is not hopeless. Not by a long shot.* And neither are you.

Hopelessness comes from believing the lie that your situation will never get better. That's exactly what the devil wants you to think. However, the Bible says, "Those who hope in [God] will not be disappointed" (Isaiah 49:23). We need to believe that life can be different— that no circumstance is hopeless. Jesus said, "What is impossible with man is possible with God" (Luke 18:27).

I SEE A CLOUD

In the book of 1 Kings is a story about a prophet named Elijah. God had caused a three-and-a half-year drought in Israel because His people had followed foreign gods and depended on resources other than Him. Miracle after miracle occurred during those three and a half years, but I want to focus on what happened at the end of the drought.

Elijah sent a message to King Ahab to let him know the 42-month dry spell was coming to an end. Let's take a seat on Mount Carmel with Elijah and see what happened next (1 Kings 18:41-46).

> Elijah said to Ahab, "Go, eat and drink, for there is the sound of a heavy rain."
>
> So Ahab went off to eat and drink, but Elijah climbed to

the top of Carmel, bent down to the ground and put his face between his knees.

"Go and look toward the sea," he told his servant. And he went up and looked.

"There is nothing there," he said.

Seven times Elijah said, "Go back."

The seventh time the servant reported, "A cloud as small as a man's hand is rising from the sea."

So Elijah said, "Go and tell Ahab, 'Hitch up your chariot and go down before the rain stops you.'"

Meanwhile, the sky grew black with clouds, the wind rose, a heavy rain started falling and Ahab rode off to Jezreel. The power of the LORD came on Elijah and, tucking his cloak into his belt, he ran ahead of Ahab all the way to Jezreel.

How do you think the servant felt when he went down from the mountain to the shore the first time and didn't see a cloud in the sky? Do you think he was nervous telling Elijah the bad news? This prophet had just had 850 prophets of Baal killed. He was not someone you wanted to give bad news to.

What about the second time?
What about the third time?
What about the fourth time?
What about the fifth time?
What about the sixth time?

I would have probably said to the prophet, "Mr. Elijah, I think you heard God wrong. Maybe you spoke too soon when you told King Ahab to go start celebrating. Man, there's nothing there. The sky's as blue as the ocean below it. God's not doing anything. And besides, I'm getting tired running up and down this mountain. This is hopeless!"

Ignoring the servant's complaint, Elijah says, "Go again."

The servant turns around, takes a deep breath, and makes another trek down the mountain.

"Hmm." He scratches his chin as he stands on the shore and ponders the sky. He returns up the mountain where Elijah is still sitting with his head between his knees. "Well, I saw a little something this time. It's not very big—just a little cloud—about the size of a man's hand. It's not very big, but it's something."

It's not very big, but it's something. That's all the faith you need to move from believing the lie that a situation or a person is hopeless to believing the truth that nothing is impossible with God. A cloud as big as a man's hand, the faith as big as a mustard seed.

Here's a question to ponder: Was God working the entire time the servant was running up and down Mount Carmel, or did He make the cloud appear suddenly on the seventh trek? I think God was working the entire time; the servant just couldn't see it.

I'm not much of a meteorologist, but I do remember a little bit about rain cycles from elementary school. Water falls from the sky in the form of rain, snow, or ice into oceans, rivers, and lakes. The sun heats the water, and it evaporates or turns into an invisible gas called water vapor. The vapor rises from the earth into the atmosphere, cools, and forms droplets called condensation. Little droplets get together and form bigger droplets. Eventually those droplets form clouds. When the droplets get too heavy, they fall back to the earth as precipitation into oceans, rivers, and lakes. Then the cycle starts all over again.

God was working on the servant's first run down the mountain; he just couldn't see it. That water cycle was heating up. Jesus said, "My Father is always at his work to this very day, and I too am working" (John 5:17). Just because you can't see God working doesn't mean He's not. Oh, the devil will say God's forgotten you, but He hasn't.

God said, "Can a mother forget the baby at her breast and have no compassion on the child she has borne? Though she may forget, I will not forget you!" (Isaiah 49:15).

HOPELESS MESSES BECOME HEAVEN'S MIRACLES

God tells us we will have difficulties in this life. Jesus said, "In this world you will have trouble. But take heart! I have overcome the world" (John 16:33). How will we handle difficulties? What will we do? I can tell you what the enemy wants you to do. He wants you to give up, to quit. During difficult times he will tell you the situation is hopeless: the disease is incurable, the loss irrecoverable, the decision irrevocable, the brokenness irreparable, the loss irretrievable, the sadness inconsolable, and the circumstances irreversible. And it's a lie.

All through the Bible, we see examples of God transforming seemingly hopeless situations into miraculous victories. Jonah was swallowed by a large fish. David was thrown in a lions' den. Shadrach, Meshach, and Abednego were tossed into a fiery furnace. Moses and the two million Israelites stood at the edge of the Red Sea with thousands of Egyptian soldiers on their heels. Job lost his children, his health, and his wealth—everything except his grumpy wife. Joseph was sold into slavery. Naomi lost her husband and both of her sons.

With each one of these apparent hopeless situations, God showed up and His people were shored up. Seemingly hopeless situations are the raw material for God's miracles. Oh, friend, we are never without hope. God is always at work. Geri saw that firsthand. Here's her email to me:

> Dear Sharon,
>
> Twelve years ago, my home burned down and we lost everything. Ten months later, my husband died. He was only 40 and I was 37. We had two teenage boys. I felt as though my life was over, but eight years later, I remarried. After this, life only got worse. My new husband and son were always at odds with each other. I remember sitting on the bathroom floor at my job sobbing and believing the only way out was to fall asleep and never wake up. I had the perfect plan and it almost worked.
>
> Our family had started attending church again. I had attended in the past, but had fallen away from my relationship with God. There was a woman at the church who listened to God and intervened in my suicide attempt. God literally reached down and saved my life. It was amazingly obvious that He put circumstances in place to keep me from following through with what I had planned.

I surrendered my life to Jesus and began to pray that God would change me. That was three years ago, and I can honestly say my life is wonderful. My husband came to Christ and will be baptized in a few days. God brought me out of the pit, and I praise Him for all He has brought me through.

> Seemingly hopeless situations are the
> raw material for God's miracles.

I read this email and whispered a prayer of praise. I was so thankful that God had stopped Geri from taking her life. That's Satan's ultimate goal, you know. "The [enemy] comes only to steal and kill and destroy" (John 10:10). Suicide is a permanent solution to a temporary problem. There is always hope.

HOPELESS INTO GRATEFUL

For 12 long years, she had been bleeding. Over 4380 days. Lydia had gone from doctor to doctor to try to stop the flow, but as the years progressed the problem only worsened. Each day was a reminder of the emptiness she felt as her very life ebbed from her body.

I've lost my family, my friends, my energy, and now all my money. My very womanhood, the ability to conceive and suckle a child at my breast flows out of my body and leaves me a barren wasteland. And the pain? The constant cramping feels as though my womb is being squeezed by an invisible hand.

"Unclean." That's what the priests say I am. No one is supposed to even touch me unless they are willing to go through a cleansing process afterward. The house I live in, the chair I sit in, the utensils I cook with—all ceremonially unclean. Oh, how I long for a human touch. A hug. A kiss. A pat on the back. A baby's cheek against my own.

"Oh, God," Lydia prayed. "I've tried everything. My life is hopeless."

God smiled down at His daughter of Abraham and noticed her name on Jesus's celestial calendar. Today was the day.

Sitting all alone in a darkened room, she heard a ruckus outside her window.

"It's Jesus!" someone shouted. "Jesus is coming!"

Jesus, she whispered to herself. *Maybe He could heal me. I know I'm not supposed to go out in public. Certainly I cannot speak to this man or any man on the street. What can I do?*

Quickly, she devised a plan. She wrapped a veil around her face with only enough of an opening for her eyes to peer out. She snuck out of her home and merged with the throng of people trying to catch a glimpse of the much-acclaimed healer and teacher. Gathering all the courage she could muster, she pushed her way through the crowd in hopes of getting close enough just to touch the hem of His robe.

"Jesus!" a man called from the crowd. Like the parting of the sea, the multitude gave way for the synagogue ruler to pass. Everyone knew Jairus. He was important.

Jesus turned as Jairus fell at His feet and begged. "My little daughter is dying," he began. "Please come and put your hands on her so she will be healed and live."

Lydia looked on as Jesus extended His hand to this distraught father, compassionately helped him to his feet, and apparently changed course to go with him. It was then she made her move.

Shoring up courage and confidence, she began muttering to herself. "If I can just touch His clothes, I will be healed. I know it. I just know it. I can't let this opportunity slip away." While unsure of herself, she was confident in Him. Her faith overcame her fear, and she pressed forward.

Like a runner stretching for the finish line, Lydia reached through the crowd and brushed her fingers against the hem of His garment. Just as her faith reached out to touch Jesus, God's healing power reached down to touch her. Immediately, she felt a surge of power flow through her body and the flow of blood come to a halt.

She knew it. She felt it. The flow stopped...and then Jesus stopped.

"Who just touched My clothes?" He asked.

While unsure of herself, she was confident in Him.

Lydia kept her eyes fixed on the ground as a jumble of thoughts scrambled through her mind. *I'm unclean and not supposed to be out in public. I'm not supposed to touch anyone. What am I going to do? If I remove my veil, people with recognize me. I'm not supposed to talk to a man in public.* She wanted to run, but her feet were suddenly rooted to the ground.

"You see the people crowding against You," His disciples answered, "and yet You can ask, 'Who touched Me?'"

Jesus ignored the disciples' comments and continued to pan the crowd in search of the person who had purposely touched His robe. He felt the power flow from His body like a current. He knew what had happened. Jesus could always sense the difference between the press of the curious and the touch of the faithful.

Silence hung like a low-lying cloud. No one said a word.

Finally, Lydia couldn't hold it in any longer. She turned to Jesus and fell at His feet. With trembling voice and a geyser of gratitude, her confession gushed forth.

"Master, I have had an issue of blood for over 12 years. No one has been able to help me. I've lost my family, my friends, my finances, and my hope. But when I heard You were passing through, I just knew that You, oh Lord, could heal me. I know I'm not supposed to touch anyone. I know I am unclean in all regards. Please forgive me for the intrusion. But Jesus, I am healed! As soon as I touched the hem of Your robe, the blood ceased to flow! Thank You, Jesus! Thank You, Jesus!"

While others began to back away from her "uncleanness," Jesus reach forward and embraced her faith.

"Daughter, your faith has healed you. Go in peace and be freed from your suffering."

Oh, how I love this story in Mark 5:25-35! What woman among us hasn't felt the wretchedness of rejection, the shame of suffering, and the humility of hopelessness? And yet Jesus singles this one woman out of a crowd of curious thrill seekers to change her seemingly hopeless situation into a miraculous transformation.

The woman has been referred to as "the woman with the issue of blood." She was defined by what was wrong with her; not by what was right. I've given her the name Lydia and turned her story into a narrative to help us remember that she was a real woman just like you and me, not just a character in a story. This woman's feelings of hopelessness are visceral. You can feel them.

The world had told her to give up and shut up because she was messed up. Doctors had given her no hope. Her family had abandoned her. The culture had labeled her. She was physically, financially, emotionally, and spiritually drained—bankrupt in every way.

Then one day Jesus came to town. Hope surged through her veins. "If I just touch his clothes, I will be healed" (Mark 5:28). She reached. She touched. She was healed.

"Daughter, your faith has healed you," Jesus said. "Go in peace and be freed from your suffering" (Mark 5:34).

When we first met this woman, she was fearful and forgotten. Jesus commended her courage, called her "Daughter"—a name she would not soon forget. He turned her feelings of hopelessness into a message of hope. She went to Him in secret, but left telling everyone what He had done. Jesus wants to do the same for you and me.

"Guide me in your truth and teach me, for you are God my Savior, and my hope is in you all day long" (Psalm 25:5).

DADDY'S GOT YOU

It was a bit too early. Little Tripp was snug in his mommy's womb and not quite ready to meet the world. But the doctors decided it was time for his grand debut.

My niece, Emily, developed preeclampsia in her last weeks of pregnancy. The doctors waited as long as they could, but decided it was best if Tripp were welcomed into the world sooner rather than later. Emily was placed on magnesium to prevent the preeclampsia convulsions, and induced for preterm labor. And while Tripp's birth was God's poetry in motion, he arrived with a few side effects of the magnesium on his 5 pound 12 ounce body.

Toxic magnesium levels.

Relaxed smooth muscle activity.

Reluctance to eat.

Irregular heart rate.

The nurses swept Tripp away to the neonatal intensive care unit soon after his first cry. While we prayed for him and his mom, Stu, his dad, stayed right there with him—exactly where Emily wanted him to be.

Tripp was hooked up to several monitors and had a feeding tube in his nose. At one point, his heart rate began to drop dangerously low from the 120-160 of a newborn.

100...90...80...70...

Stu held little Tripp's hand and began to speak. "We love you, Tripp. Daddy's right here with you. God's right here with you. I'll always be with you. I know this is a scary place, but this is the best place for you right now. I've got you. You get strong. Don't give up. I've got your hand. You're going to be okay.

"Mommy loves you. She can't come in here right now. She's got to get well too. But she loves you. Try to block out your surroundings and look at me. People everywhere are praying for you. Keep fighting, little man. You are God's miracle to us."

As Stu spoke words of love and encouragement, Tripp's heart rate began to climb—70...80...90...100...120. In a few minutes the blood coursed through his veins at a quickened pace, pumped by two hearts joined by fingers of love.

 I don't know where your heart is today. Perhaps like little Tripp's it's running a little sluggish. I'm not talking about your physical heart, but your spiritual heart, your emotional heart. Sluggish from sadness. Despondent from disappointment. Barely beating because of being beaten by life. Hopeless because life just isn't turning out the way you hoped it would and you're out of options.

Here's what I want you to imagine. See yourself in Tripp. See your heavenly Father in Tripp's earthly father. God is talking to you. Reaching for your hand.

"I love you, daughter. I'm right here with you," God's saying to your heart. "I'll always be with you. I know this world is a scary place, but this is the best place for you right now. I've got you. You get strong. Don't give up. I've got your hand. You're going to be okay. Try to block out your surroundings and look at Me. People everywhere are praying for you. Keep fighting, little one. You are My miracle."

Tripp left the NICU after seven days. Healthy and strong.

And, friend, you're going to make it too. Reject the lie if the enemy tells you anything different.

GOD CHANGES OUR PERSPECTIVE

When I was pregnant with my son, I had severe morning sickness for almost the entire nine months. However, I knew it would come to an end with a baby's cry and a precious bundle in my arms. But what if you don't know what the outcome of your struggle will be? What if you don't have the end in sight? What do you do then?

Sometimes God doesn't improve our difficult situation all at once. Most of the time we experience a gradual unfolding of His divine plan. Shannon Woodward said this about healing: "Healing, I've learned, is hidden work. It's the touch of God on the tender, raw places of your soul. It's something you don't feel all at once, something you can't see. You don't mark that day on a calendar. You just look back over the weeks and months and realize you don't hurt the way you used to."[1]

One of the words used to describe God in the Old Testament is *ezar*, one who comes alongside to rescue or help. Yes, He could rescue us from our circumstances, and many times He does. But He can also rescue us *in* our circumstances. Paul and Silas found themselves in a difficult situation. They were behind bars for teaching the good news of Jesus's resurrection and delivering a demon-possessed girl from an evil spirit. The girl could no longer tell fortunes, and her employer was furious about his loss of income. Paul and Silas were arrested, flogged, and locked in the inner chambers with their feet in stocks.

What did they do as they sat bloodied, condemned, and chained? They began singing and praying. Yes, singing! Suddenly, as the other prisoners were listening to the music, God made a little disturbance of His own. A violent earthquake shook the foundations of the prison and the doors flew open. Everybody's chains fell off (see Acts 16).

When we begin to praise God in our circumstances, others watching and listening are blessed as well. Who knows, your trust in God may be the vehicle through which others are freed from their personal chains.

God says, "Was my arm too short to deliver you? Do I lack the strength to rescue you?" (Isaiah 50:2). Your difficult circumstances may feel too deep to climb out of, too high to reach up to, or too wide to stretch your arms around. But the arm of God is never too short to reach down and pull you out, reach up and draw you near, or reach around you and hold you close.

I don't want to give the impression that if we hang on long enough, or have enough faith, every difficult situation will turn out the way we hoped. That is simply not true. Everyone is not healed on this earth. Every marriage is not restored. Every closed womb does not bear a child.

If God did everything we wanted Him to do, He wouldn't be God. We would.

God tells us, "As the heavens are higher than the earth, so are my ways higher than your ways and my thoughts than your thoughts" (Isaiah 55:9). Man trying to understand the mind of God is like an amoeba trying to understand the mind of man. It's not going to happen. But we can cling to this truth: "All the ways of the LORD are loving and faithful toward those who keep the demands of his covenant" (Psalm 25:10). Sometimes God changes our circumstances for us; sometimes He changes us in the circumstances.

Sometimes God changes our circumstances and sometimes He changes how we view them. Peace comes not with changing your feelings in a difficult situation, but by changing your focus. No matter what lies the devil tells you and wants you to repeat to yourself, your life is never hopeless.

IT IS WELL WITH MY SOUL

I wish I could tell you each time life throws me a curveball, I strike up a chorus of "It Is Well with My Soul." I wish I could tell you that when my baby died, I hummed "Jesus Loves Me." Or that when the pregnancy test came back negative for the thirty-sixth time, I sang "Victory in Jesus." I wish I could tell you the day my father looked me in the eyes and couldn't remember my name because of Alzheimer's disease, I whistled Laura Story's "Blessings." But that hasn't been the case. I have grieved. I have mourned. I cried out to God in discouragement and pain.

But through many trials and tears, God has taught me to say, "It is well, it is well with my soul." How? By replacing the lies with the truth. Oh, the situations didn't change. My baby is still in heaven rather than in my arms, I never birthed another child, and my father was not healed from Alzheimer's. The circumstances didn't change, but my perspective did.

I began to see that my baby was with Jesus. I began to see that God had a greater plan for my life that involved spiritual children all around the world. I began to see that my heavenly Father would never forget my name.

When we sing and praise God amid the jail cell of discouragement, the chains fall off and the doors fly open. Being grateful amid disappointment isn't denial; it is choosing to view our circumstances from God's perspective rather than from our own.

I really dislike the phrase "It is what it is." Rarely is that true. Rarely are things as they appear to be. God is always working behind the scenes. We just can't see it.

I think it only fitting to end this chapter with the story of Horatio Spafford. He was born on October 20, 1828, in North Troy, New York. Horatio was a successful lawyer in Chicago who was devoted to the Scriptures and his relationship to Jesus Christ. Sometime in 1871, just after Spafford had invested greatly in real estate, a devastating fire swept through Chicago, wiping out his holdings and his life savings. Just before the fire, he experienced the death of his only son.

Two years after the fire, Spafford planned a vacation to Europe for him and his family. He wanted to provide a respite for his wife and children and at the same time assist evangelist D.L. Moody with his campaigns in Great Britain. But at the last minute, just before their ship was to set sail, Spafford was called away on a business matter. He put his wife and four daughters on the *SS Ville du Havre* and kissed them good-bye with a promise to join them in a few days. But on November

22, the ship carrying Spafford's family was struck by an English vessel and quickly sank to the bottom of the Atlantic. In 12 short minutes, 226 lives met their watery graves; among them were all four of Spafford's daughters.

After the survivors were shuttled safely to shore in Wales, Spafford's wife cabled her husband with two simple words: "Saved alone." Spafford left Chicago immediately to bring his grieving wife back home. As he passed near the place where his daughters took their last breaths, amid his intense grief, he penned the words to one of my favorite hymns.

It Is Well with My Soul

When peace, like a river, attendeth my way,
When sorrows like sea billows roll;
Whatever my lot, Thou hast taught me to say,
It is well, it is well with my soul.

REFRAIN:
It is well (it is well),
With my soul (with my soul).
It is well, it is well with my soul.

Though Satan should buffet, though trials should come,
Let this blest assurance control,
That Christ hath regarded my helpless estate,
And hath shed His own blood for my soul.

My sin, oh, the bliss of this glorious thought!
My sin, not in part but the whole,
Is nailed to the cross, and I bear it no more,
Praise the Lord, praise the Lord, O my soul!

And Lord haste the day when my faith shall be sight,
The clouds be rolled back as a scroll;
The trump shall resound, and the Lord shall descend,
Even so, it is well with my soul.

• • • • •

RECOGNIZE THE LIE: *My life is hopeless.*

REJECT THE LIE: *That is not true.*

REPLACE THE LIE WITH TRUTH:

We know that in all things God works for the good of those who love him, who have been called according to his purpose (Romans 8:28).

15

God Doesn't Really Love Me

LIE: *God doesn't really love me.*

TRUTH: *God says he loves me with an everlasting love; he has drawn me with unfailing kindness* (Jeremiah 31:3).

hen I was a little girl, my father spent most of his waking hours working at his building supply company, observing construction sites, or socializing with his colleagues and associates. Even though his place of business was only a few blocks from our home, his heart was miles away in a place I could not find. My father didn't drink alcohol every day, but when he did, it consumed him. He was filled with a rage that always seemed to be simmering just beneath the surface of his tough skin. But when he drank, that lava of rage erupted out onto those around him.

As a child, many nights I crawled into bed, pulled the covers tightly under my chin or over my head, and prayed that I would hurry and fall asleep to shut out the noise of my parents fighting. Occasionally I'd tiptoe over to my pink ballerina jewelry box, wind up the music key in the back, and try to focus on the tinkling sound that came as the ballerina twirled with arms overhead.

I was afraid of my father. Even when he was sober, I kept my distance.

At the same time, I observed how other daddies cherished their little girls. I saw them cuddle them in their laps, hold their hands while walking in the park, or kiss their cheeks as they dropped them off at school in the mornings. Deep in my heart, a dream was birthed. I dreamed that one day I would have a daddy who loved me—not because I was pretty or made good grades or could play the piano well, but just because I was his.

A DREAM COME TRUE

In the Old Testament, God has many names, but in the New Testament, Jesus used the name "Father" more than any other. It's the name He invites us to use to address the Creator of the universe. Think about that for a moment. The God of all creation, who always has been and always will be, who is all-knowing, all-powerful, and present everywhere at once—that same God invites you to call Him Daddy! He said, "I will be a Father to you, and you will be my sons and daughters" (2 Corinthians 6:18).

For many, the idea of God being their father may not be a pleasant one. We tend to project our experiences with our earthly fathers onto our expectations of our heavenly Father. Some never knew their earthly fathers, some had abusive fathers, some were deserted by their fathers, some had loving and endearing fathers, and some lost their fathers because of sickness or catastrophe. But even the best earthly fathers have feet of clay and will disappoint their children.

No matter what your experience has been with your earthly father, the truth is your heavenly Father is the perfect parent who loves you, cares for your every need, is interested in all you do, skillfully guides you, wisely trains you, never deserts you, generously supplies for your needs, is always available to you, and cherishes you as His precious child. He loves you with an everlasting love. He is especially fond of you.

GOD'S UNCONDITIONAL LOVE

Unfortunately, we live in a world of performance-based acceptance. We grow up believing, "If I make good grades, my parents will be proud of me. If I keep my room clean, my mom will approve of me. If I make the team, my friends will admire me. If I make myself pretty, the boys will like me. If I cook great meals, keep the house clean, and perform well in bed, my husband will love me. If I meet my deadlines, make no mistakes, and get to work on time, my boss will reward me. If I call my mother three times a week, visit her once a week, and spend every Christmas and Thanksgiving at her house, then she will approve of me. If I..."

From the time we are children, we look to people to make us feel valuable. Parents, peers, teachers, boyfriends, employers, and church folks become our measuring sticks. When we measure our worth by the approval of others, we are only as valuable as our last compliment or accomplishment.

Performance-based acceptance will always leave us clamoring for acceptance at every turn. But, friend, God does not love us on the merit of our behavior. He loves us just because we're His.

I love these words Paul wrote to the Ephesians:

> Even before he made the world, God loved us and chose us in Christ to be holy and without fault in his eyes. God decided in advance to adopt us into his own family by bringing us to himself through Jesus Christ. *This is what he wanted to do, and it gave him great pleasure* (Ephesians 1:4-5 NLT, emphasis added).

Why does God love us so much? Because He wants to! It gives Him pleasure.

In the Old Testament, the Israelites were commanded to follow all manner of rules and regulations. They thought if they followed the law without fail, they would be acceptable to God. But there was no way the people could remember all those rules and regulations, much less obey them.

I believe one reason God gave the Old Covenant was to show that we are helpless to earn our way to heaven on our own. No one could ever perform perfectly. It's simply not in our nature or ability to do so. "All our righteous acts are like filthy rags" (Isaiah 64:6).

So God sent His Son, Jesus Christ, who gave His perfect, sinless life as a sacrifice for our sins. Jesus's last words were "It is finished." The debt was paid in full, and we never have to perform for our acceptance again. He did what we are unable to do—once and for all. Why did God do such a thing? Why did He give His only Son so we could be forgiven, cleansed, and free from our sins? Because He loves me so much. Because He loves you so much (John 3:16).

God loves us regardless of our actions. This is difficult for our human minds to grasp because we're not naturally wired that way. This is another example of His ways being higher than our ways. His love is unconditional, unchanging, unfathomable, and immeasurable.

The Bible says, "What a person desires is unfailing love" (Proverbs 19:22). The word *desire* comes from the Hebrew word *ta'avah*, which means to greatly long for, deeply desire, or crave. It's used 32 times in the Bible, and every time it is used of God. Never once is *ta'avah* used in reference to a man or woman. Why is that? Because only God can give unfailing love.

God put the need for unfailing love in our hearts because He knew it would draw us back to Him. "Until God's love is enough, nothing else will be."[1] Christianity is the only faith that offers a personal relationship with the living God. We can't earn it or be good enough for it. It is a gift received, accepted, and enjoyed—offered to you because He loves you.

GOD CAN BE TRUSTED

I hopped up on the counter at the soda fountain and placed my five-year-old feet on the spinning stool in front of me. Dad sipped on a Coke and talked to the lady behind the counter with the red-and-white-striped apron tied around her waist.

"This is my little girl," Daddy said with a smile. "She's a little monkey."

"Why, Allan, she's just as cute as she can be."

For a moment, I thought I was.

I stood in the front yard waiting for the screaming to stop before I went back inside. Dad was drunk again, and Mom was screaming at the top of her lungs. Why couldn't he see how afraid I was? Why did he drink? Why did Mom yell? Why did they hit each other? After 17 years of these volcanic outbursts, you'd think I'd be used to it. But they always took me by surprise.

The next day came with many tears and promises. "I'll never do it again," Dad said. "I am so sorry."

But there was always a next time. I couldn't trust him.

Once we grasp the truth of God's amazing love, we come to the next question: Can I trust Him? Can I trust God with my hopes and fears, days and years? When you understand the depth of His love, the answer is always yes. Perfect love drives away all fear, kicks it out the door, gives it the boot (1 John 4:18). I love how another translation says 1 John 4:18:

> There is no fear in love [dread does not exist], but full-grown (complete, perfect) love turns fear out of doors and expels every trace of terror! For fear brings with it the thought of punishment, and [so] he who is afraid has not reached the full maturity of love [is not yet grown into love's complete perfection] (AMPC).

I could relate to the rejected Jesus and easily accept the indescribable gift He gave. I marveled at God's love. I truly did. But when it came time to trust my heavenly Father with my hopes and dreams? That was a different story. For the longest time, when conflicts arose, I became that teenage girl looking in the crowd for a daddy who wasn't there. Could I trust this heavenly Father? I wasn't so sure.

But one day God spoke to my heart in a poignant way. *Take your father's face off Mine,* He seemed to say. *I am not like your earthly father. I am your heavenly Father.*

I am always good.

I always tell the truth.

I want what is best for you.

You can trust Me.

It's easy to trust God when life is good. But when a child rebels, the bank account dwindles, or the biopsy comes back saying the tumor is malignant, we wonder. Is God really good? We know in our heads that He is, but the heart struggles to believe. The enemy peddles the lie that God is *not* good—that He's holding out on us. That's what he told Eve. *God is holding out on you. You can't trust Him. You will not die.*

Then disappointment hits and the devil says, "Told you so."

Life is filled with disappointments. And it's during those times of disappointment that the enemy sows seeds of distrust with thoughts of mistrust. Disappointment and discouragement become the breeding ground for Satan's lies to take root.

During all those years I struggled with infertility, the enemy continually taunted me with lies. *God doesn't love you,* he whispered. *If He loved you He would give you a child. You can't trust Him with your heart. You can't trust Him with your deepest longings.*

When we lost our second child due to a miscarriage, the enemy pestered me with more lies. *How could God let this happen? How could He break your heart like this? How could a loving God allow such pain?*

Have you ever felt that way? I think most of us have heard those lies at one time or another. But the truth is, if God says no in one area of our lives, it's because He has a greater yes in another.

Can you imagine how the disciples must have felt as the stone rolled in front of Jesus's tomb? *How could this happen? Where is God? We thought He was going to restore Israel?* But three days later, when Jesus rose from the grave and appeared to them in all His glory, they knew the answer. God had a greater plan. And God has a plan for you.

> "What no eye has seen,
>   what no ear has heard,
> and what no human mind has conceived"—
>   the things God has prepared for those who love him—
>   (1 Corinthians 2:9).

GOD'S BIRD'S-EYE VIEW

One summer I stood on the edge of the Grand Canyon, amazed at the magnitude of its majestic beauty. Even a wide-angle camera lens didn't begin to capture the expanse. And yet, when I flew over it the day before, I saw it from beginning to end in a single sweep.

Once again I was reminded about God's perspective of my life. I have only a few pieces of the puzzle, but God holds the box top. I have no idea what the finished portrait of my life is going to look like, but God holds the brush and knows exactly what strokes belong where.

The enemy tells us we know what's best for our own lives, and if we're honest, we think we know what's best for others as well. But the truth is we have no idea. Oh, sure, we do know the ultimate best is summed up in two words—*follow Jesus*. Jesus said, "I am the way and the truth and the life" (John 14:6).

But when it comes to the details of everyday life, I have no idea what's best for me or for anybody else. I could worry about it, but what good would that do? Worry is the opposite of trust. One definition of *worry* is "to seize by the throat with teeth and shake or mangle as one animal does another, or to harass by repeated biting or snapping."[2] That's exactly what Satan does with his prey. He seizes us by the throat and mangles our trust with repeated harassing lies beginning with "What if?"

All worry is wrapped in the lie that God is not to be trusted. If we truly believe the truth that God loves us, that God is good, that God always tells the truth, and that God wants what's best for us, then we will not worry. The future is in God's hands, and His plans are good.

"Cast all your anxiety on him," Peter wrote, "because he cares for you" (1 Peter 5:7). Another translation says it this way: "Let him have all your worries and cares, for he is always thinking about you and watching everything that concerns you" (TLB).

Like a passenger who keeps grabbing the steering wheel, we tend to grab for control in our lives. We believe the lie that we know what's best and so try to steer things the direction we think they should go. When that happens, we run off the road, take wrong turns, and often run out of gas.

I read a bumper sticker that said, "God is my copilot." If that's the case in your life, you need to switch seats.

IS GOD PUNISHING ME?

The question of why bad things happen to God's people has no easy answer. Is it God's discipline? Is it because we live in a fallen world? Is it because of our poor choices? Each one of these is a viable option, but we mustn't be too quick to assume that trials are the result of something we've done. Trials are often God's training ground for our greater good.

Yes, God does discipline His children. The Bible says, "Know then in your heart that as a man disciplines his son, so the LORD your God disciplines you" (Deuteronomy 8:5). However, every time we read about God disciplining someone in the Bible, that person knew exactly who was doing the disciplining and why He was doing it.

God disciplined Miriam for gossiping about her brother Moses (Numbers 12). God disciplined Saul for acting like a self-appointed priest (1 Samuel 13). God struck down Ananias and Sapphira when they lied about how much money they put in the offering plate (Acts 5). In each case, there was not a hint of repentance from the offenders and no question as to why they were being punished.

The Bible tells us God quickly forgives when we confess and repent. He does not keep a record of wrongs and punish us for past sins. He throws our sins into the deepest of seas and doesn't go back to fish them out. He simply does not work that way. "As far as the east is from the west, so far has he removed our transgressions from us" (Psalm 103:12).

Sometimes we must live with the consequences of our sin, and that can feel like punishment. But we must always remember that consequences are a result of our choices. Sexually transmitted diseases and unplanned pregnancies can be consequences of sexual promiscuity. Broken relationships can be the consequence of lying. Some illnesses are consequences of poor eating habits.

If you jump out of a three-story building and break your leg, you wouldn't say God was punishing you by breaking your leg. The injury is the consequence of a bad choice.

The question of why bad things happen has no pat answer. Ultimately, God is in control. His ways are higher than our ways, and we may never know the "whys" this side of heaven (Isaiah 55:9).

GOD'S NOT MAD AT YOU

Shannon is a friend of mine who questioned whether God was punishing her through infertility. She described her doctor's words as "a constant, haunting hum in her head, like a song you can't shake—a song with the power to drive you insane. His voice was inescapable. 'You're infertile,' I heard before breakfast, and again in the late afternoon when the light dipped and faded, and yet again in the black, middle-of-the-night hours when I ached for sleep but couldn't make my eyes close."[3]

Through many years of doctor visits, failed adoptions, and negative pregnancy tests, Shannon wondered if God was punishing her. When she was 19, she walked through the doors of an abortion clinic to terminate the life of her unborn child. A test before the procedure proved she was not pregnant after all, but the guilt from what she had intended to do followed her into her adult years. *Could it be that God is punishing me?* she wondered through the years of infertility. *Perhaps I'm not good enough for Him to bless me.* But it took hearing the lie from a coworker to awaken her to the truth.

> I wanted to be a powerful teacher. I wanted to make God proud. So in addition to my regular Bible reading and my scheduled prayers, I started reading Romans every week...I comforted myself with the hope that my studious diligence would pay off in the only way that mattered.
>
> Somewhere deep down, I must have believed that God would notice how smart as a whip I was and grade me accordingly. He'd remove the F I received the day I walked into that abortion clinic with its rainbow sign and its filthy floor, and he'd replace it with an A+. When he did that—when he nodded his approval and expunged my record—he'd let me know by sending the only message that could possibly convince me: He'd let me conceive.
>
> About a year after I began my Romans-fest, I began a job as a hostess in the apartment clubhouse where we lived. I'd take my Bible and notebook and sit in the center of the lounge where I could keep an eye on the pool and greet the residents who popped in.
>
> I had my tally sheet and much-marked book of Romans lying open one evening when a maintenance worker walked in to get a cup of coffee. He saw my Bible and asked what I was reading.

"Romans," I said.

He nodded. "Good book."

We talked about where we each fellowshipped for a moment, and then he made an odd pronouncement. "Yeah, I learned my lesson this week."

"How's that?"

"Last Sunday I forgot to tithe. And guess what happened Monday?"

I couldn't guess.

"I got a flat tire."

I sat waiting for the punch line, unable to track with his thinking.

"Don't you get it? The flat tire was a message: 'If you want me to bless you, you've got to keep up your end of the deal.' God will not be mocked. He was warning me."

"No, he wasn't." The words galloped out of my mouth before I could fling a rope around them.

"He sure was."

Now we were into it. I tossed all restraint aside. "You think God only blesses you when you're good?"

"Sure do. If you follow the rules, give him what belongs to him, and don't mess up, good things will happen to you. If you don't do all that, bad things follow."

"How can you even *think* that? Who taught you that garbage?"

"You calling the Word of God garbage? "'Will a man rob God...Bring the whole tithe into the storehouse...Test me in this,' says the Lord Almighty, "and see if I will not throw open the floodgates of heaven and pour out so much blessing that you will not have room enough for it"'" (Malachi 3:8,10).

"Yes...but...but to talk about God as if he's vindictive and petty and...and...like us."

"If you want to be blessed, you've got to hold up your end of the bargain." He picked up his cup, gave me a firm and dismissive nod, and marched out of the clubhouse.

I stared after him. How could a person think that way? How could you love or serve a God that petty? I couldn't figure it out. I certainly didn't know his God...

Oh, don't you?

The thought echoed in the stunned silence of my mind. For a long, horrible moment I sat and let the ramifications of that question pelt and taunt me.

But then I stood, plugged in the vacuum cleaner, and drowned out the echo.

I didn't read a word of my Bible the next day. I had a good excuse—friends from California had called earlier in the week to visit. After catching up on our lives, we said our goodnights. I didn't sleep well. Untended business tugged at me. So at 5:00 a.m., with only a few hours' sleep behind me, I took my Bible and crept into the bathroom—the only room where I could read and not disturb anyone else.

I opened my Bible to a familiar spot and sat on the floor with my back against the wall—both literally and figuratively. God had me cornered. That blasted maintenance worker had pulled all my sleepy thoughts from my mind, laid them out on the table, and slapped them awake—and now I was going to have to claim them for my own.

I *did* think of God that way. I thought I could make him owe me.

It's more than that, I heard.

So he wanted to get it all out. He wanted to fillet me, right there, and remove every cancerous thought growing on my mind.

"It's more than what?"

You think you can earn blessings—and you think you have to erase your mistakes to make me love you.

I looked at the open Bible in my lap and, suddenly, all the red marked verses began to leap off the page at me: "justified by faith...whose sins have been covered...reconciled to God...free gift...made righteous..." (Romans 3:28; 4:7; 5:10,15,19).

Then my eyes flew back a few verses to the one that finally broke through: "For while we were still helpless, at the right time Christ died for the ungodly" (Romans 5:6 NASB).

The words I'd read every week for a year breathed and sat up and stretched their arms wide, and I fell into them. And God whispered a revelation. *When you were head over heels in love with your sin, that's when I chose you. When you were as far from me as you could possibly be, that's when I said, "She's mine."*

He had planned it all. God drove me to that bathroom and set me on that floor, and when I looked around I realized where I was, and remembered that long-ago bathroom when I sat in that same position and begged him to empty my womb, he was right there to whisper what I most needed to hear:

I was there—and I wept with you.

I wasn't being punished. I wasn't paying for a mistake. God wasn't angry with me.

I pulled my Bible up tight against my chest, lifted my face toward his, and sobbed. He offered, and I let him take from me all the hatred I'd held for myself, all the fear I'd held toward him, and every doubt I'd held about my past and how it affected my future.

In the quiet of that room I heard a promise:

I will be your very great reward.[4]

God was not punishing Shannon. Her sins were forgiven and forgotten the moment she asked. She knew that now.

WHEN LOVE HURTS

"Mommy, Mommy," Steven cried. "Don't let them hurt me!"

My son was about three years old when he contracted a severe case of the flu. His slumped body snuggled listlessly in my lap like an old, worn rag doll. When I carried him into the medical clinic, the doctor quickly diagnosed dehydration and immediately sent us to the hospital.

My heart ripped apart as the nurses strapped my little boy onto a table and began placing IVs in his tiny arms. "Mommy, Mommy," Steven cried. "Make them stop! They're hurting me."

"No, honey," I tried to assure him. "They're going to make you all better."

"Mommy, help me!"

Steven cried. I cried. The nurses cried.

I could only imagine what was going through Steven's little mind. *Why are these people hurting me? Why doesn't Mommy make them stop? She must not love me. She's not protecting me. If she loved me she wouldn't let them do this. She must not care about me.*

Standing in the corner watching my little boy cry, I wondered if how I was feeling is how God feels when I'm going through a painful situation that's for my ultimate good. I cry out, "God, why are You letting this happen? Don't You love me? Don't You care about what's happening to me? Why don't You make it stop?"

It was a picture I would not soon forget. I envisioned God speaking to me in my pain. *You don't understand the reason for the pain. You might think I've deserted you, but I will never leave you. You might think I don't love you, but I love you to the height of heaven and the depth of the sea. You might think I don't care about what's happening to you, but I am orchestrating your days and care about every hair on your head. My ways are higher than your ways and My thoughts are higher than your thoughts. Yes, I do care about you and what is happening to you. In the end, this will make you better.*

C.S. Lewis, who watched his beloved wife die of cancer, put it this way: "But pain insists upon being attended to. God whispers to us in our pleasures, speaks in our conscience, but shouts in our pains: it is his megaphone to rouse a deaf world." Because God loves us, He desires our conformity more than our comfort. Allowing troubles, trials, and pain is one of the ways our loving God makes that so. No one likes to be stuck with a sharp needle; but if the needle brings healing or prevents greater suffering in the future, it's just what we need. Faith in Jesus Christ does not guarantee an easy life, but a perfect eternity.

> Faith in Jesus Christ does not guarantee
> an easy life, but a perfect eternity.

We can rejoice, too, when we run into problems and trials, for we know that they help us develop endurance. And endurance develops strength of character, and character strengthens our confident hope of salvation. And this hope will not lead to disappointment. For we know how dearly God loves us, because he has given us the Holy Spirit to fill our hearts with his love (Romans 5:3-5 NLT).

God loves you. God is good. God always tells the truth. God wants what's best for you. And you can trust Him. That's the truth.

•••••

RECOGNIZE THE LIE: *God doesn't love me.*

REJECT THE LIE: *That's not true.*

REPLACE THE LIE WITH TRUTH:

I am convinced that neither death nor life, neither angels nor demons, neither the present nor the future, nor any powers, neither height nor depth, nor anything else in all creation, will be able to separate us from the love of God that is in Christ Jesus our Lord (Romans 8:38-39).

Second Glances

*C*arrie stood before the bathroom mirror putting the finishing touches on her makeup before rushing off to the carnival with her girlfriends. It had been ten years since she and the old gang ventured to the traveling fair. A lot had happened since then. Some good. Some bad. But through all the joys and trials of the past decade, Carrie had come to know Jesus. She had traded in her religion for an intimate relationship with God.

I'm so thankful, Carrie thought. *I now know who I am as a child of God. I no longer believe the enemy's lies that I'm not good enough, that I'm worthless, or that I'm a failure. Oh, I am so grateful for the truth of Jesus that has set me free from the weight of the lies. No more shame!*

The honking horn interrupted Carrie's thoughts. She grabbed her sweater and yelled to her mom, who was in the kitchen.

"Bye, Mom. I'll be home by eleven."

"Be careful," her mom called out.

She kissed each of her kids and ran for the door before they started begging her to stay.

Carrie, Katie, Clair, and Meghan scurried from booth to booth as the carnival barkers drew them in. They laughed at new huddles of teenage boys who tried to prove their manhood by banging hammers, firing rifles, and shooting hoops. The girls tried their hand at the old games and laughed as they stuck their fingers in the water to pick up ducks. They even reminisced with clouds of sticky cotton candy that melted on contact.

"Come one, come all," the barker called. "Step right up and see yourself as you've never been seen before. The House of Mirrors, sure to entertain and amuse. Step right up."

"Come on in, little lady," the man with slicked-backed hair and a toothy grin said as he motioned to Carrie. She wondered if it was the same man from years before.

"Let's go in here," Katie said. "This'll be fun."

Carrie was whisked away with the crowd and pushed into the first mirrored room. Elongated reflections stared back, and the girls giggled at the older, taller, thinner versions of themselves. In the next room, they laughed at their stubby arms and legs and wondered where the mirrors were that took away wrinkles.

The other girls ran to a third room, but Carrie stayed behind. She was silent as she stared at what she saw staring back at her. Words seemed to appear across her chest, fading in and out in various scripted forms. *Deeply loved. Completely forgiven. Fully pleasing. Priceless treasure. New creation. Accepted. Chosen. Holy. Valuable. Redeemed. Cleansed. Free.*

She couldn't move. She couldn't breathe.

Tears of joy trickled down Carrie's smiling face. "Thank You, God, for opening my eyes to the truth. I love You so much. Because of Jesus, I am enough."

Replacing the Lies with the Truth
Quick Reference Guide

LIE: *I'm not good enough.*

TRUTH: Because of Jesus Christ and His work of redemption, I am deeply loved, completely forgiven, fully pleasing, and totally accepted by God. I am empowered and equipped by the Holy Spirit to do all God has called me to do.

> *You were washed, you were sanctified, you were justified in the name of the Lord Jesus Christ and by the Spirit of our God* (1 Corinthians 6:11).

LIE: *I'm not smart enough.*

TRUTH: I have the mind of Christ.

> *We have the mind of Christ* (1 Corinthians 2:16).

LIE: *I'm rejected.*

TRUTH: I have been chosen.

> *He chose us in him before the creation of the world* (Ephesians 1:4).

LIE: *I'm condemned.*

TRUTH: I am forgiven and free.

> *Therefore, there is now no condemnation for those who are in Christ Jesus, because through Christ Jesus the law of the Spirit who gives life has set you free from the law of sin and death* (Romans 8:1-2).

LIE: *I'm a loser.*

TRUTH: I am a conqueror.

> *In all these things we are more than conquerors through him who loved us* (Romans 8:37).

LIE: *I'm insecure.*

TRUTH: I am secure.

> *Those who fear the LORD are secure* (Proverbs 14:26 NLT).

LIE: *I'm inadequate.*

TRUTH: My adequacy is in Christ.

> *Not that we are adequate in ourselves to consider anything as coming from ourselves, but our adequacy is from God* (2 Corinthians 3:5 NASB).

LIE: *I'm inferior. I'm just a nobody.*

TRUTH: I am a child of the King.

> *To all who did receive him, to those who believed in his name, he gave the right to become children of God* (John 1:12).

LIE: *I'm insignificant. I don't matter to anyone.*

TRUTH: I have great significance as a child of God.

> *See what great love the Father has lavished on us, that we should be called children of God! And that is what we are!* (1 John 3:1).

LIE: *I'm incomplete. I need _____ to be fulfilled.*

TRUTH: I have been made complete in Christ.

> *In Him dwells all the fullness of the Godhead bodily; and you are complete in Him, who is the head of all principality and power* (Colossians 2:9-10 NKJV).

LIE: *I'm unacceptable.*

TRUTH: I am totally accepted by God.

> *Accept one another, then, just as Christ accepted you, in order to bring praise to God* (Romans 15:7).

LIE: *I'm all alone.*

TRUTH: God and His heavenly angels are always with me.

> *The angel of the LORD encamps around those who fear him, and he delivers them* (Psalm 34:7).

LIE: *I can't do anything right.*

TRUTH: I can do all things through Christ, who strengthens me.

> *I can do everything through Christ, who gives me strength* (Philippians 4:13 NLT).

LIE: *I'm worthless.*

TRUTH: The Lord has chosen me to be His treasured possession. My worth is not based on what others think of me, but on what God thinks of me—and He thinks I'm priceless.

> *Out of all the peoples on the face of the earth, the LORD has chosen you to be his treasured possession* (Deuteronomy 14:2).

LIE: *I'm too far gone. I don't think God could still love me after what I've done.*

TRUTH: Nothing can separate you from God, not even your own poor choices.

> *I am convinced that neither death nor life, neither angels nor demons, neither the present nor the future, nor any powers, neither height nor depth, nor anything else in all creation, will be able to separate us from the love of God that is in Christ Jesus our Lord* (Romans 8:38-39).

LIE: *I'm helpless.*

TRUTH: God is my strength.

> *"Fear not, for I am with you. Do not be dismayed. I am your God. I will strengthen you; I will help you; I will uphold you with My victorious right hand...I am holding you by your right hand—I, the Lord your God—and I say to you, Don't be afraid; I am here to help you"* (Isaiah 41:10,13 TLB).

LIE: *I will never figure this out.*

TRUTH: God will give me wisdom.

> *If any of you lacks wisdom, he should ask God, who gives generously to all without finding fault, and it will be given to him* (James 1:5).

LIE: *I'm a bad person.*

TRUTH: I am a partaker of God's divine nature.

> *Through [everything we need for life and godliness] he has given us his very great and precious promises, so that through them you may participate in the divine nature, having escaped the corruption in the world caused by evil desires* (2 Peter 1:4).

LIE: *My sin is unforgivable.*

TRUTH: God has forgiven me of all my sins.

> *If we confess our sins, he is faithful and just and will forgive us our sins and purify us from all unrighteousness* (1 John 1:9).

LIE: *I'm used goods.*

TRUTH: I am a new creation—God's temple.

> *Don't you know that you yourselves are God's temple and that God's Spirit dwells in your midst?* (1 Corinthians 3:16).

LIE: *I'm powerless.*

TRUTH: I have been given the power of the Holy Spirit.

> *I pray also that the eyes of your heart may be enlightened in order that you may know...his incomparably great power for us who believe* (Ephesians 1:18-19).

LIE: *I'm an outcast.*

TRUTH: I have been adopted into God's family.

> *In love he predestined us for adoption to sonship through Jesus Christ* (Ephesians 1:4-5).

LIE: *I'm weak.*

TRUTH: I am strong in the Lord. His power is working in me.

> *The LORD is the strength of my life* (Psalm 27:1 NKJV).

LIE: *I'm condemned.*

TRUTH: I am forgiven.

> *There is now no condemnation for those who are in Christ Jesus* (Romans 8:1).

LIE: *I'm all alone.*

TRUTH: Jesus is always with me.

> *God has said, "Never will I leave you; never will I forsake you"* (Hebrews 13:5).

> *Jesus came to them and said, "...And surely I am with you always, to the very end of the age"* (Matthew 28:18,20).

LIE: *I'm such a failure:*

TRUTH: I am a child of God who sometimes fails.

> *Thanks be to God! He gives us the victory through our Lord Jesus Christ* (1 Corinthians 15:57).

LIE: *I'm not safe.*

TRUTH: God will protect me.

> *The name of the LORD is a fortified tower; the righteous run to it and are safe* (Proverbs 18:10).

LIE: *I can't take this any longer.*

TRUTH: I can endure.

> *Everyone born of God overcomes the world. This is the victory that has overcome the world, even our faith* (1 John 5:4).

LIE: *I can't get past my past.*

TRUTH: God makes all things new. I am a new creation.

> *If anyone is in Christ, the new creation has come: The old has gone, the new is here!* (2 Corinthians 5:17).

LIE: *I can't resist temptation.*

TRUTH: Through the power of the Holy Spirit, I can resist temptation.

> *No temptation has overtaken you except what is common to*

*mankind. And God is faithful; he will not let you be tempted
beyond what you can bear. But when you are tempted,
he will also provide a way out so that you can endure it*
(1 Corinthians 10:13).

LIE: *I can't let anyone know about my past.*

TRUTH: There is incredible power in my personal story of forgiveness and deliverance. It is the enemy who wants me to keep it quiet.

> *They triumphed over [Satan] by the blood of the Lamb and
> by the word of their testimony* (Revelation 12:11).

LIE: *I just can't help myself.*

TRUTH: I can stop this sinful habit through the power of Christ.

> *We know that our old self was crucified with him so that the
> body ruled by sin might be done away with, that we should
> no longer be slaves to sin—because anyone who has died has
> been set free from sin* (Romans 6:6-7).

LIE: *I can't trust God to take care of my needs.*

TRUTH: I can trust God to take care of my needs.

> *My God will meet all your needs according to the riches of his
> glory in Christ Jesus* (Philippians 4:19).

LIE: *I don't believe God hears my prayers.*

TRUTH: God always hears my prayers.

> *This is the confidence we have in approaching God: that if
> we ask anything according to his will, he hears us. And if we
> know that he hears us—whatever we ask—we know that we
> have what we asked of him* (1 John 5:14-15).

LIE: *I don't need God on this one. I can handle this one on my own.*

TRUTH: I can't do anything significant apart from Christ working through me.

> *"I am the vine; you are the branches. If you remain in me and I in you, you will bear much fruit; apart from me you can do nothing"* (John 15:5).

LIE: *I don't have what it takes to succeed in life.*

TRUTH: God has given me everything I need to do all He has called me to do.

> *His divine power has given us everything we need for a godly life through our knowledge of him who called us by his own glory and goodness* (2 Peter 1:3).

LIE: *I don't have enough faith.*

TRUTH: God has given me all the faith I need. I simply need to exercise it and believe.

> *God has allotted to each a measure of faith* (Romans 12:3 NASB).

> *"Truly I tell you, if you have faith as small as a mustard seed, you can say to this mountain, 'Move from here to there,' and it will move. Nothing will be impossible for you"* (Matthew 17:20).

LIE: *I'll never do anything significant with my life.*

TRUTH: God has wonderful plans for my life.

> *We are God's handiwork, created in Christ Jesus to do good works, which God prepared in advance for us to do* (Ephesians 2:10).

LIE: *I'll never recover from this horrible circumstance. Life will never be the same.*

TRUTH: God will cause all things to work for good in my life.

> *We know that in all things God works for the good of those who love him, who have been called according to his purpose* (Romans 8:28).

LIE: *Nobody ever prays for me.*

TRUTH: Jesus prays for me continually.

> *Christ Jesus who died—more than that, who was raised to life—is at the right hand of God and is also interceding for us* (Romans 8:34).

LIE: *Nobody knows what I'm going through.*

TRUTH: Jesus understands what I'm going through.

> *We do not have a high priest who is unable to sympathize with our weaknesses, but we have one who has been tempted in every way, just as we are—yet he did not sin* (Hebrews 4:15).

LIE: *Nobody loves me.*

TRUTH: God loves me greatly.

> *This is love: not that we loved God, but that he loved us and sent his Son as an atoning sacrifice for our sins* (1 John 4:10).

LIE: *God won't forgive me this time.*

TRUTH: God will forgive me when I confess, repent, and ask.

> *Because of the LORD's great love we are not consumed, for his compassions never fail. They are new every morning; great is your faithfulness* (Lamentations 3:22-23).

LIE: *God isn't really good.*

TRUTH: God is good all the time.

> *You are good, and what you do is good* (Psalm 119:68).

LIE: *God's love for me is related to my performance.*

TRUTH: God's love for me is not based on my performance but on the finished work of Jesus Christ.

> *It is by grace you have been saved, through faith—and this not from yourselves, it is the gift of God—not by works, so that no one can boast* (Ephesians 2:8-9).

LIE: *I am too weak.*

TRUTH: God's power is made perfect in weakness.

> *"My grace is sufficient for you, for my power is made perfect in weakness"* (2 Corinthians 12:9).

LIE: *God has forgotten me.*

TRUTH: God will never forget me.

> *"Can a mother forget the baby at her breast and have no compassion on the child she has borne? Though she may forget, I will not forget you! See, I have engraved you on the palms of my hands"* (Isaiah 49:15-16).

LIE: *God doesn't care about me.*

TRUTH: God knows the number of hairs on my head and is concerned with every aspect of my life.

> *"Even the very hairs of your head are all numbered. So don't be afraid; you are worth more than many sparrows"* (Matthew 10:30-31).

LIE: *I have reason to fear.*

TRUTH: God will protect me. I do not need to be afraid.

I sought the LORD, and He heard me, and delivered me from all my fears (Psalm 34:4 NKJV).

LIE: *I want to obey God, but it's too hard.*

TRUTH: God will never ask me to do anything He will not give me the power to do.

What I am commanding you today is not too difficult for you or beyond your reach (Deuteronomy 30:11).

LIE: *I need _____ to feel complete.*

TRUTH: I am complete in Christ.

In Him dwells all the fullness of the Godhead bodily; and you are complete in Him, who is the head of all principality and power (Colossians 2:9-10 NKJV).

LIE: *My marriage is hopeless.*

TRUTH: Nothing is impossible for God. He can heal my marriage.

What is impossible with man is possible with God (Luke 18:27).

LIE: *This is an impossible situation. It cannot be fixed.*

TRUTH: God can fix any situation.

Jesus looked at them and said, "With man this is impossible, but not with God; all things are possible with God" (Mark 10:27).

LIE: *My finances are hopeless.*

TRUTH: God can take care of my finances if I seek Him first.

Seek first his kingdom and his righteousness, and all these things will be given to you as well (Matthew 6:33).

LIE: *It's my body. I can do what I want.*

TRUTH: My body is God's temple.

> *Do you not know that your bodies are temples of the Holy Spirit, who is in you, whom you have received from God? You are not your own; you were bought at a price. Therefore honor God with your bodies* (1 Corinthians 6:19-20).

LIE: *He's not a Christian, but I'm going to marry him anyway. I'm sure it will all work out.*

TRUTH: God has commanded believers not to marry unbelievers.

> *Do not be yoked together with unbelievers. For what do righteousness and wickedness have in common?...What does a believer have in common with an unbeliever?* (2 Corinthians 6:14-15).

LIE: *I deserve better.*

TRUTH: I deserve hell. God doesn't owe me anything. I owe Him everything.

> *Do nothing out of selfish ambition or vain conceit, but in humility value others above yourselves...have the same mindset as Christ Jesus: Who, being in very nature God, did not consider equality with God something to be used to his own advantage; rather, he made himself nothing, taking the very nature of a servant, being made in human likeness* (Philippians 2:3,5-7).

LIE: *The devil made me do it.*

TRUTH: The devil can't make me do anything.

> *The one who is in you is greater than the one who is in the world* (1 John 4:4).

LIE: *I'd be happy if I just had _____.*

TRUTH: My joy comes from knowing God.

> *I have learned to be content whatever the circumstances* (Philippians 4:11).

LIE: *I must pay for my sins.*

TRUTH: Jesus paid for my sins.

> *"The Son of Man did not come to be served, but to serve, and to give his life as a ransom for many"* (Matthew 20:28).

LIE: *It's my life. I can do what I want.*

TRUTH: My life now belongs to God.

> *You were bought at a price. Therefore honor God with your bodies* (1 Corinthians 6:20).

LIE: *I have no purpose in life.*

TRUTH: God has great plans for my life.

> *What no eye has seen, what no ear has heard, and what no human mind has conceived—the things God has prepared for those who love him—* (1 Corinthians 2:9).

LIE: *This problem is too big. It cannot be fixed.*

TRUTH: No problem is too difficult for God.

> *O Sovereign Lord! You made the heavens and earth by your strong hand and powerful arm. Nothing is too hard for you!* (Jeremiah 32:17 NLT).

LIE: *I should be worried.*

TRUTH: I don't need to be worried. God is in control.

> *Do not be anxious about anything, but in every situation, by prayer and petition, with thanksgiving, present your requests to God. And the peace of God, which transcends all*

understanding, will guard your hearts and your minds in Christ Jesus (Philippians 4:6-7).

LIE: *I feel dirty.*

TRUTH: I have been cleansed and made pure and holy.

You were washed, you were sanctified, you were justified in the name of the Lord Jesus Christ and by the Spirit of our God (1 Corinthians 6:11).

LIE: *God doesn't hear my prayers.*

TRUTH: God hears my every prayer.

The LORD is near to all who call on him, to all who call on him in truth. He fulfills the desires of those who fear him; he hears their cry and saves them (Psalm 145:18-19).

LIE: *I don't deserve to be forgiven.*

TRUTH: No one deserves to be forgiven. God's forgiveness is a gift.

It is by grace you have been saved, through faith—and this is not from yourselves, it is the gift of God— not by works, so that no one can boast (Ephesians 2:8-9).

LIE: *I'll never change. I'll always be a mess.*

TRUTH: God will finish what He started in you.

He who began a good work in you will carry it on to completion until the day of Christ Jesus (Philippians 1:6).

LIE: *God could never use me.*

TRUTH: God can and will use me to accomplish His purposes for my life.

"You did not choose me, but I chose you and appointed you so that you might go and bear fruit—fruit that will last" (John 15:16).

LIE: *If someone doesn't like me, then something is wrong with me.*

TRUTH: Not everyone will like me. Not everyone liked Jesus.

> *He was despised and rejected by mankind, a man of suffering, and familiar with pain* (Isaiah 53:3).

LIE: *I can dress the way I want. If a man is tempted, that's his problem.*

TRUTH: I must not dress in a way that causes a brother to be tempted.

> *Do not cause anyone to stumble* (1 Corinthians 10:32).

LIE: *I can't trust God to take care of me.*

TRUTH: I can trust God to take care of me.

> *"Do not worry about your life, what you will eat or drink; or about your body, what you will wear... seek first his kingdom and his righteousness, and all these things will be given to you as well"* (Matthew 6:25,33).

LIE: *I need _____ to be happy and secure.*

TRUTH: My happiness and security come from knowing Jesus.

> *Because the Lord is my Shepherd, I have everything I need!* (Psalm 23:1 TLB).

LIE: *I used to be a Christian, but I lost my salvation.*

TRUTH: I did not do anything to earn my salvation. It is all about what Jesus did, not what I do. Therefore, I cannot lose my salvation because of poor performance.

> *"I give them eternal life, and they shall never perish; no one will snatch them out of my hand"* (John 10:28).

LIE: *I have rights.*

TRUTH: The way to joy is to lay down my rights.

> *Have the same mindset as Christ Jesus: Who, being in very nature God, did not consider equality with God something to be used to his own advantage; rather, he made himself nothing, taking the very nature of a servant, being made in human likeness* (Philippians 2:5-7).

LIE: *I will never figure this out.*

TRUTH: God will direct your steps.

> *Trust in the LORD with all your heart and lean not on your own understanding; in all your ways submit to him, and he will make your paths straight* (Proverbs 3:5-6).

Bible Study Guide

T his Bible study guide is designed to enhance the message of *Enough: Silencing the Lies that Steal Your Confidence.* Each lesson will dig a little deeper into the topic for the coinciding chapter. Remember, because of the finished work of Jesus Christ on the cross and His power and presence in your life...you are enough.

LESSON ONE: HOUSE OF MIRRORS

If you are doing this Bible study in a group, consider having each person tell her story of how she came to Christ. You might want to spread it out over several weeks.

1. If you could write words on a mirror to describe how you saw yourself as a teenager, what would they say? Is it different from how you see yourself today?

2. What does 2 Corinthians 5:17 say happened to you when you accepted Christ?

3. What do the following verses say about your true identity in Christ? *[handwritten: ✝]*

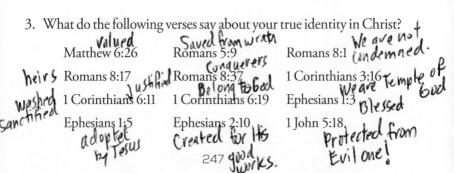

Handwritten annotations on verses:
- Matthew 6:26 — *valued*
- Romans 5:9 — *Saved from wrath*
- Romans 8:1 — *We are not condemned.*
- Romans 8:17 — *heirs*
- Romans 8:37 — *Conquerors / Justified*
- 1 Corinthians 3:16 — *We are Temple of God*
- 1 Corinthians 6:11 — *washed / sanctified*
- 1 Corinthians 6:19 — *Belong to God*
- Ephesians 1:3 — *Blessed*
- Ephesians 1:5 — *adopted by Jesus*
- Ephesians 2:10 — *Created for His good works.*
- 1 John 5:18 — *Protected from Evil one!*

4. Before Jesus began His earthly ministry, God wanted to ensure the world knew exactly who Jesus was and just how His heavenly Father felt about Him. Read Luke 3:15-22 and note what God said when Jesus came up out of the water. You are my beloved Son in whom I am well pleased.

5. God has great plans for you. Did you know that? Read and record 1 Corinthians 2:9. In your own words, write what God's says about the plans He has for you.

6. Before we can accomplish all that God wants us to do, we must know who we are. Read 1 John 3:1 and fill in the blanks. I am God's child, whom He loves.

LESSON TWO: REALIZE THE ENEMY'S TRUE IDENTITY

1. In chapter 2, we looked at the enemy's true identity. Read Ezekiel 28:12-17 and Isaiah 14:12-15 and list everything you learn about Satan's fall.

    Bible scholars have long pondered these passages, uncertain whether they point specifically to Satan's fall from heaven or simply to earthly kings.* Whether these passages were written about Satan or earthly kings, Satan was pulling the puppets' strings.

2. Look up the following verses and note what you learn about how the devil works.

    John 8:44   2 Corinthians 4:4   2 Corinthians 11:14

    Ephesians 6:11-12   1 Peter 5:8

3. Look up in a dictionary the following words the Bible uses to describe the enemy and note what you learn about the enemy's tactics. Give an example of each one.

    a. Murderer (John 8:44)

---

* *Zondervan NIV Bible Commentary, Volume 1: Old Testament*, ed. Kenneth L. Barker and John R. Kohlenberger III (Grand Rapids: Zondervan, 1994), 1070.F.

    b.   Deceiver (2 Corinthians 11:14)

    c.   Accuser (Revelation 12:10)

    d.   Liar (John 8:44)

4. According to the following verses, what did Jesus come to do?

    1 John 3:8   John 10:10   Luke 4:18-19

    Destroy works of devil.   *Give life*

5. I know we're only at the beginning of this study, but I have great faith that we're going to experience incredible victory. So rather than wait until the last lesson together, let's start the party. Read the following verses and note what you learn about the victory we have in Jesus.

    1 Corinthians 15:57   2 Corinthians 2:14   1 John 5:4

LESSON THREE: RECOGNIZE THE LIES

1. As mentioned in chapter 3, the only way to recognize the lies is to know the truth. Read Ephesians 6:10-18 and list the pieces of the armor and what they were used for.

2. In those days, soldiers wore loose-fitting tunics (picture a big sheet with armholes). The belt pulled all the loose ends together and held the tunic closed. How does truth pull all the loose ends of our lives together and prepare us for battle?

3. How is God described in the following verses?

    Psalm 31:5   Isaiah 65:16   Numbers 23:19

4. How is Jesus described in the following verses?

    John 1:14   John 1:17   John 14:6

5. How is the Holy Spirit described in the following verses?

    John 14:15-17   John 16:13   Matthew 10:17-20

6. Read the following verses and note how living in the truth affects your life. Give an example of each.

   Psalm 40:11   Psalm 43:3   John 8:32

   John 8:51

7. What did David pray in regard to the truth?

   Psalm 25:4-5   Psalm 26:2-3   Psalm 51:6

8. What are our inner parts? Mind & heart

9. Pilate asked an important question just before Jesus was sentenced to death (John 18:38). Suppose someone asked you that same question. How would you respond? God is the source of truth

10. Let's go back to question 2. How does the belt of truth hold our lives together? What happens when we don't have the belt of truth fastened securely in place? We believe the devil's lies.

LESSON FOUR: REJECT THE LIES

1. In chapter 4 we learned about how to reject the lies. Go back and read Ephesians 6:10-18 and note once again the pieces of the spiritual armor we're to wear every day. What was the purpose of the shield? How does faith in God's truth protect us from the lies Satan shoots?

2. The shields were often covered with leather and soaked in water. When a fiery dart hit the waterlogged shield, it was extinguished on contact. What is water compared to in the following verses?

   Ephesians 5:26   John 4:10-13

3. How can immersing ourselves in God's Word help extinguish the fiery lies of the enemy?

4. Look up Hebrews 11:1 and note the definition of *faith*. Now paraphrase that in your own words. What does faith look like in your own life?

5. The Greek words for *faith* and *believe* are closely connected. *Pisteuo* is translated *believe*. It is a verb. *Pistis* is translated *faith*. It is a noun. How are these two words different and how are they similar? Can you have one without the other?

6. What kept the Israelites out of the promised land (Numbers 13:17– 14:35; note especially 14:11)? Could your unbelief in regard to what you believe about yourself be keeping you out of your promised land?

7. Our faith is made stronger by confessing what we know. Read the following and note what the writers knew to be true. How would each of these truths combat particular lies?

Romans 8:28	2 Timothy 1:12	James 1:2-3
1 Peter 1:18-19	1 John 4:13	1 John 4:16
1 John 5:18-20		

We have two mini-shields at the ends of our arms. The next time you hear a lie, either audibly or in your mind, reject it. Hold up your hand as if blocking the lie and say, "That's not true."

LESSON FIVE: REPLACE THE LIES WITH TRUTH

Right after Jesus was baptized, the Holy Spirit led Him into the desert to be tempted by Satan. The devil knew exactly who Jesus was and why He came. In the wilderness he challenged Jesus, as if to say, "If you are God's Son, prove it."

1. What were the three temptations recorded in Luke 4:1-13, and how did Jesus preface each rebuttal?

2. Read Romans 12:2. How are we transformed?

When you begin replacing the lies with truth as I mentioned in chapter 5, you will simultaneously be renewing your mind by changing the way you think to line up with God's Word. The word *transformed* implies a process. The moment we accept Jesus Christ as our Lord and Savior, our dead spirits come to life and we are a new creation (2 Corinthians 5:17). However, the transformation of the mind, will, and emotions is a process.

3. Read Colossians 3:16. What do you think it means for something to "dwell" in you?

     a. To dwell means to live at a place, to camp out, to think about constantly. How does that relate to dwelling on the truth?

     b. Notice the verse (in the NIV and others) begins with the word *let*. What does that imply about our part in dwelling on the truth?

4. Read Philippians 4:8 and note what we are to dwell on.

5. Go back to Colossians 3:16 and back up a verse to 3:15. What will rule in our hearts when we dwell on the truth?

     a. To "rule" means to act as an umpire. How is God's Word like an umpire in our lives? Give some examples.

     b. The more time we spend in the truth, the more clearly we can discern God's voice and the more accustomed we grow to detecting the umpire's voice.

6. One way we renew our minds is by meditating on the truth. I think of meditation as mental and spiritual rumination. Read the following and note what you learn about meditation. Especially note what the writer meditated on.

     Psalm 77:12   Psalm 119:15   Psalm 119:48

     Psalm 119:97   Psalm 145:5

7. What are the results of meditating on the truth?

    Proverbs 6:20-22   Joshua 1:8-9   Psalm 1:2-3

8. What is the result of keeping our minds on God's truth (Isaiah 26:3)?

9. Turn to the "Quick Reference Guide" and choose five lies you have often believed about yourself. Now write the following on five different index cards:

    a. *Recognize the lie:* (Write the lie you have believed.)

    b. *Reject the lie:* (Write the powerful sentence, "That's not true.")

    c. *Replace the lie with truth:* (Write the corresponding truth to dispel the lie.)

10. For the next six weeks, meditate on the truth you have recorded. Put the cards in a place where you will see them often, and speak the truth out loud.

LESSON SIX: I'M NOT GOOD ENOUGH

1. All through the Bible we read of men and women who felt that they were not good enough. As a review, what did Moses say when God called him to speak to the Pharaoh and ultimately lead the Israelites out of Egypt (Exodus 3:10-11; 4:10)?

2. What was God's reply to Moses (Exodus 3:12; 4:11-12)?

3. Much like Moses, Jeremiah felt he was not good enough to do what God had called him to do. Read Jeremiah 1:4-10. What was Jeremiah's main concern? What was God's response?

    If you have been telling yourself that you are not good enough, it's time to have a talk with yourself about yourself.

    Some say only crazy people talk to themselves, but I tell you the truth: If I didn't talk to myself, I would go crazy. There is something very powerful about the words we speak to ourselves. Let's look together at the power of our words to ourselves.

4. Read Romans 10:17. What is made stronger when we *hear* the truth? Don't assume this means when you hear the truth spoken by someone else. It could be when you hear it spoken by yourself to yourself.

5. David talked to himself often. Read the following and note his internal conversations. What did he say to himself?

   Psalm 57:8   Psalm 62:5   Psalm 103:1-2,22

6. What do the following proverbs teach us about the power of our words?

   Proverbs 12:18   Proverbs 18:21   Proverbs 21:23

7. From where do our words flow (Luke 6:45)?

8. My grandmother would say, "What is down in the well will come up in the bucket." How does that relate to Luke 6:45?

9. Our spoken words have more power than our unspoken thoughts. Read Matthew 17:20. What part does speaking play in the exercise of our faith?

10. Read 2 Corinthians 4:13 and fill in the blank: "I have believed; therefore _____."

11. What do your words reveal about what you believe?
    Here are some words I want you to say to yourself about yourself today: "Because of the finished work of Jesus Christ on the cross and His power and presence in me...I am enough."

LESSON SEVEN: I'M WORTHLESS

1. Today, let's take a look at your great worth. Read Genesis 1:26-27. In whose image were YOU created?

   The word *image* is the Hebrew word *tselem,* and in the context of Genesis 1: 26-27 means something made in the likeness of something else. "It is literally a shadow which is the outline or representation of the original."* While we are not made in the physical likeness of God, we are created in His spiritual likeness. We reflect God on this earth, as the moon reflects the sun.

2. What does the truth that you are made in God's image say about your worth?

3. What does Psalm 8:5-8 tell you about your worth?

4. Let's look at two women and one girl who would have been considered the lowest of the low in their culture: Hagar and the widow at Zarephath, and a demon-possessed little girl. Read Genesis 16. How did God show Hagar, a Gentile slave, that she was not worthless?

5. What name did she call God?

6. Read 1 Kings 17:7-16. How did God show the Gentile widow at Zarephath that she was not worthless? Remember, if God could send ravens to feed Elijah, He certainly could have kept water in the brook.

7. Read Mark 7:24-30. This is the only miracle Jesus did on His trip to Tyre. It appears that He went there for the specific purpose of healing this Syrophoenician woman's daughter. What does this tell you about the worth of a little girl to God? Also see Luke 8:40-41,49-56.

---

* James Strong, *Strong's Exhaustive Concordance* (Grand Rapids, MI: Baker Book House, 1987), #6754.

8. How do the following verses show your great worth to God?

   Isaiah 49:15   Romans 5:7-8   Romans 8:6-8,32
   1 John 3:1

9. It's a common saying that an object is worth as much as someone is willing to pay for it. What price did God pay for you (1 Corinthians 6:19-20; 7:23; Romans 5:8)?

LESSON EIGHT: I'M SUCH A FAILURE

Almost every significant leader in the Bible failed at one time or another, yet those failures did not prevent them from being used mightily by God. They repented, dusted off their messy robes, and tried again. Let's look at a few.

1. Read Genesis 12. God instructed Abraham to leave his country and go to a place He would show him. Rather than trust God to protect him and provide for him during the famine, what did he do?

2. How did God use Abraham regardless of his failure?

3. Read Exodus 2:11-15. Did Moses fail or succeed at his mission to save his people? What do you think he thought of himself?

4. Read Exodus 3:1-10. Considering what God called Moses to do in these verses, what did He think of Moses's apparent failure?

5. Read 2 Samuel 11. When David should have been out in the field of battle with his men, where was he and what did he do?

6. How did David react when he was confronted with his failure (2 Samuel 12:1-13)?

7. Read Psalm 51 and make note of the specifics David prayed during this time of failure.

8. In the end, what did God later say about David, Israel's greatest king (1 Samuel 13:14; Acts 13:22)?

   David failed, but he was not a failure...and neither are you.

9. What did Jesus tell Peter he was to do after his predicted failure (Luke 22:31-32)?

   Some of our most valuable lessons are learned during a time of apparent failure. If we learn the lesson, then I'd call that a great success.

10. Read 2 Corinthians 1:3-6. What are we to do with the lessons we learn during a time of apparent failure?

11. What does Proverbs 24:16 teach us about what a righteous person does when she falls?

   You are not a failure when you fail. You are a child of God who failed and gets back up to try again.

LESSON NINE: I'M SO UGLY

For some of us, the lies we've believed have become strongholds in our lives—lies we've been holding on to that are now holding on to us. The lie of "I'm so ugly" can be one of those lies. In this lesson, let's stop and think about what a stronghold is and how to tear it down. A stronghold can consist of many lies or one deeply engrained lie that has framed how you see yourself.

1. Read 2 Corinthians 10:3-5. Using your dictionary, define a *stronghold*. What are the strongholds mentioned in these verses?

2. What are the weapons we have at our disposal to tear down the strongholds in our lives?

   If you believe any one of the lies mentioned in this book, it could be a stronghold in your life. Flip to the "Quick Reference Guide" and place a check (in pencil) by any of the lies you believe about yourself. (We're using pencil because I have every confidence that you'll be erasing those checks.)

3. Let's look at a literal stronghold. All that stood between the Israelites and the promised land was a walled city called Jericho. What was God's battle plan for destroying the city walls (Joshua 6:1-6)?

4. If you were among the group, do you think you would have been skeptical of such a plan? What was the result of their obedience (Joshua 6:20-21)?

Let me ask you again: Do you believe any lie about yourself that's keeping you from entering your personal promised land? Do you need to march around the lie, saying the truth, believing the truth, or even shouting the truth? Go ahead. Give it a try. March around the lie of "I'm so ugly" with the truth of "I am God's workmanship" and watch the walls come tumbling down.

5. One of the reasons Jesus came was to set captives free. Read 2 Corinthians 3:17. "Where the Spirit of the Lord is, there is _____."

6. On the Sabbath, Jesus stood up in the synagogue and read Isaiah 61:1-2. Why do you think He read those particular verses?

7. Then with all eyes on Him, what did He declare (Luke 4:20-21)?

8. Jesus did set us free from the penalty of sin, but many Christians are still in bondage to strongholds. What does Galatians 5:1 warn against?

9. Jesus came to set captives free, no matter what prison has them bound. What is the promise of John 8:32?

10. In closing, list 20 amazing features of your body that you are grateful for.

LESSON TEN: I WOULD BE HAPPY IF...

It is interesting that God used someone in chains to show us how to be set free from the lie of "I would be happy if..." Read Philippians and answer the following questions.

1. Where was Paul when he wrote this letter to the Philippians (Philippians 1:11-14)?

2. What was Paul's attitude in the middle of his situation (1:18-26; 3:1; 4:1)?

3. What had Paul learned through the ups and downs of his life (4:11-13)?

4. Just to put Philippians 4:13 in perspective, what are a few of the situations Paul had been through before he came to this conclusion (2 Corinthians 11:22-28)?

5. Twice Paul said he had "learned" how to be content (4:11-12). What does it mean to you that he used the word *learned*?

   I'm sure that Paul was disappointed that he was in prison. You can be disappointed and content at the same time. However, he refused to be defined by his discontentment, but by the truth that he was in God's will.

6. Let's look at some folks that were mumbling, "I'd be happy if" in the Old Testament. God brought the children of Israel out of slavery and into freedom. What do the following verses tell you about their contentment level?

   Exodus 15:24; 16:2,7-8; 17:1-3; 32:1

   Numbers 11:1-2,4-6

7. What was the final outcome of the Israelites' lack of contentment and gratitude for God's provision and protection (Numbers 14:20-23)?

8. God gave Solomon great wealth. Was he content? Peruse the book of Ecclesiastes for your answer.

9. What is God's warning and promise found in Hebrews 13:5?

10. What was Jesus's warning in Luke 12:15?

11. What is the promise of Psalm 37:3-4?

LESSON ELEVEN: I CAN'T FORGIVE MYSELF

In chapter 11, we looked at the idea of forgiving ourselves. The Bible never mentions the idea of "forgiving ourselves," but rather of accepting God's forgiveness when we ask.

1. Read and record the following verses. Even though some of them may have been mentioned in the chapter, it will do your soul good to actually write them out.

Psalm 103:12	Isaiah 1:18	Jeremiah 31:34
Hebrews 10:17	Romans 8:1	1 John 1:9

2. What did Paul say about his own sin (1 Corinthians 15:9)?

3. What did Paul say about his sin once he came to Christ (2 Corinthians 5:17)?

4. What did Jesus say was the reason His blood was poured out for us (Matthew 26:28)?

5. What do you think it says to Jesus when a person doesn't accept the forgiveness that Jesus died to give, but continues to walk in shame and condemnation?

6. Where does that condemnation originate (Revelation 12:10)?

7. Read, record, and memorize Galatians 5:1. You are forgiven and free!

LESSON TWELVE: I CAN'T FORGIVE THE PERSON WHO HURT ME

In our last lesson, we looked at accepting God's grace and forgiveness by letting go of shame and condemnation. Now let's look at how we extend that same gift of forgiveness to others.

In Genesis 25:19–31:20 is the account of two brothers, Jacob and Esau. Jacob was a trickster who tricked Esau into giving him his birthright and his father into giving him the blessing due the firstborn. Esau wanted to kill Jacob, so he fled to live with his uncle. After twenty-two years, God told Jacob to return to his family. When he arrived, his brother met him not with weapons, but with forgiveness.

1. What did Jacob say about seeing Esau's face of forgiveness (Genesis 33:1-12)?

2. How is looking in the face of forgiveness like looking into the face of God?

3. What are we to put on, according to Ephesians 4:24? Glorifying God means reflecting Him in all we do. How does forgiveness glorify God?

4. What do the following verses teach us about forgiving those who have hurt us? Some were included in the chapter, but it will do your heart good to look them up in your own Bible.

   Matthew 6:12-15; 18:21-22,32-35   Mark 11:25-26

   Ephesians 4:26-27, 31-32   Colossians 3:12-13

5. What did Paul tells us to get rid of in Ephesians 4:31-32? Use a dictionary to define each word. How do they relate to unforgiveness?

6. What were Jesus's final words on the cross?

7. In chapter 12, we looked at Matthew 18:23-35. Read it again in your own Bible. How can you apply that parable to your own life?

8. Read John 8. What were Jesus's final words to the Pharisees about the stones they held in their hands? Are you holding any stones in your hands? If so, what have you learned about letting them go?

9. When Jesus gave His disciples a pattern for prayer, what did He say about forgiveness (Luke 11:4)?

10. Is there someone you need to forgive today?

LESSON THIRTEEN: I CAN'T HELP MYSELF

1. The lie of "I can't help myself" is denying the power of the Holy Spirit in us and lack of self-control by us. Perhaps we can't help ourselves by ourselves, but we have the power of the Holy Spirit available and accessible. Read Galatians 5:22-23 and note the fruit of the Spirit. What is the last one listed?

2. What is the difference between a gift of the Spirit (1 Corinthians 12) and a fruit of the Spirit (Galatians 5:22-23)?

3. To what does Solomon compare a person who lacks self-control (Proverbs 25:28)?

4. In the Old Testament, cities were surrounded and protected by tall, thick walls. Some were so thick they could ride a chariot around them. With this in mind, what additional insight can you glean from Proverbs 25:28? How is a person who lacks self-control like a city with no fortification?

5. The Greek word for self-control is *egkrateia*, which means "restraining passions and appetites."*

---

* John F. MacArthur *The MacArthur New Testament Commentary: Galatians* (Chicago: Moody Publishers, 1987), 169.

Let's read the stories of two different men and see how self-control affected their lives. You might want to space this lesson out over a few days.

6. Read Judges 13–16 and note all the ways that Samson did not have self-control.

7. Read Daniel 1 and 6 and note ways that Daniel exhibited self-control.

8. What was the outcome for each man? What do you learn by comparing these two men?

9. What did God say to Cain about the sin that was crouching at the door (Genesis 4:6-7)?

   The Hebrew word for "crouching is the same as an ancient Babylonian word referring to an evil demon crouching at the door of a building to threaten the people inside. Sin may thus be pictured here as just such a demon, waiting to pounce on Cain—it desires to have him." *

10. With that in mind, what is really going on in the spiritual realm when we feel the urge of "I can't help myself"?

11. The Hebrew word for "master" is *mashal* and means "to rule, have dominion, governor, gain control."† God would never command us to do something that He would not give us the power to do. Read and record this promise from God (1 Corinthians 10:13).

12. Read, record, and memorize Philippians 4:13. You can do it! I know you can.

---

* Kenneth Barker, *NIV Study Bible*, gen. ed. (Grand Rapids, MI: Zondervan Publishing House, 1984), 12.

† http://biblehub.com/hebrew/4910.htm

LESSON FOURTEEN: MY LIFE IS HOPELESS

There's one thing I know: The devil wants you to lose hope. Remember, he is a liar and the father of lies. In Christ, you have a great hope.

1. Before we begin, look up the definition for the words *hope* and *hopeless.*

2. Read John 10:10. What does the devil want to do in your life? Interestingly, a common thread of suicide victims is the loss of hope...that life will never be any different than it is at this moment. How is that a lie and Satan's ultimate goal?

3. What is Jesus's ultimate desire for you?

4. Read and record Psalm 43:5. What was David's prescription for hopelessness?

5. Read the following verses and note the promise of each:

Exodus 14:14	Jeremiah 29:11	Isaiah 40:31
Psalm 91:1-16	Philippians 4:19	Proverbs 23:18

6. Read the following and note where David tells us to place our hope: Psalm 25:5; 33:22; 37:9; 52:9; 62:5; 71:5; 119:74.

7. What did Moses tell the Israelites when they were up against what seemed like a hopeless situation (Exodus 14:14)? Do you believe that the Lord will fight for you as well? What is the promise of Hebrews 13:8?

8. What did Solomon tell us in Proverbs 23:18? This is not wishful thinking but the truth. God is faithful to His Word, even when we are not.

9. After Jesus died on the cross, how did His followers feel (Luke 24:16-22)?

One thing Jesus's resurrection teaches us is that we are not people without hope no matter how bleak the situation may seem.

10. What do the following verses from Psalms teach us about where our hope comes from? Psalm 31:24; 33:18,20; 42:5; 71:5; 119:114; 147:11?

11. Read 2 Corinthians 9:8 and underline the first four words. Write them down on a card and tuck it in your Bible.

12. I get it—sometimes we can feel so hopeless we don't even know how to pray. How do the following verses comfort even when we are at that low point?

Romans 8:26-27,34   John 17:20-23   Hebrews 7:25

Here is my prayer for you today: *May the God of hope fill you with all joy and peace as you trust in him, so that you may overflow with hope by the power of the Holy Spirit* (Romans 15:13).

LESSON FIFTEEN: GOD DOESN'T REALLY LOVE ME
I look at the title of chapter 15, and I want to shout, "Oh yes He does!"

1. What did Paul pray for the Ephesians (Ephesians 3:14-19)?

2. Paul wouldn't pray for them to know something that they already knew. What does that tell you about our capacity to understand God's great love for us?

3. How does John describe who God is (1 John 4:8)?

4. Read the following verses and note what you learn about God's love for you.

Psalm 136:26   Isaiah 49:15-16   Romans 5:8
Romans 8:35-39   1 John 3:1   1 John 4:9-10

There is nothing you can do to make God *not* love you. Seriously. Nothing. It's who He is. It's what He does.

5. Did you know God is crazy about you? The apostle John knew Jesus loved him. How did he refer to himself in his Gospel (John 13:23; 19:26; 21:7,20)?

6. That's how you can begin introducing yourself. Give it a try. *I am* (your name goes here*), the one Jesus loves.*

    Take some time today to summarize what you have learned from this study.

Your heavenly Father has so much planned for you. He has big dreams for your life. But He's waiting for you to put away the lies, to start seeing yourself as He sees you, and to walk in the confidence of a woman who knows she is deeply loved, completely forgiven, fully pleasing, and totally accepted by God. You are empowered and equipped by the Holy Spirit to do all God has called you to do.

Go back to the "Quick Reference Guide" and look at the lies you checked earlier. Can you erase them now? I hope so.

NOTES

CHAPTER 1: HOUSE OF MIRRORS

1. Sharon Jaynes, *Take Hold of the Faith You Long For* (Colorado Springs, CO: Baker Books, 2016), 22.

CHAPTER 2: REALIZE THE ENEMY'S TRUE IDENTITY

1. Steven Furtick, *Crash the Chatterbox* (Colorado Springs, CO: Multnomah, 2014), 56.

2. Neil Anderson, *Living Free in Christ* (Ventura, CA: Regal Books, 1993), 124.

3. https://www.barna.com/research/most-american-christians-do-not-believe-that-satan-or-the-holy-spirit-exist/

4. John MacArthur, *The MacArthur Bible Commentary* (Nashville: Thomas Nelson Publishers, 2005), 1704.

5. Dr. Lynda Hunter, *Who Am I Really?* (Nashville: Word Publishing, 2001), 30.

6. Peter H. Davids, *The Epistle of James* (Grand Rapids. MI: Eerdmans, 1982), 161.

7. Francis Frangipane, *The Three Battlegrounds* (Marion, IA: River of Life Ministries, 1989), 36.

CHAPTER 3: RECOGNIZE THE LIES

1. http://www.clevelandclinicwellness.com/programs/NewSFN/pages/default.aspx?Lesson=3&Topic=2&UserId=00000000-0000-0000-0000-000000000705

2. William Backus and Marie Chapian, *Telling Yourself the Truth* (Minneapolis: Bethany House Publishers, 2000), 3.

3. Kenneth Barker, *Study Bible, gen, ed,* (Grand Rapids, MI: Zondervan, 1995), 12.

4. www.airsafe.com/events/celebs/jfk_jr.htm

5. www.airlinesafety.com/editorials/JFKJrCrash.htm (Eric Nolte, "Heart Over Mind: The Death of JFK, Jr.").

6. Ibid.

7. Robert McGee, *The Search for Significance* (Tulsa, OK: Rapha Publishing, 1990), 155.

CHAPTER 4: REJECT THE LIES

1. Beth Moore, *Breaking Free* (Nashville, TN: LifeWay Press, 1999), 184, 194.

2. Markus Barth, *Ephesians 4-6, the Anchor Bible, vol. 34A* (Garden City, NY: Doubleday, 1974), 763.

3. John MacArthur, *The MacArthur Bible Commentary* (Nashville, TN: Thomas Nelson, 2005), 1706.

4. *Inspiring Quotations, Contemporary and Classical, comp.* Albert M. Wells Jr. (Nashville: Thomas Nelson Publishers, 1988), 209.

5. Timothy Keller, *The Reason for God: Belief in an Age of Skepticism* (New York: Riverhead, 2008), 171.

CHAPTER 5: REPLACE THE LIES WITH TRUTH

1. Paul Meier, "Spiritual and Mental Health in the Balance," in *Renewing Your Mind in a Secular World,* John E Woodbridge, ed. (Chicago: Moody Press, 1985), 26–29.

2. http://sethgodin.typepad.com/seths_blog/2006/07/belief.html

CHAPTER 6: I AM NOT ENOUGH

1. Henry T. Blackaby and Richard Blackaby, *Experiencing God Day by Day* (Nashville, TN: Broadman and Holman Publishers, 1997), 109.

2. Sharon Jaynes, *Take Hold of the Faith You Long For* (Grand Rapids, MI: Baker Books, 2016), 69–72.

3. I first heard the idea of God filling in your blanks from a sermon by Pastor Steven Furtick at Elevation Church, in Charlotte, NC.

4. Beth Moore, *The Beloved Disciple* (Nashville: LifeWay Press, 2002), 87.

5. Renee Swope, *A Confident Heart* (Grand Rapids, MI: Revell, 2011), 88–89.

CHAPTER 7: I'M WORTHLESS

1. C.S. Lewis, *The Weight of Glory* (New York, NY: Harper Collins), 46.

2. Alan Loy McGinnis, *Bringing Out the Best in People* (Minneapolis: Augsburg, 1985), 32.

3. John MacArthur, *The MacArthur Bible Commentary* (Nashville, TN: Thomas Nelson, 2005), 1364.

4. Mark Buchanan, *Your God Is Too Safe* (Sisters, OR: Multnomah, 2001), 153–54.

CHAPTER 8: I'M SUCH A FAILURE

1. Renee Swope, *A Confident Heart* (Grand Rapids, MI: Revell, 2011), 122.

2. Lysa TerKeurst, *Unglued: Making Wise Choices in the Midst of Raw Emotions* (Grand Rapids, MI: Zondervan, 2012), 32–33.

3. Dr. Neil T. Anderson, "Daily In Christ," posted August 10, 2010, http://www.crosswalk.com/devotionals/dailyinchrist/544718/

4. Brennan Manning, *Abba's Child: The Cry of the Heart for Intimate Belonging* (Colorado Springs: NavPress, 2004), 26.

5. Those words were first spoken by John Bradford, a sixteenth-century reformer and martyr who uttered them from behind bars in the Tower of London when he saw a criminal going to execution for his crimes. http://en.wikipedia.org/wiki/John_Bradford

CHAPTER 9: I'M SO UGLY

1. https://www.dove.com/us/en/stories/about-dove/our-research.html

2. Ibid.

3. John Eldredge, *Wild at Heart* (Nashville, TN: Thomas Nelson Publishers, 2001), 16–17.

4. Michele Cushatt, *I Am: A 60-Day Journey to Knowing Who You Are Because of Who He Is* (Grand Rapids, MI: Zondervan, 2017), 39–40.

5. Ibid., 41.

6. http://www.desiringgod.org/articles/you-are-god-s-workmanship

7. Bruce Marchiano, *Jesus, the Man Who Loved Women* (New York, NY: Howard Books, 2008), 16–17.

8. http://www.statisticbrain.com/barbie-doll-statistics/

9. Nancy Stafford, *Beauty by the Book* (Sisters, OR: Multnomah Publishers, 2002), 118.

CHAPTER 10: I WOULD BE HAPPY IF...

1. Shannon Woodward, *Inconceivable* (Colorado Springs: Cook Communications Ministries, 2006), 9.

2. C.S. Lewis, *The Weight of Glory* (New York: HarperCollins, 1949, 1976, revised 1980), 26.

3. This has often been attributed to Blaise Pascal. What he really said was the following: "What else does this craving, and this helplessness, proclaim but that there was once in man a true happiness, of which all that now remains is the empty print and trace? This he tries in vain to fill with everything around him, seeking in things that are not there the help he cannot find in those that are, though none can help, since this infinite abyss can be filled only with an infinite and immutable object; in other words by God himself" (148/428). http://theconstructivecurmudgeon.blogspot.com/2006/05/incorrect-pascal-quotes.html

4. William D. Mounce and Robert H. Mounce, *The Zondervan Greek and English Interlinear New Testament* (Grand Rapids, MI: Zondervan, 2008), 382, 1098.

5. Judith S. Wallerstein, Julia M. Lewis, and Sandra Blakeslee, *The Unexpected Legacy of Divorce* (New York: Hyperion, 2000), 310.

6. Eric Weiner, *The Geography of Bliss* (New York: Twelve, Hachette Book Group USA, 2008), 148.

7. https://www.census.gov/newsroom/press-releases/2015/cb15-47.html

8. C.S. Lewis, *The Silver Chair* (New York: Macmillan Publishing Company, 1953), 15–17.

CHAPTER 11: I CAN'T FORGIVE MYSELF

1. Beth Moore, *Beloved Disciple* (Nashville: LifeWay Press, 2002), 141.

2. Diane Dempsey Marr, *The Reluctant Traveler* (Colorado Springs, CO: NavPress, 2002), 155.

3. Brennan Manning, *The Ragamuffin Gospel* (Sisters, OR: Multnomah, 1990), 26.

4. Bob and Audrey Meisner, *Marriage Under Cover* (Winnipeg, MB, Canada: Milestones International Publishers, 2005), 138.

5. 1 John 3:19-20 (MSG).

6. Joyce Meyer, *Beauty from Ashes* (Tulsa, OK: Harrison House, 1994), 75.

7. Neil Anderson, *Living Free in Christ* (Ventura, CA: Regal Books, 1993), 110.

CHAPTER 12: I CAN'T FORGIVE THE PERSON WHO HURT ME

1. Diane Dempsey Marr, *The Reluctant Traveler* (Colorado Springs, CO: NavPress, 2002), 113.

2. Spiros Zodhiates et al., eds., T*he Complete Word Study Dictionary: New Testament* (Chattanooga, TN: AMG publishers, 1992), 229.

3. Beth Moore, *Living Beyond Yourself* (Nashville: LifeWay Press, 1998), 120.

CHAPTER 14: MY LIFE IS HOPELESS

1. Shannon Woodward, *Inconceivable* (Colorado Springs: Cook Communications Ministries, 2006), 11.

CHAPTER 15: GOD DOESN'T REALLY LOVE ME

1. Renee Swope, *A Confident Heart* (Grand Rapids, MI: Revell, 2011), 55.

2. *Random House Unabridged Dictionary*, 2nd ed. (New York: Random House, 1992), s.v. "worry."

3. Shannon Woodward, *Inconceivable* (Colorado Springs: Cook Communications Ministries, 2006), 17.

4. Ibid., 151–54.

Acknowledgments

There are so many amazing people who have worked together to make this project possible. A special thanks to the Harvest House family: Bob Hawkins Jr., who continues his father's dream of reaching the world for Christ with the printed word; LaRae Weikert, who has the uncanny ability to make everyone feel like they are her best friend; Terry Glaspey, who is an amazing listener, encourager, and friend; and Betty Fletcher, editor extraordinaire.

• • • • •

I am especially thankful for two friends who encouraged me on when I felt that I wasn't good enough, my Girlfriends in God: Gwen Smith and Mary Southerland. God has used these two women to impact my life in amazing ways.

I'm also forever thankful for my prayer team—Karen Shiels, Van Walton, Sandy Fulginiti, Barbara Givens, Kathy Mendietta, Linda Butler, Bonnie Schulte, Cynthia Price, Cissy Smith, Bonnie Cleveland, Pat Smith, and Linda Eppley—and for the many friends who shared their stories in order to expose the lies we believe and the truth that sets us free.

• • • • •

This book would not be a reality without my "in-house editor," my precious husband, Steve. Thank you for believing in me and giving me the love and encouragement I needed to press on.

• • • • •

Most of all, I am thankful for my heavenly Father who loves me, the Holy Spirit who empowers me, and my Savior, Jesus Christ, who set me free.

About Sharon Jaynes

Sharon Jaynes is an international conference speaker and bestselling author of 22 books including *The Power of a Woman's Words, Becoming the Woman of His Dreams, The 14-Day Romance Challenge,* and *Take Hold of the Faith You Long For.* Her books have been translated into several languages and impact women for Christ all around the world.

Sharon served as vice president and radio cohost for Proverbs 31 Ministries for ten years. She is currently on Proverbs' *Encouragement for Today* devotion writing team and She Speaks Writers and Speakers teaching team. Sharon is also the cofounder of Girlfriends in God, a nondenominational conference and online ministry that seeks to cross generational, racial, and denominational boundaries to bring the body of Christ together as believers.

For those who know Sharon best, she is a simple Southern girl who loves sweet tea, warm beaches, and helping women live fully and freely as a children of God and coheirs with Christ. She and her husband, Steve, call North Carolina home. They have one grown son, Steven.

Sharon is always honored to hear from her readers. You can connect with her through her

> **Blog:** www.sharonjaynes.com
>
> **Email:** sharon@sharonjaynes.com
>
> **Facebook:** www.Facebook.com/sharonjaynes
>
> **Instagram:** www.instagram.com/sharonejaynes
>
> **Twitter:** www.twitter.com/sharonjaynes

Sharon also has a special Facebook page for those who want to join daily to pray for their husbands at www.Facebook.com/ThePraying WivesClub.

To learn more about Sharon's books, resources, and ministry, or to inquire about having Sharon speak at your event, visit www.sharon jaynes.com.